Economic Issues in American History

Gary M. Walton
Washington State University

Roger LeRoy Miller
University of Miami

Canfield Press CP San Francisco
A Department of Harper & Row, Publishers, Inc.
New York, Hagerstown, London

Interior and cover design, biography art: Bill Yenne

ECONOMIC ISSUES IN AMERICAN HISTORY
Copyright © 1978 by Gary M. Walton and Roger LeRoy Miller

Library of Congress Cataloging in Publication Data

Walton, Gary M.
    Economic Issues in American History

    1.   United States—Economic conditions. I. Miller,
Roger LeRoy, joint author.   II.   Title.
HC103.W33   330.9'73   77-22072
ISBN 0-06-389127-1

78 79 80   10 9 8 7 6 5 4 3 2 1

Contents

Part V   Economic Life in Modern America, 1920-1980

Preface

American history encompasses the extensive interplay of political, social, psychological, and economic phenomena. In this short book, we offer an interpretation of American history through the eyes of the economist. Herein the reader will find a nontechnical reappraisal of America's economic experience presented in light of the latest and most thorough research. The smallness of this book clearly indicates that we are not offering a complete or in-depth study of all aspects of American history or even American economic history. We have had to be selective, giving only the essential economic and historical transitions in chronological fashion.

By interspersing controversial issues between chapters, we hope to capture the reader's interest and allow him or her to take a closer, undistracted scrutiny of the topic at hand.

Biographies have also been included at the beginning of each historical period. In them we portray such diverse figures as Eliza Lucas—one of America's first female entrepreneurs, Jay Gould—the financial wizard, and John L. Lewis—the great leader of organized labor. To a degree, these biographies personify both the period and the roles these key figures played in our economic past; they give an essential human quality to our economic history.

Economic jargon has been kept to a minimum. Theory necessarily forms the basis of the analysis, but it is couched in narrative form. In this manner, we hope to enliven the subject of economic history and to display its relevance for a better understanding of the world today. Finally, we think this approach also allows the inquiry to be enjoyable.

We are greatly indebted to a number of key reviewers for this project, including Dr. Harry N. Scheiber of the University of California at San Diego, Dr. Albert Fishlow of the University of California at Berkeley, and Dr. William Carlisle of the University of Utah.

G.M.W.
R.L.M.

Part I
Introduction

1. Great Junctures in American Economic Life

Dying For a Foothold

There is an old quip that the Quakers came to America to do good and ended up doing well. The grain of truth to this resides partly in the fact that the Quakers were not among the very first to arrive on American shores. For those hardy souls who arrived first, it could hardly be said that they "did well."

The first British outpost in North America was set up by Sir Walter Raleigh in the 1580s, for the purpose of harassing the Spanish treasure fleets. It was located at Roanoke, North Carolina, and it stands as one of history's teasing mysteries because after a short absence, Raleigh's captain, John White, returned in 1590 to find no trace—living or dead—of anyone.

This "lost colony," as it is known in history, forcefully accents the great hardships faced by newcomers to America. A majority of the earliest settlers in the seventeenth century died within two years of their arrival. Starvation, disease, Indian attacks, and other calamities were commonplace.

In 1607 the Plymouth Company landed a group of settlers near the mouth of the Sagadohoc River in Maine. Those who survived the winter ordeals packed up and returned to England. In that same year, the London Company landed a party of 105 at Jamestown, Virginia. Of these, 67 died within the first year, but 800 new arrivals in 1609 added to their numbers. By the spring of the next year, frontier hazards had cut their number to 60! These disheartened few were actually heading down river to leave for England when new supplies and more settlers on three ships arrived to change their plans. In this way, Jamestown eventually won the dubious honor of being the first permanent British settlement in North America.

Much of the problem was that the earliest settlers had not yet discovered any commercial enterprise to enrich them materially or any way to provide for themselves, and many were more adventurers than settlers. Vital energy and time was often futilely spent on get-rich-quick schemes; for example, in 1607 and 1608 shiploads of mica and yellow ore were sent to England. Later, the word came back: They were worthless.

In 1622 an Indian uprising near Jamestown resulted in the massacre of 347 settlers. The very next year another 500 died from disease, and this prompted a "royal investigation" of the state of things in the colony. The investigation revealed that 6,000 people had left England for Virginia between 1607 and 1623. Of these, 4,000 had perished.

There can be little doubt that the human costs of taking the colonial frontier were enormous. As the distinguished historian, Charles Andrews, has said, "This was the 'Starving Time' for Virginia, just as there were to be starving times for Bermuda, Plym-

Introduction

outh, and Barbados, when men suffered and died, because they had not yet learned the art of colonization, and had come to America inadequately supplied and equipped and unfamiliar with the method of wresting a living from the wilderness."[1]

There can be little doubt that during the earliest years the white man's economic vitality in North America was at the barest minimum to sustain life. Certainly it was below that of the resident Indians and provided only the fewest essentials of a subsistence livelihood.

After Independence

New Standings, 1776

From these meager beginnings, the standard of living soon began its upward march. By the eve of the American Revolution, the white population was near 2.5 million people and the number of blacks was nearly .5 million.

By 1776, the white population had an average income that rivaled that of the wealthiest, most advanced countries in the world. Average income per person in England was the highest in the world, with France, Holland, and the thirteen colonies close behind. Because of the relative preponderance of very wealthy individuals in England, average incomes there were higher than in the colonies. However, if the wealthy classes and slaves are excluded and only the average incomes of the common white people are compared, the thirteen colonies were perhaps the richest area in the world. Indeed, North America was the best poor person's country, not only then, but for decades to follow. It was in the British North American colonies that wages were highest and land most abundant.

Material standards of living, not to mention political and social rewards, were radically different for blacks and whites, because almost all of the

blacks were slaves. Their material comforts were low, although they were adequate for the maintenance of a reasonably healthy and vigorously growing domestic black population.

It is difficult to overemphasize the fact that the level of income per free person at the time of the birth of the United States was extraordinarily high. With painstaking care, Alice Hanson Jones has estimated average colonial wealth holdings per free person in 1774. Her estimate of 76 pounds sterling in 1973 dollars converts to $2,860, because one pound sterling in 1774 had the buying power of just over $38 in 1973.[2] This average wealth level suggests a range of annual average income per free person in the colonies that was between $600 and $950.[3] Most likely it was close to $750. As Table 1−1 vividly shows, the thirteen colonies were quite advanced in comparison to countries today. Few countries today enjoy annual incomes on an average that match or exceed those achieved in the thirteen colonies on the eve of the revolution. Indeed, countries comprising more than two-thirds of the world population today live with average annual incomes below that earned by the free people in the colonies over two hundred years ago.

Two Centuries of Economic Growth

The extraordinary rise from starvation levels to relative comfort for the average free citizen by 1775 was followed, of course, by another two centuries of improvement in the standard of living. For the time following 1840, the year of our first national in-

---

[1] Charles M. Andrews, *The Colonial Period of American History*, Vol. 1 (New Haven: Yale University Press, 1934), pp. 110−111.

[2] U.S. Bureau of the Census, *Historical Statistics: Colonial Times to 1973*, Series Z, 169−212. Washington, D.C.: U.S. Government Printing Office, 1976, p. 1175.

[3] Wealth is, of course, the value of possessions at a particular moment in time. To convert this to a stream of earnings for a year, we use contemporary and historical relationships between the capital stock and output (or income). These vary to a degree but generally range between a ratio of 3 to 1 and 5 to 1; hence, the $600 and $950 range.

TABLE 1−1. Population and Gross National Product (GNP) Per Capita by Income Group, 1973.

Income groups	Number of countries	Population (millions)	Average GNP per capita U.S. dollars
Less than $200	43	1,151	120
$200 to $499	52	1,184	280
$500 to $1,999	53	531	1,000
$2,000 to $4,999	28	654	2,860
$5,000 and over	12	316	5,970

Selected countries with per capita income of less than $200

Bangladesh	Indonesia	South Vietnam
Burma	Kenya	Sudan
Cambodia	Laos	Uganda
Ethiopia	Nepal	Vietnam (Democratic Republic of)
India	Pakistan	Zaire

Selected countries with per capita income of $200 to $499

Angola	Ecuador	Morocco
Antigua	Egypt (Arab Republic of)	New Hebrides
Bolivia	Honduras	Nigeria
China (People's Republic of)	Jordan	Paraguay
Columbia	Korea (Democratic Republic of)	Philippines
Congo (People's Republic of)	Korea (Republic of)	Rhodesia

Selected countries with per capita income of $500 to $1,999

Algeria	Guatemala	Nicaragua
Argentina	Hong Kong	Panama
Barbados	Hungary	Portugal
Brazil	Iran	Saudi Arabia
Bulgaria	Iraq	South Africa
Chile	Jamaica	Spain
Costa Rica	Malaysia	Turkey
Cuba	Malta	Venezuela
Greece	Mexico	Yugoslavia

Selected countries with per capita income of $2,000 to $4,999

Australia	France	Netherlands
Austria	German Democratic Republic	New Zealand
Belgium	Israel	Norway
Czechoslovakia	Italy	Poland
Finland	Japan	United Kingdom
		USSR

Selected countries with per capita income of $5,000 and over

Canada	Iceland	United States
Denmark	Kuwait	Sweden
Germany (Federal Republic of)	United Arab Emirates	Switzerland

Source: *World Bank Atlas: Population, Per Capita Product, and Growth Rates* (Washington, D.C.: IBRD, 1975), p. 8.

come estimate, it is possible to calculate with fair precision the nation's record of economic growth. We generally express economic growth in terms of rates of change of real per capita income. This rate, although not steady, followed a long-run trend of approximately 1.6 percent per year. This implies a doubling every 43 years in average yearly income per person, after correction for changes in the purchasing power of the dollar. That is, for much of our history each new generation of Americans could expect on an average to command almost twice the material standard of living that the former generation had enjoyed. This is not to say that each generation was twice as happy or even that they experienced considerably more enjoyment. But in terms of goods and services there was nearly twice as much to go around for each person and, as shown in Table 1−1, the U.S. remains one of the leading economies in the world today. When viewed in this context, the American economic record is truly impressive. And it must be remembered that not only were Americans producing more goods and services (per person) with each passing generation, they were also enjoying more leisure time. □

EQUALITY AND INEQUALITY: MYTHS AND REALITIES

Equality at the Beginning

"With liberty and justice for all" is a phrase we know so very well. Perhaps it even expounds, in brevity, the American ideal. But does "justice for all" imply merely equal rights before the law, or does it mean more than this—equal rights to good health, equal rights to job security, equal pay, equal leisure; in short, does it mean equal income?

Some people believe that the distribution of income that results from participation in a market economy such as ours is inherently unjust and that ideally income should be distributed equally. Actually, in the earliest years of colonial life in America, the principle of strict economic equality was forcefully attempted.

Jamestown Revisited

The Jamestown colony originally operated as a collective, both in terms of communal production and shared consumption. Belief in the ideal of "fairness" and "equality," however, was not shared by all. Many individuals inevitably shirked assigned tasks, and the human characteristic of self-interest discouraged incentives to work and to innovate. To see why, consider the following hypothetical case.

Suppose one of a hundred equally industrious workers suddenly decides to work half as hard as the others. Daily output then falls by 0.5 percent. If each receives an equal share of the total product, the shirker loses almost nothing in consumption, and yet he

eases the burden of his work dramatically. And with each new shirker, the total product falls and falls. Alternatively, suppose a worker decides to work twice as hard. Total output then rises by about 0.5 percent. For twice the work, this worker receives hardly any more to consume. Under such circumstances, greater work effort is seldom realized. Now, suppose there are various tasks and one worker thinks of a way to perform a task better and more quickly. With collective production methods, he gains little, because now the time freed is not rewarded to him alone; he must use the time saved to help others in other tasks for the sake of equality. As a consequence, collective production methods and shared consumption often result in relatively low levels of output and limited growth, especially when material gain is the main incentive to work.

Such was the situation in Jamestown in the early years. Single men complained of working, without due reward, for other men's wives and children. The strong and industrious were aggrieved at obtaining no more in food, clothes, and supplies than others capable of much less work. Wives considered tasks benefiting others than their own families a form of enslavement. And since land was owned in common, incentives to care for and improve it were generally lacking. Only with private holdings could individuals expect the *full* return for their efforts to improve the land.

Despite the introduction of tobacco in 1612, which led to commercial production for market, the organizational difficulties stemming from collective enterprise resulted in continued complaints and low levels of output per worker. The clash of the egalitarian ideal with the economic reality of individual self-interest quickly became apparent, however. By 1614, the first step towards private holdings (with 3-acre limits), was taken. In 1619, the **headright system** was introduced. This granted fifty acres of land to anyone paying his or her ocean passage to Virginia. Another fifty acres could be obtained if the person paid the way for someone else. In 1623, the year of the "royal investigation," all holdings were converted to private ownership. The noble but troubling age of economic equality in America was over.[1]

Inequality

Differences in ability, inheritance, legal status, work effort, and just plain luck soon led to a distribution of wealth in the thirteen colonies that was far from egalitarian. Not only did differences in people's wealth holdings sharply accent the differences in social classes in the colonies, epitomized in the contrast between master and slave, but they also revealed very sharp differences in wealth possibilities among the major geographical regions.

As shown in Table I–1, in the years just preceding the birth of the nation, the southern colonies were more than twice as wealthy (per free person) as the middle colonies and New England. This higher relative standing shows up not only in the category of slaves, where we might ex-

Table I–1. Average Private Physical Wealth per Free Person, 1774 (Pounds Sterling).

	New England	Middle Colonies	Southern Colonies	Total Thirteen Colonies
Land	£27	£28	£55	£38
Servants and Slaves	0	2	58	21
Livestock	3	5	9	6
Farm tools and household equipment	1	1	3	2
Crops and perishables	1	3	5	3
Consumer durables	4	4	6	5
Other	2	3	1	2
Totals	£38	£46	£137	£76

Note: New England—New Hampshire, Massachusetts, Rhode Island, and Connecticut; middle colonies—New York, New Jersey, Pennsylvania, Delaware; southern colonies—Maryland, Virginia, North Carolina, South Carolina, Georgia.

Source: U.S. Bureau of Census, *Historical Statistics Colonial Times to 1973*, Series Z. (Washington, D.C.: U.S. Government Printing Office, 1976), p. 1175.

[1] Although eventually abandoned, collective activity in early New England had fewer negative results. Undoubtedly, this was because of a more cohesive society there, based on common religious principles (Puritan beliefs). Similarly, the Mormon pioneers, and to a degree their descendants, fruitfully combined collective enterprise with individual motivation. Again, these successes apparently result when strong religious or social forces tend to counter individual motivation based on self-interest.

pect it, but also in all of the other classifications of wealth.

Although we presently do not have careful documentation of the distribution of wealth in the southern colonies, it seems fairly obvious that the South displayed the greatest degrees of wealth inequality. Southern whites averaged the highest wealth holdings per free person in the entire thirteen colonies, and yet the South domiciled 90 percent of the nation's slaves. In the late colonial period, Virginia's population, for instance, was 45 percent black; in South Carolina, the black proportion was 70 percent. It seems fairly clear that the disparity in wealth holdings between free persons and slaves was widest in the South and that despite their large numbers, the share of total wealth going to those in bondage was only a tiny fraction of the whole. The blacks in Virginia probably received less than 10 percent of the wealth; in South Carolina, they might have held a little more than 10 percent. Yet, as noted above, their proportions of these populations were 45 percent and 70 percent, respectively.

A more systematic view of wealth distribution is possible for New England and the middle colonies. In these regions, slaves were few, and most people had the legal right to share at least poten-tially in the economic opportunities provided by work and enterprise. As Table I−2 reveals, however, the distribution of wealth per free person in New England and the middle colonies was far from equal. In New England, the poorest half of the population had only 11 percent of the wealth. The richest tenth had almost four times that share. The degree of inequality was comparably less striking in the middle colonies, but clearly, by the time of the Declaration of Independence, economic equality was purely a myth.

Degrees of economic inequality were highest in the major urban centers, such as Boston, where the richest 30 percent of the population held between 80 and 90 percent of the wealth. But even in the countryside and in the newly settled frontier areas, inequality was the rule, with the top 30 percent typically holding about 60 percent of the wealth. Clearly economic inequality in America existed before the age of industrialization. Inequality has been a reality of American economic life for almost our entire history.

Inequality at Maturity

The degree of inequality apparent at the birth of the United States has not been erased. Indeed, during the century following the American Revolution, wealth concentration actually rose. By the late nineteenth century, the distribution of wealth and income had tended to stabilize; there was a modest rise

Table I−2. Distribution of Physical Wealth in New England and the Middle Colonies in 1774.

Cumulative Proportion of Wealth held by	Percent of Total Wealth	
	New England	Middle Colonies
Poorest 10% of population	less than 1%	less than 1%
Poorest 20% of population	1	2
Poorest 50% of population	11	23
Richest 20% of population	60	47
Richest 10% of population	40	32

Source: Alice Hanson Jones, "Wealth Estimates for the New England Colonies about 1770," *Journal of Economic History*, 32, 1 (March, 1972): 119, and "Wealth Estimates for the American Middle Colonies, 1774," *Economic Development and Cultural Change*, 18, 4, (July 1970).

of inequality in the 1920s, a reversal in the 1930s, and another reversal around 1945.

As portrayed in Table I—3, the distribution of income in the United States remains unequal even today. While the richest 20 percent of the population receives more than 42 percent of money income, the poorest 20 percent receives less than 6 percent of money income. Because this distribution has remained fairly stable (in the long run) over the last century, the path to enrichment has been primarily, although not exclusively, by economic growth. This winding, colorful story is of great interest, even from the days of Columbus. ☐

Table I—3. Distribution of Income, 1974.

Families	Percentage of Money Income Share
Top 20 percent	42.1
Fourth 20 percent	23.0
Third 20 percent	17.2
Second 20 percent	12.1
Bottom 20 percent	5.6

Source: U.S. Bureau of Census.

Definition of New Term

Head-right System: A plan that granted fifty acres of land to anyone paying his or her ocean passage to Virginia, with a provision that another fifty acres could be obtained if the person paid the way for someone else.

Part II
The Colonial Era

A Pioneering Effort In Early Agriculture

Eliza Lucas

(1723-1793)

Entrepreneur

In 1737, Lieutenant-Colonel George Lucas, who was stationed in Antigua in the Caribbean, departed for South Carolina with his ailing wife and three daughters. Shortly after settling there, diplomatic negotiations broke down between England and Spain and, with hostilities renewed, Colonel Lucas was recalled to duty in Antigua.

Since Mrs. Lucas was in poor health, responsibility for the family's affairs in South Carolina fell to the oldest daughter, Eliza, who was then sixteen. Not only did she admirably discharge her duties, but she also revolutionized agricultural production in South Carolina.

For her, planting was no mere weekend or holiday business. Having three plantations to oversee, she was rivaled by none in her industriousness and ingenuity.

Like other colonists she spent much time and energy trying to discover which crops were best suited for the soil and climate. Happily, in July 1739, she wrote, in a "coppy book of letters to my Papa": "I wrote my father a very long letter on his plantation affairs . . . on the pains I had taken to bring the Indigo, Ginger, Cotton, Lucern, and Cassada to perfection, and had greater hopes from the Indigo." Within three years her hopes were realized and, almost singlehandedly, she successfully introduced and entrepreneured indigo production in the mainland colonies.[1] Additionally, as an active member of the local agricultural society, she helped disseminate her findings to other planters.

Indigo was used as a blue dye to color textiles, and, as a complement to textile production it was deemed so valuable in England that Parliament eventually granted a subsidy for its production. By 1770, indigo ranked fifth among the major commodities exported from the thirteen colonies. Three decades earlier, only Eliza had been producing it on the mainland.

In South Carolina, rice and indigo overshadowed all other forms of commercial commodity production. Part of the reason for this was that indigo also complemented rice production. Whereas rice was grown in the low-lying, swampy regions, indigo was grown in high, dry areas. Moreover, the harvesting and planting time for these two crops did not conflict. Consequently, different soil types and work seasons for each permitted plantations to more fully utilize their land and their slaves.

By the time of the Revolution, exports per capita from South Carolina were greater than those from any of the other thirteen colonies. Eliza Lucas, more than any other single person, must be credited with this relative standing. In the process of enriching her family and other South Carolina planters, she hastened the settlement in early America.

Eliza Lucas was certainly one of North America's first great entrepreneurs. ☐

---

[1] Many earlier experiments with indigo had been attempted in the southern colonies, but without success.

A Man of Common Sense

Benjamin Franklin (1706-1790)

Statesman, Printer, Scientist, and Writer

"Remember that *time* is money. He that can earn ten shillings a day by his labour, and goes abroad, or sits idle, one half of that day, though he spends but sixpence during his diversion of idleness, ought not to reckon *that* his only expense; he has really spent, or rather thrown away, five shillings besides." Such were the words of Benjamin Franklin in his *Advice to a Young Tradesman*, published in 1748. A better example of keen understanding of the opportunity cost of one's time would be hard to find.

To be sure, his aphorisms must have been colored by his strict Calvinist upbringing. The true Calvinist was a driven man, described by British economist R. H. Tawney as: "Tempered by self-examination, self-discipline, self-control, he is the practical ascetic, whose victories are won not in the cloister, but on the battlefield, in the counting house, and in the market." Calvin himself referred to God as the "great task maker" and looked around for tasks man should undertake. Ben Franklin claimed that he was a freethinker, but the continual exhortations he got from his father—for example, "Seest thou a man diligent in his business. He shall stand before kings"—must have had some effect.

Young Ben was born and raised in Boston. Family funds were insufficient for him to aim at Harvard, so he turned his hand to printing and went to Philadelphia in 1723, then decided he needed to perfect his printing knowledge in London, where he spent two years doing so and living like a bohemian. Within a few years, he began to prosper as a master printer. His simple style and great clarity in writing also started to bring in rewards. *Poor Richard's Almanac*, published annually between 1732 and 1757, was one of Franklin's most profitable enterprises, selling 10,000 copies a year. At the tender age of twenty-three, Franklin wrote his first words on economics: *A Modest Inquiry into the Nature and Necessity of a Paper Currency* (1729). Coincidentally, Franklin was the first one to start printing Pennsylvania's paper currency, and he stayed in this business for quite some time.

Franklin was a crusader and also a good businessman. He introduced printing and newspaper publication to many communities throughout the colonies. He also helped start the present University of Pennsylvania in 1751. Then he was named Deputy Postmaster General of the colonies.

Ben Franklin was also one of the first advertisers in America. When he started his *General Magazine*, he became disappointed that businessmen did not believe that advertising could bring better results. Franklin himself advertised his own Pennsylvania Fire Place. The copy he wrote was persuasive: He criticized ordinary fire places because they caused drafts that made "women . . . get cold in the head, rheums, and defluxions, which fall into their jaws and gums have destroyed early many a fine set of teeth."

During the Revolution, Franklin helped draft the Declaration of Independence, which he signed. He was also the diplomatic agent sent to France for the new republic. Then he was chosen commissioner in 1781 to negotiate peace with Great Britain. Finally, he took part in the Constitutional Convention.

To practical men, especially the officers of savings banks ("a penny saved is a penny earned"), Ben Franklin seemed the summation of good sense and morality. To others, he appeared to be a colorless and materialistic opportunist. But as John Adams once said, his "reputation was more universal than that of Leibniz, Newton, or Voltaire, and he was the first civilized American." □

The Colonial Era

2. The Age of Exploration and Spanish Colonization

Europe in 1492

On the eve of Columbus's voyage to the "New World," the wealth and commerce of Europe centered in the coastal regions of the Mediterranean. The most important hubs of commerce were the northern Italian city-states of Venice, Florence, Genoa, and Milan. For centuries these city-states were the funnels of trade between Asia and Europe. Like magnets, they linked three great overland routes from Asia to the markets of Europe. By their superior know-how, commercial skills and locational advantages, Italian traders were able to dominate most of the world's long-distance trades.

In contrast to the earlier centuries of the Middle Ages, the late sixteenth century was a time of material expansion. This period witnessed the growth of trade, both in volume and in value. In the long-distance trade, the most important items were expensive manufactured products: light cottons and silks from India and China and jewel-toned rugs from Persia. Even delicate items such as glass from Damascus and porcelain from China were carried on the long routes to the markets of Europe. Another extremely important item in the long-distance trade was spices such as cloves, nutmeg, ginger, and cinnamon. These were eagerly sought to redeem European diets from monotony, and pepper was vital as a meat preservative in these warm climates.

Short-distance trade within Europe was burgeoning as well. Here again Italian merchants reigned supreme, especially in the handling and delivery of Mediterranean goods. A brisk traffic in grain, salt, salted fish, and other bulk commodities such as cheese, wine, and oil arose in the late fifteenth century. By this time, the Mediterranean had become a bustling trade arena.

Clearly the types of commodities carried on the long-distance trade were quite different than those on the short-distance trade. The commodities from distant areas were typically expensive relative to their bulk and weight. This characteristic was due to the high land transportation costs. No cheap water route had yet been discovered to Asia. Nevertheless, Europe was reaching out, and seafaring voyages to the more distant areas were taking place as the decades passed. Of the many motives spurring seafaring adventures into the Atlantic, the primary one was to tap the riches of the long-distance trade from Asia. The most vigorous adventurers in this endeavor, however, were not the Mediterranean city-states. Why should they seek out new paths, since they were already comfortable astride the traditional routes?

The Atlantic Pioneer

The great Atlantic pioneer of that time was Portugal. Indeed, it was almost an accident of history that an Italian sailor in the employ of Spain made the most crucial of all the landfalls. By the time Columbus set sail in 1492, Portugal could already claim more than seven decades of Atlantic exploration and discovery. It was Portugal that discovered Madeira and the Canary Islands, settled the Azores, and made the great daring adventures along the western coast of Africa. Since as early as 1415, the chain of Portuguese adventures had been given firm and persistent backing by Prince Henry the Navigator, the younger son of the King of Portugal. For almost four decades, he led Portugal through a vibrant period of exploration, and each new probe into the Atlantic added to the seafaring experience and to the stockpile of knowledge about winds and currents. New trades developed in the islands, and in Africa new discoveries were made as the Portuguese relentlessly pushed further and further southward along the African coast. Finally, in 1488, Bartholomew Dias reached the Cape of Good Hope. He might have sailed on into the Indian Ocean, but a mutinous crew stopped further exploration. It was nine years later that Vasco da Gama reached India by the all-water route. The rate of return on the capital invested in that expedition approached 6000 percent—certainly a lucrative investment. There can be little doubt that in the perspective of that time da Gama, not Columbus, could claim credit for the more celebrated and rewarding discovery. By the turn of the century, Portugal controlled a rich trading realm. The cargoes of spices from Asia; gold, ivory, and slaves from Africa; and sugar from the Atlantic Islands all swelled her coffers.

Of course, the all-water route to the East Indies offered military possibilities as well as economic opportunities. The traditional vessels of the Indian Ocean were no match for the well-armed ships of Portugal. Taking advantage of their military superiority, the Portuguese frequently attempted to block the traditional flows of goods to the Italian city-states in the Mediterranean and to win trading concessions from rulers in the East. It was their ambition to monopolize the trade from the Far East. Despite disruptions, the trade flows along the traditional routes persisted, and Portugal's military excursions in the Far East went in vain. Although

haltingly successful, these ventures proved extremely costly in the long run, and their anticipated goal of complete monopoly was never realized. In the process, Portugal's limited resources were severely strained, and many soldiers, slaves, and ships were lost. Actually it was not until 1600 that the preeminence of Venice in the eastern trade was destroyed. This was accomplished by the Dutch East India company. The coup was made by economic means: by superior efficiency in shipping and in commercial organization. Superior warfare technology and strength also helped, but they played a secondary role.

Shifts in the Center of Wealth

As the realm of Portuguese trade expanded, the relative economic position of the Mediterranean began to slip back. The volume of trade in the Mediterranean continued to increase in absolute terms throughout the sixteenth century, but not in proportion to the size of the Atlantic trade. The centers of commerce and wealth and the balance of power were shifting steadily to the nations bordering the Atlantic Ocean.

In addition to Portugal's colorful seafaring adventures that initiated new southern and far eastern trades, other developments in the North Atlantic were reinforcing the shift of European economic activity. New discoveries of fishing grounds such as that resulting from John Cabot's expedition from England to Newfoundland in 1497 spurred fishing activity in the North. The main force of Northwest European expansion, however, was in the older, established trades. To a disproportionate degree, trade expanded in the cold-zone products—grain, salt, salted fish, woolen cloth, furs, iron, timber, and naval stores. These bulky staple items could withstand the high cost of transportation, since they were transported almost entirely by sea, and unlike the Asian all-water trade, in which vessels were typically full only on the return to Europe, the trade between the Baltic and the northwestern Atlantic regions fully utilized ships in both directions. This had the effect of lowering the average cost of freight and thereby encouraging trade, even in these heavy, bulky products.

As markets widened and trade increased throughout Europe and the rest of the world, greater **regional specialization in production** took place. Areas increasingly specialized in products that they could produce most efficiently and traded these for other goods produced more cheaply elsewhere. In this way, there were **gains from exchange**, and people became better off in terms of material wealth. In addition, the growth of market exchanges during this period encouraged greater **division of labor**. Individual workers slowly but steadily took on specialized tasks, instead of performing all tasks necessary to produce an item from start to finish. As each worker specialized in one or a few steps of the line of production, output per worker increased.

Antwerp

As the volume of trade increased in sixteenth-century Europe, this led to the dazzling preeminence of Antwerp. At this time Antwerp became the **entrepôt** of trade between the traditional city-states of northern Italy, Germany, England, and Holland. Antwerp prospered as the distribution center for German wares of silver, copper, lead, and zinc and for Italian, Flemish, and English manufactures. Both its shipping and commercial services flourished, and, like a magnet, it pulled in merchants from all over Europe.

The rise of Antwerp was critically linked to the rise of the Atlantic trade. Its commercial superiority was determined primarily by its willingness to enforce contracts and reduce risks of exchange and by its advantageous location. Like the Italian city-states of an earlier era, Antwerp now sat astride the great crossroads of trade. New discoveries of copper, lead, zinc, and silver deposits in southern Germany, Hungary, and Poland further stimulated trade throughout western Europe. The expansion of population and growing **urbanization** also increased demand. Moreover, insurance coverage became more common, and market exchanges became less risky. By the late fifteenth century, the Netherlands had become one of the most densely populated and economically advanced areas in Europe.

Antwerp's zenith was reached around 1560, when it contained a population in excess of 100,000. In the West, only Paris, London, and Seville matched or surpassed Antwerp in size. Trading activity was continuous throughout the year, but four lengthy trade fairs annually provided periods of financial settlement.

Wars and the division of the Netherlands between 1572 and 1585 finally ended Antwerp's supremacy. Its decline paralleled the weakening prosperity of central Europe, which had been sapped by peasant wars in religious and dynastic struggles throughout the middle of the century. By this time, the silver mines of central Europe were cutting back production. The value of silver was decreasing. Now, for the first time, the treasures of America became a truly critical factor in shaping the economic landscape of Europe. The influx of American silver undercut silver production in Europe. The flows of Spanish-American treasure made Cadiz the attractive new entrepôt. In addition, it provided the sinews of war and whetted the Spanish crown's appetite for empire.

The voyages of discovery, together with the swelling tides of commerce, were now exerting heavy pressure on the balance of power in Europe. By the late sixteenth century, dramatic shifts had already occurred. The minor short-run effects of this discovery were giving way to highly significant long-run effects. Although contemporary Europeans had lightly dismissed Christopher Columbus' discovery, later observers were beginning to understand what we know so well: Columbus had placed a bounty of riches at the feet of Spain. He had given Spain an empire that won the envy of Europe.

Spanish Colonization

The first Europeans to secure a foothold in the New World were the Spanish. They colonized primarily for the dual purpose of extracting wealth and christianizing the native Indians. To accomplish this double objective, they introduced a practice entitled **encomienda** (commendation), which had been developed earlier in the Canary Islands shortly after the Spanish took over there. To "civilize" the native population and to convert the Indians to Christianity, each populated community was placed under the "protection and authority" of a Spanish overseer. In return for the overseer's "services" and direction, the villagers had to pay tribute in the form of labor services. Of course, the day-to-day direction of *encomienda* rested with the overseers. They were little influenced in any practical way by the remote authority of the Spanish Crown or the Catholic Church. Therefore, in practice, many abused the system for personal gain. They forced people to give many hours of labor in slave- or prison-gang fashion.

The first several decades of Spanish colonization were concentrated in the islands of the Caribbean. It was there that *encomienda* was the most damaging, with effects even more harsh than slavery. Because the overseers had no rights of ownership in the natives, they had little incentive to care for them properly. Nevertheless, they had "legal claim" to their labor services and this gave ample incentive to work them relentlessly. The combination of poor care, bad nutrition, overwork, and the spread of European diseases (mainly smallpox, typhus, and measles) virtually wiped out the islands' populations. For instance, within several decades the native population of Española, which today forms the nations of Haiti and the Dominican Republic, fell from approximately 300,000 to several hundred. The populations of Cuba and Puerto Rico suffered similar declines, and other areas, such as the Bahamas and some of the leeward islands that were not settled, had their populations stripped to work the mines of Puerto Rico. The excesses of this system on the islands were gradually curbed on the mainland, and *encomienda* was finally outlawed in 1549. Nevertheless, harsh treatment and disease continued to take their toll. Within two decades of Cortez's conquest of Mexico in 1518–1519, the preconquest population of twenty-five million there had been halved. It

has been estimated that in 1500 the population of Spanish America approximately matched that of western Europe. By 1600, the relative numbers were merely one-tenth of Europe's. The forced exchange of Christianity for bullion and treasure was costly for the natives of Spanish America.

The dramatic decline of the native population was offset only to a minor degree by Spanish settlers. By 1650 there were about one-half million residents who were white or predominantly white. Most of these were Spanish born males of working age, since few women and children were attracted to the New World. Although black slaves had begun to be imported as early as 1503, it was not until the seventeenth century that large numbers arrived in the New World. By the mid-seventeenth century, approximately one-half million black slaves from Africa were working the sugar islands of the Caribbean. In addition, there were another one-half million people of mixed blood. However, in all of Mexico and the central regions of Peru and Bolivia, there now remained only two million pure-blooded Indians.

New Crops

Although the great treasure flows and the striking demographic shifts were the most dramatic changes brought by the Spanish, important cultural and organizational changes also affected the daily lives of people in the Americas. Imported European techniques, commodities, and animals altered economic activity in America. Despite Spanish attention to the mining of precious metals, the basic structure of the economy remained agrarian. This sector was sharply influenced by new European crops, including wheat, barley, rye, sugar, onions, cabbage, peas, apples, and peaches. Having only the llama, the dog, and the turkey as original livestock, the natives discovered that horses, cattle, and oxen afforded possibilities for heavy plowing and better land transportation. In addition, these European livestock were accompanied by hogs, chickens, and sheep, which led to herding activities and improved diets. Of course, European advances in metallurgy and the use of guns and powder had significant effects as well.

In return, a variety of new crops was also introduced to the Europeans. These included tobacco, Indian corn, or maize, beans, peanuts, white potatoes, squash, pumpkins, tomatoes, chocolate, vanilla, and avocados. But none of these items became commercially vital. The first cash crop of any significance in the trans-Atlantic trade did not develop until almost a century after Columbus. That crop was sugar, produced in the depopulated islands of the Caribbean. The new labor supply used to produce sugar in these islands was imported. By the mid-seventeenth century, the islands were crowded with African slaves working Spanish-run sugar plantations.

The character of Spanish settlement was altered to a degree by this new cultivation. The extraction of mineral treasure by forced labor had been on a "take and go" basis. The sugar plantations, however, required permanent settlement. Forced labor was still used, but now the roots of Spanish occupation sank deeper and became more lasting. As the plantations prospered, both Spanish immigrants and African slaves poured in, and implanted agrarian capitalism. In this way, the commercial link between the New and the Old World was solidly forged.

Treasure

One of the most important developments, of course, stemmed from the treasure flowing from America. Paralleling these Spanish treasure flows was a tremendous rise in prices in Europe. In terms of gold and silver, it was a price inflation without parallel in history. Some have argued that this inflation was the critical factor in the rise of commercial capitalism. Such an assertion deserves careful scrutiny, as we give it in Issue II. □

Definitions of New Terms

Regional specialization in production: Regional specialization in production results from the opportunity to trade and from different conditions for production among areas. Each region will tend to produce and trade more of the items they can produce at lowest cost (relative to other regions).

Gains from exchange: Gains from exchange are produced when the personal value or satisfaction of the goods received exceed the personal value or satisfaction of the goods (or money) given in exchange. Note that in most voluntary exchanges both parties to the exchange gain; that is, they "feel" better off from the trade.

Division of labor: In division of labor, individual workers take on specialized tasks instead of attempting to do everything necessary to produce a product or service.

Entrepôt: An entrepôt is a main center for trade and commercial activity, such as New York today, or Antwerp in the sixteenth century.

Urbanization: When a larger fraction of the total population lives in towns and cities (urban centers), urbanization is said to exist.

Encomienda: *Encomienda* is an arrangement whereby Spanish overseers extracted labor services from the native population. It was similar but not identical to slavery.

CAPITAL FLOWS

Spanish colonization involved numerous special features. Perhaps none was so unique as that involving the direction and magnitude of capital flows. Ordinarily, one might suspect that the taking of a new frontier would require substantial subsidization from the older, established regions and commercial centers. To be sure, in the first years of Spanish conquest Spanish nobles and merchants did supply financial support for ships and stores. By 1506, however, several Spanish colonists had accumulated sizable fortunes from gold mines worked on the islands of Española. These in part financed the exploration and settlement of Cuba, Jamaica, and Puerto Rico. In turn, the profits from investments in Cuba supported a series of mainland expeditions that after 1516 led to the conquest of Mexico by Cortez. Further conquests were financed by wealth extracted from Mexico. In this stepwise fashion, fortunes acquired in the Americas led to further expansion and widened the Spanish hold on the new frontier. Consequently, it was only in the first decade or two after Columbus' discovery that Spain made any significant net investment in America. By the mid-sixteenth century, investments were steadily and sizably proceeding in the opposite direction.

These capital flows had profound repercussions in Europe. The flow of gold and silver from America to Europe is illustrated in Figure II–1. The lion's share of these Spanish imports was in silver and came after 1516. Compared to the supply of money at the beginning of the sixteenth century, these imports approximately tripled the total supply of money in Europe.

Besides raising Spain to a position of military dominance, the influx of treasure led to higher and higher prices throughout Europe. Inflation became the order of the day. Spanish prices swept upward, and, in 1600, were 340 percent above their level in 1500. Similarly, England experienced a rise of almost 260 percent over the century, and France experienced one of 220 percent.

The Hamilton Thesis

The phenomenal impact of American treasure on European prices, commerce, and growth has been analyzed in a pioneering study by Earl J. Hamilton. Hamilton summarized his conclusions as follows:

> It is difficult . . . to see how anything else could have been more important than the great lag of wages behind prices in certain economically advanced countries during the price revolution. Capitalism required *capital*, and it would not be easy to imagine a more powerful instrument for provid-

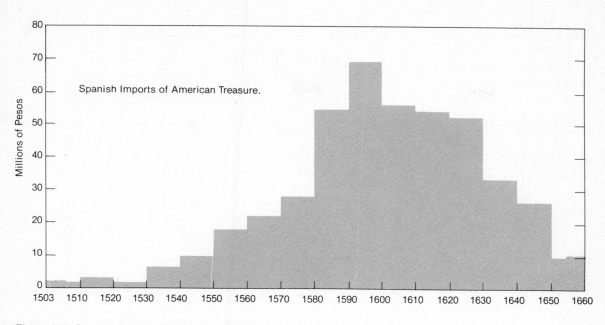

Figure II-1. Spanish Imports of American Treasure.

Source: Earl J. Hamilton, *American Treasure and the Price Revolution in Spain, 1501-1650* (Cambridge, Mass.: Harvard University Press, 1934).

ing it than forced saving through a highly favorable price-wage ratio. The high rates of profit when prices were rising and wages, the chief cost, were lagging gave a strong inducement to invest savings in productive enterprise. Rising prices penalized delay in investment and by lowering the effective rate of interest encouraged borrowing for investment in anticipation of earnings. In short, rising prices and lagging wages provided capital and gave strong incentives to use it capitalistically. Other things anywhere near equal, capitalism could hardly have failed to flourish.[1]

[1] Earl J. Hamilton, "Prices as a Factor in Business Growth: Prices and Progress," *The Journal of Economic History*, 69, 2 (Fall 1952): 338–339.

In short, Hamilton argues that the influx of treasure drove up both prices and wages, but prices more rapidly. As **real wages** declined, income and wealth was distributed increasingly to the favor of merchants and capitalists. Since these classes supposedly had unusually strong inclinations to save and invest, this led to higher rates of capital formation and ultimately to economic growth throughout Europe.

A great deal of the evidence strongly supports Hamilton's thesis. The large increase in the money supply and the tremendous rise in prices are

certainly without doubt. As shown in Figure II-2, real wages in Spain, England, and France fell dramatically over the course of the sixteenth century. Tables II-1 and II-2 show the same downward spiral in real wages for a longer period. On closer examination of Tables II-1 and II-2, however, we see that the upward march of prices relative to wages did not favor industrial or manufactured goods. Hamilton's analysis did not go far enough and was left at too aggregate a level. As we can see from the separated indexes in Tables II-1 and II-2, the main cause of the general price index rising was the soaring prices of food and items related to agriculture. The prices of finished goods rose less than the prices of raw materials. Consequently, the redistribution of wealth was not so much from workers to capitalists as from the nonagricultural to the agricultural sectors.

In light of the high rates of population growth, it is not surprising to observe a redistribution of income between these sectors. Increasingly, land became relatively more scarce in Europe: Labor-land ratios increased with the rise of population. In all likelihood, average output per agricultural worker declined, as output from additional workers fell to very low levels. Large increases in the supply of labor tended to hold wages down, while the swelling population exerted upward pressures on prices for agricultural goods. Meanwhile rents on land soared higher and higher as agricultural prices rose. As a result, it was landowners, not merchants or industrial capitalists, who gained from the relative price movements of the period.

It is important here to dis-

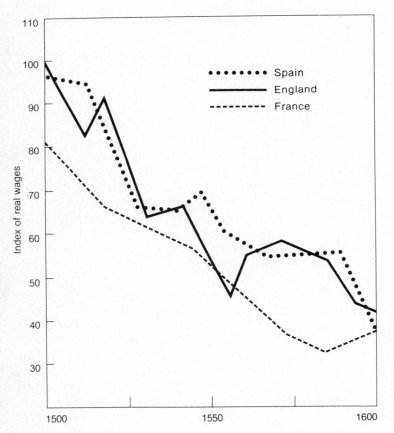

Figure II-2. Indexes of Real Wages in Sixteenth Century England, Spain, and France.

Source: E. H. Phelps-Brown and Sheila V. Hopkins, "Builders' Wage-Rates and Population: Some Further Evidence," *Economics* 2b, no. 101, pp. 18-38.

The Colonial Era

Table II—1. Indexes of Price and Wage Trends in England, 1500—1702 [(1451—1500) = 100].

	1521—1530	1551—1560	1583—1592	1613—1622	1643—1652	1673—1682	1693—1702
Total Prices	113	132	198	257	331	348	339
Unprocessed Agricultural Products	132	179	262	402	478	466	518
Assorted Industrial Products	110	116	150	176	217	200	239
Wood and Wood Products	87	119	185	259	300	420	395
Imported Food Products	151	119	146	124	151	— —	163
Wages	93	88	125	134	175	205	233

Source: David Felix, "Profit Inflation and Industrial Growth: The Historic Record and Contemporary Analogies," *Quarterly Journal of Economics*, 70 (August 1956): 446.

tinguish between *relative* and *absolute* price changes. The influx of treasure and the consequent increase in the money supply did spur inflation. This had the tendency to push *all* prices higher, over time. But general inflation—a rise in average prices—tells us little about changes in relative prices. Some prices moved up faster than others, and for these differential movements we need to look at the conditions of supply and demand for various goods and productive resources.

The general forces of inflation fail to explain differences in relative price movement, but relative price changes lie at the heart of Hamilton's thesis.

The influx of American treasure did not by itself cause a redistribution of income among economic classes or sectors that led to economic development. It did, however, enrich Spain relative to other nations, at least temporarily. But there is little indication that this advantage raised the productivity or

soundness of the Spanish economy. The flood of wealth may even have encouraged Spain to undertake the many ill-fated military ventures that eventually led to its decline. With the exhaustion of American mines around 1650, Spain's vital resource influx dried up, and Spain quickly slipped to a second-rate power in the league of nations. No empire of similar dominance has ever undergone such a rapid rise and fall. No other has rested on such a temporary base. □

Table II—2. Indexes of Price and Wage Trends in France, 1500—1700 [(1451—1500) = 100].

	1501—1525	1526—1550	1551—1575	1576—1600	1601—1625	1626—1650	1651—1675	1676—1700
Total Prices	113	136	174	248	189	243	227	229
Selected Agricultural Products	136	163	250	429	259	402	345	315
Assorted Manufactures	96	130	122	144	129	143	133	161
Wages	92	104	103	113	113	127	127	125

Source: David Felix, "Profit Inflation and Industrial Growth: The Historic Record and Contemporary Analogies," *Quarterly Journal of Economics*, 70 (August 1956): 446.

Definition of New Term

Real wages: Real wages consist of money wages and payments after corrections are made for changes in the purchasing power of money.

3. Opening Up North America

The First British Colonies

Compared to other nation-states, England was slow to colonize. By the time the British established their first settlements on the mainland, the Dutch were already in North America and in the East and West Indies, the Spanish had been in North and South America for over a century, and the French were already in Canada and the West Indies. The first English attempts at colonization were clear-cut failures. Sir Humphrey Gilbert and Sir Walter Raleigh failed dismally in their attempts in the 1580s to establish bases in Newfoundland and the Carolinas. As noted in Chapter One, Raleigh's outpost in Roanoke, North Carolina, was designed to harass Spanish treasure ships, but, after a necessary departure for supplies, Raleigh's captain returned to find no one or no records whatsoever. Roanoke is therefore referred to as the "lost colony."

As also mentioned in Chapter One, it was not until 1607 that the Virginia Company of London succeeded in establishing the first permanent colony at Jamestown, Virginia. By 1620, the Plymouth Company had established the first New England colony, and in 1630 the Massachusetts Bay Company established a second outpost in New England. Then followed Rhode Island, Connecticut, New Hampshire, and the rest. It was not until 1732 that the last of the thirteen colonies, Georgia, was established.

Mercantilism and the Quest for Empire

Colonization was pursued for the purpose of strengthening the parent nation-states, and it greatly affected the balance of power among the nation-states. As we observed with Spain and as we know today, the basis of power is economic strength. At the time of British colonization in North America, the policies of mercantilism were the order of the day.

Mercantilist policies put into practice the idea that the greater the wealth that a nation had, the more power it had. Wealth and precious metals were viewed as one, and, in order to increase the inflow of precious bullion, governments encouraged exports and discouraged imports. When exports exceeded imports in value terms (a "favorable balance of trade"), the difference was paid in gold or silver (specie). Accordingly, government intervention took the forms of taxing goods coming into a nation, of expanding colonial territory, and of providing incentives to encourage the sale abroad of domestically produced goods. In other words, there was an attempt to force exports from the mother country to be greater than imports. However, mercantilist precepts ignored a common principle: Both parties gain from voluntary trade, whether that trade be between individuals, states, or nations. As an afterthought, we might say that the goal that government intervention should have had was the increase in both exports and imports—a balanced increase in all trade with all nations. But in the hostile world of that era, it was best to develop and trade with one's own colonies. Trade with other nation-states risked the possibility of being cut off from needed goods by war (which was frequent) or by an adverse change in policy.

Differences in Colonization Techniques

Whereas Spain was able to exploit an existing population, using the infamous *encomienda* system, the British (and others) were unable to force the elusive North American natives into slavery. Nor were there any get-rich-quick opportunities, despite hopes to the contrary. Only permanent settlement and commercial production (for export) could wring wealth from this region.

Even though some of the original English colonies were started with government help, most of them were private ventures in which the English Crown did not directly participate. The lure of profits induced joint stock companies, such as the Virginia Company and the Plymouth Company, to raise money to finance these colonies. The stockholders felt they were entitled to a return on their investment. As it turned out, however, there were dismal financial failures. For instance, capital costs for Jamestown before 1624 exceeded $200,000, but none of this principal or any interest was ever repaid. Several colonies, such as Maryland, founded by Lord Baltimore, and Pennsyvania, founded by William Penn, were started as individual proprietorships. They, too, were unable to turn a profit. They tried to secure revenues from the settlers by annual payments, called quit rents, but these generally proved futile to collect.

It may seem incongruous that the original profit-seeking entrepreneurs who set up colonies in the New World were unable to profit or generate large rewards. After all, wasn't the New World filled with untold natural riches? Weren't there abundant lands full of timber and rich soil? Yes, indeed—but it takes more than one factor of production to yield a product.

The Problem of Scarcity

Land was abundant, but labor was scarce. So was capital. Originally there were few tools, very little equipment (such as those needed to clear land), and almost no manufacturing implements. Normally, when land is abundant relative to labor and capital, as in early America, land is relatively low-priced. Labor and capital were relatively scarce and, hence, relatively high priced. The colonists originally could do little with the raw land except work some of the already-cleared areas that the Indians had abandoned. Later, as tools, horses, and other livestock were imported, and better crop-planting methods were developed, more land was tilled. But even then there was a limit to output because that depended primarily on the number of hands available.

Ways to Get Workers

There was always a problem of obtaining inexpensive labor, and several methods were used to induce more people to come to the New World. By peopling North America, England was assured strong colonies, a greater empire, and more power. Basically England employed four methods to attract laborers to the New World.

Head Rights. Many, although not all, of the British colonies lured workers by offering "head rights" of land ownership. Under the head right system, approximately fifty acres were promised to each person who paid his own way to the colonies; an additional fifty acres was due one who paid the way for others. But, because the costs of transport were exorbitantly high, relatively few individuals could afford the expense.

Land Grants. Whole groups of settlers could obtain land grants for organizing their own communities. Generally, this happened when a religious minority wanted to escape persecution in Europe. The Pilgrims are a good example.

Indentured Servants. These were servants who in exchange for passage to America agreed to work for periods ranging between four and seven years. They were given the right to select their destination in America, and at the end of their work period these volunteers of bondage were sometimes given some land, a little money, and a few farm implements to start out on their own. Sometimes prisoners were sent to America as indentured servants. Generally, these prisoners were of a special type: They came from debtors' prison and were not therefore criminals, as we define criminals today.

Migration. Although migration was a major source of labor in the earlier years, the largest numbers crossed the Atlantic in the eighteenth century. Nearly 100,000 Germans came between 1710 and 1770, most of them to Pennsylvania, and between 100,000 and 125,000 Irish and Scots also arrived, with the Scots tending to prefer the South. Many English came as well, but the largest English migration took place in the seventeenth century. The total of 250,000 to 300,000 whites who came between 1700 and 1775 contributed between 15 to 20 percent to the total increase of the white population. Consequently, the primary source of the white population's increase, from as early as the mid-seventeenth century, was due to natural factors. Compared to Europe, the costs of fuel, food, and housing were low, which encouraged earlier marriages and larger families. In addition, mortality rates were lower in North America, especially infant mortality. Once past infanthood, a male could expect to live to sixty, on an average. Because of the high incidence of death from childbirth, colonial women averaged only forty years of life.

Slavery. Last, but not least, there was slavery, and slaves were first introduced to North America by Dutch traders in 1619. Eventually slaves were imported in British and American ships. Of course, slavery expanded most in the relatively warm climate of the South, where the plantation system grew up. Although just beginning on the mainland colonies, elsewhere in the seventeenth century slavery was expanding at a rapid rate, especially in the islands of the Caribbean.

Slavery was actually unimportant in North America for almost the first century of settlement. Before 1730, for example, there were fewer than 100,000 slaves in the mainland colonies. But by the Revolution that figure had grown to over 450,000. The slave trade during this time was booming, and the total number of incoming blacks matched that of whites. Accordingly, the black population, which was around 4 percent of the total in 1700, grew to more than 20 percent by the time of the American Revolution. The import of slaves was a more important source of relative increase in the black population, but by 1700 the natural rate of increase was more important than slave imports in adding to the total number of blacks in North America.

At the end of the colonial period, the concentration of blacks in the population varied widely among the colonies. In the northern colonies, they averaged less than 5 percent of the population, but in the rich fields of South Carolina their proportion was 70 percent, and it was 47 percent in Virginia, and 33 percent in Maryland. In contrast, the proportion of blacks in the British and French sugar islands of the Caribbean approached 90 percent.

What to Produce and Where?

At first, of course, there was little question of how the colonists should spend their working time. It was either produce or die. Later on, however, it was no longer a question of just surviving but of rising above the subsistence level. Historically, this has been accomplished by finding one's *comparative advantage*. It was obvious in most of the colonies, at least at first, that their comparative advantage lay mainly in agricultural production. And so almost all of the population was engaged in this endeavor. The colonists were not self-sufficient, however. They may have been able to produce the agricultural products they wanted, but there were certain manufactured goods that they could obtain only by trade with other countries.

Of course, the most obvious country to trade with was England. The colonists spoke the English language, were familiar with their customs and the system of prices, and could do business in a relatively easy manner. In other words, the *transactions or business costs* involved in trading with England were generally less than those with other countries.[1] As the English trades and other overseas trades developed, specialization in production in the various colonies became more and more apparent.

The South

The South had a relatively large population. By 1770, there were over 1.4 million southern colonists as opposed to nearly 600 thousand in New England and a similar number in the middle colonies.

The South developed exports that were complementary to English production. These included tobacco, indigo, rice, and other items that were not produced in England. By 1770, over one-half of the exports of the colonies were accounted for by southern production. In fact, even thereafter, trade with England was dominated by southern staples.

Tobacco. Tobacco use in England spread slowly. It was first introduced by traveling Spaniards, but King James I dubbed the habit "a vile and stinking custom." Nevertheless, Sir Walter Raleigh and others popularized it, and when it was found that good-quality tobacco could be grown in Maryland and in Virginia more cheaply than in most other parts of the world, the English were delighted. Even the English Crown was glad to be free of Spanish tobacco imports—so happy, in fact, that England banned its production at home and gave the Chesapeake Bay area monopoly rights to tobacco production in the empire.

It is easily understood why slavery and the plantation system developed once it was found that tobacco could be grown in the warm southern climates. Tobacco cultivation required only very crude implements and much unskilled labor. If the old land lost its fertility, there was much new land available. The plantation system, with its large numbers of slaves, was well suited for such production. Here the task system could be used, and supervision over each slave's "piecework" was relatively easy.

Developments in tobacco production showed that mercantilism was not only pervasive among the great nation-states of that time, it also was practiced by the southern colonies themselves. A free enterprise environment sometimes was thought to hinder the wealth of the southern colonists. For example, by community effort, one-half of the Virginia tobacco crop was burned in order to maintain prices in 1639, and in 1733 the growing of tobacco was again restricted.

Actually, the burning and restricting of tobacco was not as foolish as it may sound. Planters believed that the demand for tobacco, like that of many agricultural products today, was relatively **price inelastic**; that is, the quantity purchased is relatively unresponsive to price changes. Therefore, a rise in the price of tobacco would not lead to a drastic reduction in the quantity demanded. Conversely, a fall in the price would not lead to a drastic increase. Given this type of demand situation, a bumper crop of tobacco could only be sold if the southern colonists were willing to accept an extremely large decrease in the price. To avoid this in 1639, planters burned portions of their tobacco crop. As we shall see later, such "burnings" have been periodic occurrences in our history.

Rice. Rice became a major export crop of South Carolina by 1700. It was grown in low-lying fields and sometimes in swamplands. These could be irrigated with some control by allowing tidewater rivers to flood them. Like tobacco, it required a warm climate and considerable unskilled labor. Of all the mainland colonial products, it was the most conducive to a plantation system.

---

[1] A very close, and sometimes superior, competitor in certain trades was Holland. As discussed later, the English legislated trade controls to counter this competition.

The Colonial Era

Indigo. Indigo, another major crop of South Carolina, was first introduced on the mainland in 1743 by Eliza Lucas, one of America's first female entrepreneurs. She had imported the plants from the Caribbean. Indigo was useful to the British as a dye for the textile industries. Because of their influence in Parliament, the British paid a special subsidy, or bounty, to indigo producers. In other words, any colonist who produced indigo was assured a specific subsidy payment from the British in addition to whatever the crop fetched in sale on the open market in Britain.

Indigo proved to be a useful and convenient crop to grow because it was complementary to rice in its use of labor services; that is, the peak seasonal periods, when most of the unskilled workers were needed in the indigo fields, were different from the peak seasonal periods when the workers were engaged in the rice fields.

Naval Stores. The southern colonies, and other colonies as well, produced significant amounts of accessories and materials for ships, or *naval stores*, as they were called. These were items such as pitch, tar, and turpentine, which were true forest derivatives.

The Middle Colonies

The middle colonies comprised the fertile agricultural areas of Pennsylvania, Delaware, New York, and New Jersey. Here livestock and grain could be more cheaply produced than in New England or the South. That is, the middle colonies' comparative advantage lay in the production of various grains and livestock. There was much less direct trade with England from these colonies, because their comparative advantage was essentially the same as that of the English, and England also produced these goods relatively cheaply. The middle colonies, in fact, tended to import more than they exported to England. What they did to balance their trade deficit was to trade with southern Europe, the West Indies, and other colonies. Nevertheless, often this was not enough, and English merchants commonly granted short term loans (of a revolving type) to finance trade.

New England

The New England area consisted mainly of very small farms that produced only for local town markets. The comparative advantage of the New England colonists lay in their proximity to ocean waters, which were filled with fish, and in their vast forest lands. Hence, they exported ship timbers, especially pine for ship masts, and whale oil and codfish. Later on, the New England colonists became extremely efficient shipbuilders, and many New Englanders became world traders and sailors directly in competition with the mother country. In fact, their most important economic activity was providing shipping services, which they provided throughout the Atlantic, the Caribbean, and other seas.

Technology

The colonial era was one of painstakingly slow progress in technology. Adapting crops to the best-suited soils (and climates) raised output per acre and per worker in agriculture and capital accumulation and other learning-by-doing efforts did as well. But compared to later times, there was little advance in knowledge, and, especially within agriculture, the mainstay of colonial economic activity, there were no apparent technological improvements. The types of tools used, the care of animals, and the methods of agricultural production in general showed only minimal signs of change.

This was typical of other sectors as well. Few breakthroughs in knowledge led to advances in output relative to inputs. Yet output did increase relative to inputs as market participation increased, as business and economic organization improved, and as risks declined. For instance, cost reductions in shipping led to a fall in freight rates by almost one-half between 1675 and 1775. Most of this decline was due to the elimination of piracy and because of shorter port times for ships. As piracy was eliminated, dual-purpose defense and cargo carrying vessels were gradually converted to simple all cargo-carrying vessels. They used simpler rigs and eliminated armaments and men to "man the guns." And once the British Navy had ousted most of the pirates from the western Atlantic, insurance rates tumbled. In addition, growth in the volume of trade led to centralized warehousing of goods, which reduced long and costly delays in ports. This saved on crew costs and reduced underutilization of capital.

Vessel characteristics similar to those of the Dutch flute (first produced in 1595) diffused and spread once piracy was eliminated. This obstacle to **technical diffusion** was eliminated near the turn of the eighteenth century. Rapid changes in shipping, such as those just mentioned, soon followed, but **technological change**, in the sense of advances in knowledge, did not take place. Rather, change was the result of applying known techniques to new and now favorable circumstances. In general, this was characteristic of many of the improvements of the colonial era.

Overseas Trade

From the very beginning, the colonists depended on overseas trade. Even by the late colonial period, overseas trade comprised between 15 and 20 percent of American incomes. This figure was probably even higher during the early colonial period.

Throughout the colonial era, the colonies were not allowed to trade unimpeded in the world market, and the intensification of British controls on colonial trade finally spurred the outbreak of the Revolution.

Restricting the Colonies

The earliest general restrictions on colonial activity dated back to 1660 with the passage of the Navigation Acts. These acts were passed in response to the Dutch supremacy in shipping and trade. As mentioned earlier, in 1595 the Dutch developed a commercial sailing boat called the *flute*, which was

as good as any trading ship to be developed for centuries. To oust the highly efficient Dutch from British trades, the Navigation Acts imposed the stipulation that only English ships (including ships of its colonies) could be used for trade within the British Empire. Since the colonies were part of this empire, the laws applied to them also.[2]

In addition, other acts led to the control of trade flows, but the effects of these controls are left to the following Issue, which discusses whether or not the colonists were being exploited by the British Crown.

The period from 1763 onward was a period of intensification of British restrictions, repeated crises, and ultimately, revolt. After the Seven Years War (1756–1763) between the English and the French, a series of edicts on the political and economic freedom of the colonists were handed down by the British Crown. For example, the Proclamation of 1763 declared that no colonial settlement was allowed west of the Appalachians. In order to raise money in the colonies to pay for the wars that Britain had waged to a significant degree on their behalf, the Sugar Act of 1764 assessed a tax of three pence per gallon on molasses.[3] However, much opposition arose in the colonies, and very little of this duty was ever collected. The colonists were unsympathetic to the plight of the British treasury.

Still attempting to obtain money from the colonies, the English promulgated the Stamp Act of 1765, providing for internal taxation—or, as the Stamp Act Congress in 1765 called it, "Taxation without representation." As a result of a boycott in the colonies, the British backed down and William

---

[2] Note that aspects of this Navigation Act were to be repeated years later, with the passage of the Jones Act in the United States, which is in effect today and which requires that shipping among American ports must be done in American flag carriers. For results of that act, note how expensive food and manufactured goods are today in Hawaii. The shipping costs are much higher than they would be without the Jones Act.

The Sugar Act replaced the earlier "Molasses Act" of 1733, which had higher duties but was widely evaded and seldom enforced. This authoritative neglect set an important precedent in the relations between England and America.

The Colonial Era

Pitt made his famous appeal to the Parliament to repeal the Stamp Act and also to modify the Sugar Act. It is important to note that the Stamp Act crisis generated a feeling of unity within the colonies, because the Act applied uniformly to all of them. When the Townsend Acts were passed in 1767, imposing duties on glass and lead in paint, and on other items, the colonists again followed with a boycott of English commodities. The results were impressive. By 1769, purchases of British goods were reduced by about 50 percent. This caused the British to back down again and to retreat into an uneasy truce that lasted until the Boston Tea Party of 1773. This escapade was in response to Parliament's attempt to aid the British East India Company, which was facing financial difficulties. Parliament had given the company the exclusive rights to the sale of tea in the colonies and allowed tea to be directly shipped from the East—previously it had to be brought to England first and then reexported. The result was a fall in the price of tea (and presumably happier customers in the colonies), but this hurt the traditional handlers of tea in the colonies and also smugglers.

Many highly vocal colonists loudly responded that they did not want a British monopoly on the sales of that product, and several showed their wrath by dumping a shipload of tea into Boston harbor.

Essentially, the period of negotiation ended in 1773. The colonists first found out that they were a fairly unified group after the Stamp Act was countered by the Stamp Act Congress. They also found strength in their ability to boycott British goods. The colonists demanded and eventually won their sovereignty. The "shot heard 'round the world" on April 19, 1775, finally led to political independence. A question remains, however, regarding their economic situation. Were the mercantilist restrictions placed on the colonies by the British Crown actually detrimental to their economic health? □

Definitions of New Terms

Price inelastic: A characteristic of demand in which a price rise leads to a less than proportionate decrease in quantity demanded.

Technical diffusion: Technical diffusion is the spread of new or known techniques from one firm to another or from one use to another.

Technical change: Technical change is an advance in knowledge that permits more output to be produced with an unchanged amount of inputs.

MERCANTILIST RESTRICTIONS

The Navigation Acts

In the seventeenth century, the Netherlands was the supreme maritime nation. By around the turn of the eighteenth century, the English had surpassed the Dutch on the high seas. How was this accomplished?

A series of ocean battles was important, but a primary factor was the English Navigation Acts. These were devised to exclude the highly efficient Dutch shippers from carrying and handling trade within the British Empire.

The Navigation Act of 1661 was directed at shipping and restricted all British Empire trade to British (including colonial) ships. A foreign ship could land goods in England, but only from its own country, not from its own colonies or elsewhere. A British ship was one built, owned, and at least three-quarters crewed by British (including colonial) citizens.

Other acts in 1660 and 1663 regulated the movement of many goods. Imports into the colonies from continental Europe were required to pass through England first. Certain items, such as salt and wine from Spain, were made exceptions and could be shipped directly. Most of the vast array of colonial imports from the continent, however, had to be landed in England and then reloaded before heading on to America. In addition, key colonial products were to be shipped only to England: at first, tobacco, sugar, and indigo. Others were later added to the list, mainly naval stores such as pitch, tar, turpentine, and masts and yards. These were called **enumerated articles** and could be reexported to the continent only after landing in England. Of course, this procedure made transportation and other distribution costs much higher.

Some of the mercantilist controls encouraged production of certain "essential" items. Other laws actually prohibited production. Indigo and some of the naval stores were subsidized by a per unit bounty. Various other manufactures were outlawed. For instance, the production of finished woolens outside of England was outlawed in 1699. Later, in 1732, imports of fur hats (mainly beaver) from the colonies, were forbidden, as was finished iron, in 1750.

The Economics of British Controls

While a simple tabulation of the mercantilist restrictions on colonial trade might lead one to conclude that the colonists were being exploited, this assumption is not necessarily correct. All aspects of the problem must be considered. The colonists, of course, generally only saw the negative side of British rule. As dispassionate observers, however, we should be able to weigh not only the costs that were incurred because of English rule, but also the benefits. Moreover, we cannot reflect only on what actually happened. For a valid analysis, we have to compare what actually happened with what realistically *could* have happened. Would the colonists have been better off if they had been independent at an earlier date? Otherwise stated, would the levels of material well-being in the colonies have been higher if independence had been secured at an earlier date? To address this question, we must first assess the costs of the restrictions and then consider the benefits of membership in the British Empire.

Assessing the Effects of British Controls

Manufacturing Restrictions

The least consequential of the mercantilist restrictions were those on manufactures. It is hardly surprising to find that these were imposed by Parliament in response to pleas from various vested interest groups at home (the English woolen, hat, and iron manufacturers). They wanted to stop "undesirable" competition elsewhere in the British Empire. Actually, the Woolen Act was aimed pri-

marily at Ireland, but it addressed the colonies as well. American colonists were allowed to produce homespun woolens (bedding and garments), and they imported fine linens and fabrics. This was quite satisfactory to the colonists and would have resulted with or without the law. The English and other Europeans could produce these items more cheaply, so for the colonists the law was superfluous.

The restriction on fur hat production in the colonies hurt New York hatters, but this was a small group. Overall, it was inconsequential.

Interestingly enough, the restrictions on the production of finished iron were also harmless, because the law was ignored with impunity. Twenty-five "illegal" iron mills were established between 1750 and 1775 in Pennsylvania and Delaware alone, despite the ease of detection. Given the overwhelming comparative disadvantage of the colonies in most types of manufactures, these restrictions were not a significant hardship. At most, they were a minor nuisance. There is little case for inferring exploitation from these restrictions.

Shipping

The controls on shipping had mixed effects in the col-

onies. Tobacco planters and other producers lost out after 1660, as cheap Dutch shipping was no longer available. But colonial shippers gained, as did colonial shipbuilders. Shipping became a major commercial enterprise in New England and the middle colonies, and shipbuilding developed into the most important colonial manufacturing activity. By 1775, one-third of the British merchant marine had been built in the colonies. Considering both those who were hurt and those who gained, it is likely that the colonists benefited, on the average, from the controls on shipping. After independence, when American shipping was treated as foreign by the British, its exclusion from British Empire trade had catastrophic consequences. And American shipbuilders were severely hurt, too, because American-built ships were then classified as foreign.

Trade

The most costly features of the Navigation Acts to the colonists were those influencing the movement of goods. By requiring colonial imports and enumerated articles to pass first through the mother country, English ports were made more active. Of course, this was precisely the purpose of the Acts, and their stimulus made the English ports entrepôts of trade. But they also raised the costs of distribution, and this hit at the pocketbooks of the colonists, both coming and going.

The procedure used to estimate these burdens is a tedious business. Essentially, the problem is to figure out how prices and quantities would have changed on goods forcibly routed through England if direct free movement had been allowed. If direct shipment to the continent had been permitted, the prices received and quantities sold of colonial exports would have been higher. Similarly, if goods had come in directly, colonial imports from the continent would have cost less and been more plentiful.

Of course, after the Revolution direct shipment was allowed, and price adjustments resulting from this change have been studied by a number of scholars, to assess the likely magnitudes of these burdens.[1] These range from 1 to 3 percent of colonial income; that is, colonists averaged less income by a couple of percentage points because of the trade restrictions.

The Benefits of Being a Colony

We have yet to enumerate the possible benefits that the colonists reaped from being under British rule. Some of the specific benefits of mercantilist regulations have already been briefly mentioned, the most obvious being bounties on indigo, naval stores, silk, and, to a lesser extent, lumber. Although the direct payments to colonists in bounties do not indicate the actual net gain to them, we can get an upper estimate on the benefit from bounties. The data obtained by Lawrence Harper show that, in total, the bounties paid on colonial products totaled about 65,000 pounds sterling, or, at the approximate exchange ratio of pounds to dollars in those days, $325,000.[2] This particular benefit is dwarfed by an even larger one, which came from military protection.

Military Protection

Before the Revolution, the colonists had little to do with the protection of their property and life. Almost all of this was provided by the British government. In the beginning, the British helped fight the Spanish, the Indians, and the French. Moreover, American ships were allowed to sail to the Barbary Coast without fear of the infamous Barbary pirates, for Britain had in effect bought off the pirates from attacking its own ships as well as the ships of its colonies. One measure of the benefit of British protection to the colonies is obtained by looking at what the new government spent for national defense after independence. Its annual outlay was in excess of $2 million, an outlay that continued to grow as the population grew. Had the colonists become independent earlier, they would have had to provide for their own military and naval protection. The burden of defense would have been on them alone.

Additionally, Britain took care of much of the administrative work in the colonies. The colonies did not, for example, have to conduct their own foreign policy, pay for missions abroad for ministers, and the like.

When these benefits are compared with the costs, any net burden is reduced to insignificant proportions, at least on an average.

---

[1] These studies are surveyed in Gary M. Walton, "The New Economic History and the Burdens of the Navigation Acts," *Economic History Review*, 24, 3 (November 1971): 533-542.

[2] Lawrence Harper, "The Effect of the Navigation Acts on the Thirteen Colonies," in R. B. Morris, ed. *The Era of the American Revolution*. New York: Columbia University Press, 1939.

The Colonial Era

Don't Just Look at Averages

Of course, we also have to be careful about looking only at averages. We have calculated that the average net cost of British control was probably less than 1 percent. This hardly seems enough to warrant a revolution. However, the costs bore differently on different sectors of the economy. For example, the restriction of no further colonization west of the Appalachians hurt New England merchants the least and young frontiersmen the most. Not only did it eliminate the possibility of obtaining increased land for cultivation, but it also destroyed the possibility for continuing speculation in land sales. Perhaps it is not surprising that George Washington, who was one of the biggest landowners in the colonies and who had wished to own lots of land in Ohio, was one of the staunchest supporters of the Revolution.

Exploitation or Self-Determination

There is general agreement among historians that the only argument for the existence of exploitation stemmed from the indirect routing of goods and from trade controls. Note, however, that these controls were never mentioned in the list of grievances sent by the colonists to the British Crown. More importantly, they were more injurious in the seventeenth century than in 1775, and the colonists had lived with these Navigation Acts, quite harmoniously, for more than a century. Expectations, land values, and values of other assets had long since adjusted to the Acts. There is little connection between exploitation and the Revolution.

The numerous changes after 1763, however, are another matter. These changes did incite antagonism in the colonies. Many of them concerned economic matters, such as controlling the money supply and restricting settlement in western lands and the like. But in these and other concerns, especially in the question of taxation and in matters of the courts, the essence of the confrontation was who was to rule. Actually, the new nation adopted many of the British ordinances after independence, particularly those concerning land and currency. Would this have been done if these laws had imposed great burdens? The main problem was that the colonists had lived too long under conditions of relative neglect and *de facto* freedom. The British attempt to intensify control after 1763 stirred the colonists to rethink the matter of their British ties. Ironically, the defeat of the French in North America in 1763 increased the probability of independence. The threat of a French takeover was greatly reduced after 1763. When the various crises erupted, epitomized in the three boycotts between 1765 and 1775, each new British reversal prodded the colonists onward. After all, they won out on each confrontation. By 1775 they were ready, and as we know, ultimately able to free themselves from British rule. However, as we shall see in Chapter Four, independence was not a smooth road. British economic and military influence in North America did not end with the Revolution. □

Definition of New Terms

Enumerated articles: Enumerated articles were colonial exports that could be shipped only to England; after unloading, shipment elsewhere was permitted.

Part III
The Rise of a National Economy

The Man Who
Faced the Jacksonians

Nicholas Biddle

(1786-1884)

**President, Second Bank
of the United States (1822-1836)**

Faulty strategy in his fight against President Jackson and the Jacksonians certainly was not in keeping with the brilliant career that Nicholas Biddle had led up until the time he took over the presidency of the Second Bank of the United States in 1822. Biddle came from a prominent Philadelphia family. James Biddle, his father, was a U.S. Naval officer, commander of the *Ontario*, and the man who took formal possession of Oregon Country for the United States in 1818.

Young Nicholas was a precocious student; he entered the University of Pennsylvania at ten and graduated at the tender age of thirteen. He also received another degree from the College of New Jersey (now Princeton) at age fifteen. He was a student of the classics and French literature and became the editor of America's first literary periodical, *Port Folio*. In 1815 he helped prepare Pennsylvania's reply to the Hartford Convention, in which numerous proposed amendments to the Constitution had been offered. Most of these proposals attempted to limit the power of Congress and the executive. He went on later to compile for the State Department a digest of foreign legislation affecting U.S. trade.

Among his published works was *A History of the*

Expedition Under the Command of Captains Lewis and Clark, which he prepared from the explorers' notes and journals.

By the time Biddle was appointed a director of the Second Bank of the United States in 1819, he was considered brilliant, debonaire, and versatile. At the age of thirty-seven he had already been a child prodigy, a writer, a lawyer, a state senator, and a diplomat. And Biddle added to these traits tremendous pride and an uncompromising attitude toward others. These latter two qualities seemed to serve him well when he took over the presidency of the Second Bank.

As president he showed that he could discipline any other bank by forcing it to pay debts to the Second Bank of the United States and its branches in hard specie. But such behavior did not win Biddle many friends in the newer sections of the country or in the Old South.

Biddle's cavalier demeanor did not enhance his chances of winning over President Jackson's veto of the Bank's charter in 1832. Jackson claimed the Bank was unconstitutional and was merely a monopoly that used public funds to enrich a few already wealthy men. Of course, Jackson's veto prevailed and from

The Rise of a National Economy

1834 to 1836 Biddle had his bank concentrate on how to liquidate itself. This, of course, meant moving all of its capital to the East, where the banking center of the nation still lay. However, a state charter was drawn up giving it a new name and allowing it to continue in existence. With this new lease on life, Biddle attempted to peg the world price of cotton because he felt it was crucial to American credit abroad. His first cotton pool earned a cool $800,000. The second one, however, failed to the tune of over $900,000. The Bank closed its doors in 1841.

Biddle died disgraced and discredited by many, but he left behind principles that could be used later in the formulation of a true central banking system in the United States. Some observers believe that the monetary and banking reforms of Franklin Delano Roosevelt and the original creation of the Federal Reserve System were in part based on some of the principles established by Biddle. □

The Man Who Made Cotton King

Eli Whitney
(1765-1825)

Inventor and Manufacturer

In 1790, cotton production in the United States was about two million pounds. Ten years later, it had risen to thirty-five million. In the early 1790s, several northern states introduced gradual emancipation schemes, and the trend toward voluntary abolition of slavery was increasing: For example, Washington and Jefferson provided in their wills for their own slaves to be set free. This trend was soon reversed, however, and slavery in the United States grew until the Civil War.

What was responsible for the tremendous increase in the production and sale of cotton and for the newfound profitability in slaves? A simple but monumental invention—the cotton gin. And it was invented by an inveterate tinkerer, Eli Whitney.

As a boy, Eli used to putter around in his father's workshop on their family farm in Massachusetts. Eventually he started to make and repair violins in the neighborhood. When he was only fifteen, he was a manufacturer of nails in his father's shop, even hiring helpers to fill part of his orders. Then he turned to hat pins. But by the time he was eighteen, he decided he wanted more education. Working his way through Leicester Academy in Massachusetts, he finally was able to enter Yale in 1789 at

the age of twenty-three. Not able to live on the funds offered by his father, he repaired equipment and apparatus around the college. A carpenter who had lent Eli his tools remarked after watching him work, "There was one good mechanic spoiled when you went to college."

Then he decided to go into law. Having been invited as a tutor to stay with the widow of General Nathaniel Green, he overheard a conversation at one of her dinners on the Savannah plantation. The men there pointed out the deplorable state of cotton cultivation in the South. Except in certain coastal areas the only variety that could be grown was short-staple, upland cotton, which was extremely difficult to clean, requiring one whole day to obtain a pound of lint. A machine was needed to remove the tenacious seed from the cotton. In ten days Whitney had invented that machine; a cylinder barely two feet long and six inches in diameter, with rows of combing teeth to separate the lint from the seeds and a brush with a fan to remove the clean cotton. This little model was fifty times as efficient as hand labor. News of the cotton gin soon spread, and the curious and interested flocked to find out what it was all about. It was soon stolen, carried off, and copied. Given the ease of duplication and weakly enforced patent laws of the time, there was little Whitney could claim for his efforts and ingenuity.

Nevertheless, his invention changed the entire history of the South, and indeed, the United States. Most southern planters went into cotton production, and land that was once considered worthless soon became valuable. Slaves were now a much sought-after part of the cotton production process, and the price of field hands doubled in twenty years.

Whitney did not stop with the cotton gin, however, and in later years, he invented another process that perhaps proved to be even more important for the history of the United States. Whitney looked at the manufacture of firearms and decided he could do better. Having never built a gun before, he brashly contacted Treasury Secretary Oliver Wolcott in 1798 and took on the task of manufacturing 10,000 or 15,000 stand of arms at a price of $13.40 each. Whitney proposed to make the guns by a new method and in so doing invented the standardization of parts. He once wrote, "One of my primary objects is to form the tools so the tools themselves shall fashion the work and give to every part its just proportion—which when once accomplished, will give expedition, uniformity, and exactness to the whole. . . . The tools which I contemplate are similar to an engraving on a copper plate."

After a slow start, Whitney perfected his method. He was able to use relatively unskilled mechanics to fashion the precise parts that when put together made a very good gun. As it was, Whitney took eight years to fulfill a contract that he promised would be done in two. During this period he had to withstand prejudice and ridicule, but in the end he won out, and his method of machine milling of parts that could be used interchangeably revolutionized the entire manufacturing process used throughout the world. As late as 1840 the British were amazed at the use of interchangeable parts, which had already begun to revolutionize industry in America.

College apparently did not spoil the mechanic in Eli Whitney. ☐

4. From Unification to Secession: Nonagricultural Development

The year 1776 produced the Declaration of Independence, but it was not until 1783 that the Treaty of Paris formalized the termination of hostilities with England. During the Revolution, the new nation was continuously faced with the economic problems of war—among the most pressing of which was how to finance it.

Financing the War

Even though the total cost of the war for the United States was only $100 million—taking probably less than 10 percent of national income per year from 1775 to 1783—the Continental Congress had great difficulty raising even that sum. The very weak Articles of Confederation did not give the Continental Congress the power to tax. However, Congress was able to borrow almost $8 million in gold from abroad, over three-fourths of it coming from France and the remainder from Holland and Spain. Domestically, about $10 million was raised through loans from individuals and businesses. By requisitioning money from the states, the Congress obtained only $6 million, because the states usually ignored the requests. From the viewpoint of any particular state, it often seemed wise to hold back and let the other states pay. When each acted this way, of course, little revenue was raised.

Continental Dollars

The Continental Congress authorized an issue of almost $200 million in paper currency during the four-year period commencing in 1775. But during that period this paper money actually accounted for little more than $40 million in terms of gold. Since nobody was really sure whether these "Continentals" were going to be redeemed in gold or silver after the Revolution, their value steadily declined. Congress was not empowered to declare that these notes could be used as legal tender. Instead, it merely asked the states to penalize persons who refused to take them in exchange for goods and services. By 1781, Continentals were worth 1/500th of their original face value. Part of this **devaluation** was caused by people's uncertainty and lack of faith in the government, but a large part was caused by the tremendous increase in the number of them issued.

Generally, there is a relationship between large changes in the money supply and the price level. This has been called the **quantity theory of money and prices.** Basically, it states that, for a relatively fixed amount of output, if people do not alter their habits about using money (or cash), changes in the money supply will lead to proportionate changes in the price level. (Remember this in reference to the sixteenth-century influx of American gold and silver into Europe.) Before the Continentals fell precipitously in value, however, other schemes did allow the government to purchase substantial amounts of war materiels.

Struggling Under the Articles of Confederation

When peace was resumed, the Treaty of Paris gave the United States all of the territory west to the Mississippi between Canada and Florida, in addition to the right to navigate the Mississippi. However, this was worth little, since at that time Spain controlled the mouth of the river at New Orleans. Additionally, the United States received fishing rights within British territorial waters in the North Atlantic.

Except for these highlights, there were few bright spots. The United States suffered many economic hardships stemming from the war and independence, and the Articles of Confederation added to the difficulties because of its weak political framework.

The first major peacetime goal was to reopen trade with overseas areas. Here the United States faced great problems, for American ships could no longer trade legally with the British West Indies, and ships built in America lost this market in England because of the Navigation Acts.

Overall exports did not bounce back to their former levels, and yet imports were vital, because Americans were far from being self-sufficient. Consequently, there was a deficit in the U.S. balance of trade with the rest of the world, as the value of exports remained below the value of imports.

In order to pay for this excess of imports over exports, the United States temporarily shipped large amounts of specie—gold and silver—to other countries. The result was a reduction in the U.S. money supply and with it a fall in prices. This caused many American merchants grave concern because they had not anticipated the intensity of the **deflation** that occurred after the Revolution. Moreover, they were hurt when the British resumed large-scale exports to the United States. In fact, the British

were accused of **dumping**—that is, selling their goods in our country at prices below cost. This undercut domestic production.

What happened in the United States was a "depression" between the years 1785 and 1786. This was limited primarily to the commercial sector and one should be careful not to equate the depressions of those years with depressions (or recessions) of more modern times. Today a depression is usually felt by the vast majority of Americans. But in those early years, most of the population was engaged in farming. The fall in prices hurt people, but few became unemployed. Changes in business activity were not generally catastrophic.

The export sector, however, did suffer. The real value of exports per capita right after the war was probably less than one-half of that just before it. As Table 4−1 shows, annual averages of real exports per capita fell by 30 percent between 1768−1772 and 1791−1792. And this lower level was still evident after several years of business recovery in the late 1780s. Most of the difficulty, as Table 4−1 indicates, was with the southern staples. The markets in Europe and elsewhere had stagnated. In addition, the United States had not yet secured much political power internationally.

Few countries had yet accepted the United States as a viable nation in the world economy. As a result, trade discussions and treaties were less fruitful than they might have been.

The Effects of Deflation

As the price level fell in the early and mid-1780s, there was growing unrest among debtors in the nation. The main problem was that these price declines were not generally expected. And when the principal and interest on loans had to be repaid, debtors found that they had to pay with dollars of greater value. In real purchasing power, they had to pay back more than they had bargained for. On the other side of the coin, of course, creditors were made better off.

Table 4—1. Average Annual Real Per Capita Exports from Colonies andRegions of the Thirteen Colonies, 1768—1772, and from States and Regions of the United States, 1791—1792. (Pounds Sterling; 1768—1772 Prices).

Origin	1768—1772	1791—1792
New England		
New Hampshire	0.74	0.23
Massachusetts	0.97	1.14
Rhode Island	1.39	1.72
Connecticut	0.50	0.62
Total, New England	0.82	0.83
Middle Atlantic		
New York	1.15	1.51
New Jersey	0.02	0.03
Pennsylvania	1.47	1.34
Delaware	0.51	0.44
Total, Middle Atlantic	1.01	1.11
Upper South		
Maryland	1.93	1.51
Virginia	1.72	0.91
Total, Upper South	1.79	1.09
Lower South		
North Carolina	0.38	0.27
South Carolina	3.66	1.75
Georgia	3.17	1.17
Total, Lower South	1.75	0.88
Total, all regions	1.31	0.99

The difficulties of adjusting to independence and new peacetime circumstances were felt unevenly throughout the nation. The 30 percent decline in real per capita exports for the entire United States between 1768—1772 and 1791—1792 was largely due to catastrophic declines in the export of the major southern staples. The northern states fared better than the southern states in their ability to recover.

Source: James F. Shepherd and Gary M. Walton, "Economic Change After the American Revolution: Pre- and Post-War Comparisons of Maritime Shipping and Trade," *Explorations in Economic History, 13* (October 1976): 413.

Shays' Rebellion and the Need to Revamp the Articles of Confederation

By 1786, in the City of Concord, Massachusetts, the scene of one of the first battles of the Revolution, there were three times as many people in debtors' prison as there were imprisoned for all other crimes combined. In Worcester County, the ratio was even higher—20 to 1. The prisoners were generally small farmers who could not pay their debts. In August of

1786, mobs of musket-bearing farmers seized county courthouses and did not allow the trials of debtors to continue. The rebels encouraged Daniel Shays, a captain from the Continental Army, to lead them. Shays' men launched an attack on the federal arsenal at Springfield, Massachusetts, but were repulsed. The rebellion did not stop there but continued to grow into the winter. Finally, George Washington wrote to a friend, "For God's sake, tell me what is the cause of these commotions? Do they proceed from licentiousness, British influence disseminated by the Tories, or real grievances which admit to redress? If the latter, why were they delayed until the public mind had become so agitated? If the former, why are not the powers of government tried at once?"

What Shays' Rebellion did was demonstrate chaos and the weakness of the government under the Articles of Confederation. In order for the nation to grow and prosper in the world economy, it was necessary that a stronger central government be organized. So the Constitutional Convention, which originated as a commercial convention, was convened in Philadelphia in May 1787. The completed Constitution went into effect in March 1789. It was a critical factor in the economic development of the nation.

The Economic Aspects of the Constitution

Article 1, sections 8, 9, and 10 contain the main economic provisions of the Constitution. These sections reaffirmed the permanent nature of private property in terms of federal support of the institution. The additional three major categories of the economic provisions were taxation, control over money and credit, and restrictions over commerce, as well as the ability of the federal government to establish treaties with foreign powers, which were to be held paramount over all laws made by the several states.

Taxation

One of the major weaknesses of the Articles of Confederation was the inability of the Continental Congress to levy taxes against the population. Although this problem was perhaps more political than economic, without the power to tax, the United States never could have had a large, organized central government.

Money and Credit

Even though state banks were allowed, the federal government now was empowered to "coin money, regulate the value thereof, and of foreign coin, in addition to fixing the standard of weights and measures."[1] Implicit in this section of the Constitution was the ability of the federal government to issue a national currency. Eventually this was important for the development of commercial activities and a market in which the buying and selling of debts and shares in companies could occur. This kind of trading occurs in a **capital market**. The Constitution also allowed the federal government to redeem the debts of the "several" (individual) states. This further allowed a capital market to develop.

Regulation of Commerce

The Constitution also decreed that all import duties should be the same for all of the several states, and further, that there would be no export duties. This was to ensure that the states did not establish barriers to trade among themselves. This was a way of fostering *inter*regional trade, as well as *intra*regional trade. The Constitution effectively gave the federal government the right to police interstate commerce, which was at that time limited mainly to coastal trade.

---

[1] This power is the basis for the forced conversion to the metric system of measurement that is soon to be made.

Recovery and the Growth of Shipping

The situation at the end of the 1780s was one of incomplete economic recovery from the depression of 1785 and 1786. In 1789 a revolution began in France. Then, in 1793, the French and English became embroiled in war. The series of battles between the two arch enemies lasted until 1815.

By necessity, both the British and French quickly relaxed their normal mercantilist restrictions. As their demand for our goods increased, American export activity soared; by 1795, exports of American goods had doubled over the 1793 level.

In addition, British and French ships, which normally carried cargo, were now deployed on sterner business. U.S. shipping was ready and able to fill the void created, and the United States quickly became one of the main shipping concerns in the world.

The United States also began to reexport numerous goods, because it was a neutral power. Goods of other nations were shipped to the United States, and then reshipped to the belligerents. For example, in 1790 the United States reexported only 3 percent of the goods imported, but by 1805, it was reexporting 60 percent.

As shown in Figure 4–1, the reexport trade grew by leaps and bounds. So too, of course, did total exports, until certain political actions in 1807 prevented further U.S. trade expansion. In 1790, almost 60 percent of U.S. trade was carried on in American ships; in the years 1805 and 1806, it was nearly 100 percent. This was, in fact, an era of unusually intense commercial and trading activity, as well as shipping activity. For Americans, the war in Europe was fortunate, at least initially. It stimulated the U.S. economy and brought prosperity to American businesses and workers.

Nevertheless, the prosperity of these times was not necessarily a basis for long-term development. There was no similar increase of prosperity in the interior of the United States, and a large nation cannot generally grow by merely becoming an efficient shipper for the rest of the world. Yet the profits made from commercial endeavors during this period were a major source of investment funds that financed later development, and the market sector of the economy was growing in importance.

The End of the Commercial Boom

England and France had a temporary peace during 1803, and the U.S. commercial shipping boom plummeted. When the European powers started fighting again, they renewed the economic stimulus for American shipping, until both belligerents decided to deny neutral ships entry to enemy ports. Nearly 1,500 American ships were seized after 1805 until Congress enacted the Embargo Act late in 1807. This prohibited American vessels from sailing to foreign ports, in the hope of forcing England and France to respect American neutrality. The results of the embargo were impressive indeed. As shown in Figure 4–1, reexports fell drastically; similarly, total exports dropped by almost 80 percent when the embargo was enacted. Pressure from merchants, sailors, and commercial interests led to the repeal of the act in 1809. Instead, the Non-Importation Act was passed prohibiting trade specifically with Great Britain, France, and their territories.

Nevertheless, further difficulties continued and eventually the War of 1812 erupted. The United States went to war with England again. It was largely a naval war, one in which the British navy blockaded the entire coast of the United States and seized more than 1,000 American ships. Exports fell to practically nothing.

The Rise of Industry

The blockading of American waters gave a strong boost to American industry. Before 1812, there had been almost no manufacturing in the United States. Only 7 percent of the population lived in urban areas. The young nation did have a small textile industry in 1800, but even by 1810 two-

The Rise of a National Economy

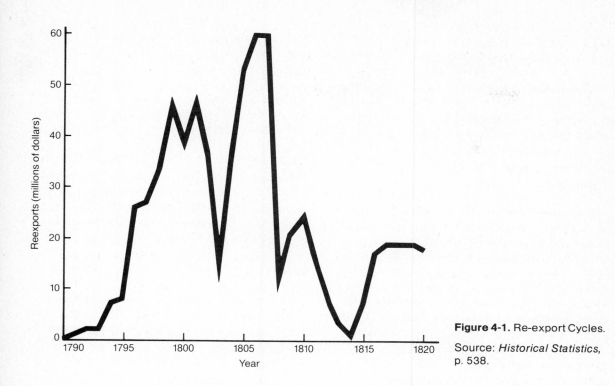

Figure 4-1. Re-export Cycles.

Source: *Historical Statistics,* p. 538.

thirds of it was based in homes. Heroic attempts by Samuel Slater developed mechanized weaving industry in Providence, Rhode Island, in the 1790s. None of the increased commercial activities or promise of fortune stirred anyone's interest until the embargo of 1807. Similar to today, resources flowed into areas where they had the highest relative rates of return. Entrepreneurs in the days before the embargo saw their highest rates of return in reexporting, shipping and general trading. Suddenly this changed. Manufacturing was the new growth sector.

The Textile Industry and Technological Adaptation

The salutary effects that the embargo had on manufacturing were quickly felt: In 1808 there were only fifteen textile mills, but by 1809, there were almost ninety. This rapid multiplication of mills demonstrated how little capital was needed to start one. Few of these new mills survived, however, after the Peace of Ghent in 1814 brought the War of 1812 to a close. Soon Britain started massive exports and was again accused of dumping. The textile industry faltered, but certain large-scale concerns, such as the Waltham system of cloth weaving, developed by Francis Cabot Lowell, survived and grew. His use of water-powered mills and a system that used relatively low-cost, well-supervised labor spearheaded the growth of the industry.

Britain was the frontrunner in the Industrial Revolution, and consequently, American businesses borrowed on English know-how for producing certain products. Most of their capital was designed for the relatively capital- and labor-abundant economy that characterized England. In contrast, therefore, the United States had to adapt their techniques to suit our situation, which by comparison was one of relative labor scarcity. Labor-saving machinery was greatly desired by American entrepreneurs. This may have led to the initial U.S. emphasis on standardized parts, such as parts for firearms. Moreover, in the early days of U.S. manufacturing development, water power was typically used instead of steam, which was more common in Britain. In the United States, water power was relatively plentiful and inexpensive compared to steam power, which tended to be more capital intensive.

Iron Production and Total Manufactures

The U.S. iron-making industry grew very slowly but eventually developed into one of our major manufacturing activities. After the introduction of puddling and rolling techniques (which had already been in use three decades in England before being used in the United States), our technology of iron making did not change until the introduction of the Bessemer converter in the late 1860s and the open-hearth furnace method in the 1870s and 1880s.

By the start of the Civil War, manufacturing had become a substantial part of national output. In fact, it had risen to 60 percent of the product generated by the agricultural sectors. By 1850, the productive capacity of the United States that was devoted to the making of *capital equipment*—machines and the like—represented a higher percentage of total production than in any other nation in the world. Prior to the Civil War, we were indeed on the way to becoming fully industrialized.

Money and Capital

Remember a key provision of the Constitution was that the federal government regulates coinage. In 1791, when Alexander Hamilton was thirty-four years old, he was appointed Secretary of the Treasury. He wielded a power in this nation that was second only to that of the president. His financial program reflected his belief in a powerful national government. He had great influence, particularly in commercial and banking sectors. In the thirtieth *Federalist* paper, he had pointed out that "Money is, with propriety, considered as the vital principal of the body politic; as that which sustains its life and motion, and enables it to perform its most essential functions." He suggested that a basic unit of value be established, and so the Mint Act of 1792 was passed. The dollar was to be that basic unit of value, and the decimal system was to be used (we fortunately didn't use the old British pounds, shillings, and pence).

Hamilton also wanted a national bank: "The tendency of a national bank is to increase public and private credit. Industry is increased, commodities are multiplied, agriculture and manufacturing flourish, and herein consists the true wealth and prosperity of a state."

First U.S. Bank

Largely due to Hamilton, the First Bank of the United States was chartered in 1791 for a period of twenty years. It was a private corporation governed by twenty-five directors and had a capital of $10 million, of which the federal government provided 20 percent. This bank served as the government's depository. It also made loans to the government and to private individuals and companies. It was profitable, averaging 8 percent per year rate of return for those who invested in it. It died, however, when its charter was not renewed in 1811; the assets of the bank were bought by Stephen Girard of Philadelphia.

This was an unfortunate time for the bank to close its doors because during the War of 1812 treasury finances were in a poor state and no central depository existed. At that time, there was a great increase in unregulated local banking. In general, specie payments were abandoned; that is, nobody was willing to pay off their debts in hard currency—gold or silver. The cry went up for a second U.S. Bank, which appeared in 1816.

The Second Bank of the United States

This bank was also chartered for a period of twenty years. It started with a capital stock three and a half times that of the First Bank and the government again provided 20 percent. Soon after it had been chartered difficulties arose as the price of cotton dropped, and farmers began to have troubles. Instead of countering these problems with expansionary activities, the bank from 1818 to 1819 contracted its deposits. This put pressure on state banks, especially in the West. At the same time, we had to pay off the debt for the Louisiana Purchase. So quite a bit of specie flowed overseas, helping contract our money supply in a way that the public did not anticipate.

Finally, there was the Panic of 1819. The bank completely stopped the payment of specie, and there were bank failures throughout the economy. The price level was falling drastically at the time. However, the extent of this crisis should not be exaggerated in a country that was highly agricultural. True, the commercial sector was hit very hard, but certainly not the largely self-sufficient agricultural sector. The first president of the bank, who was considered incompetent, was ousted after the Panic of 1819. Two later presidents, Langdon Sheves (1819-1823) and Nicholas Biddle (1823-1836) were viewed with more esteem, but Biddle too eventually faced difficulties.

Banking and Politics

Meanwhile, there were political currents in motion, particularly toward the end of Biddle's appointment. When President Jackson took office in 1829, he immediately began to attack the Second Bank of the United States. He wanted to close it, but a committee that was formed in the House of Representatives affirmed the constitutionality of the bank in spite of Jackson's request that it do otherwise. During the 1820s, the Bank had developed a sort of national currency because it had a large number of branches, and U.S. Bank notes were in circulation everywhere. The rate of exchange between U.S. Bank notes and all other bank notes was approximately stable throughout the nation. Congress apparently saw this as a good thing, and Jackson's attempt at that time to block recharter on the grounds of un-

constitutionality failed.

The Second Bank was unpopular in some quarters. Of course, it was not like a modern central bank. It could not legally regulate the reserves of commercial banks, and the support it could give to others in periods of financial crises was limited. But, by virtue of its size and the number of branches it had, it could exercise some control over the economy. For instance, it would ask for specie redemption from other banks from time to time, to keep them "honest."

Biddle's big political mistake was to apply for a recharter four years before the end of the Second U.S. Bank's original charter. His purpose was to get rechartered and at the same time to embarrass Jackson in the 1832 election and maybe cause him to lose it. Biddle backed Henry Clay in the 1832 campaign. The recharter was passed in Congress in July 1832, but it was vetoed by Jackson. For Biddle, the whole scheme backfired.

Inflation

The demise of the Second U.S. Bank brought with it many changes in the American banking scene. However, what happened after its demise was not entirely a result of that particular event. We are speaking about the inflation of 1835, 1836, and part of 1837 and about the depression from 1839 to 1843. Many historians believe that the inflation was caused by the fall of the Second U.S. Bank, which allowed for a rapid increase in the amount of paper currency available through a proliferation of wildcat banks. (These banks got their names from the fact that they were so far out in the boondocks that it was said only wildcats frequented them.) The evidence concerning the increase in the money supply and the increase in prices is fairly impressive. For example, Figure 4−2 shows that the money supply did indeed increase after Jackson's veto.

At this time Jackson began withdrawing funds from the Second Bank and placing them in state banks called "pet banks." Biddle's powers were curbed severely.

But was wildcat banking resulting from the

demise of the Second Bank the cause of the sharp money increase? No, wildcat banking with unchecked expansion of credit and paper currency did not occur. The ratio of bank-held reserves to credit outstanding did not rise. Banks on the whole were fairly cautious, and they did not overlend. What, then, caused the money supply to increase?

International Economy

The United States was part of an international economy. We adhered to a gold and silver standard, which involved shipments of gold and silver in and out of the country. These formed the basis of our circulating money supply. Moreover, there was a large increase in specie imports from Mexico. Britain and France were also periodically sending specie to the United States. The bottom line of Figure 4–2 shows that there was a tremendous specie jump between 1833 and 1837. Therefore, the demise of the Second Bank alone did not cause the inflation of 1835 and 1836.

The Second Bank Once Again

Still, the bank was a factor. In the early 1830s, people became very trusting of banks, largely be-

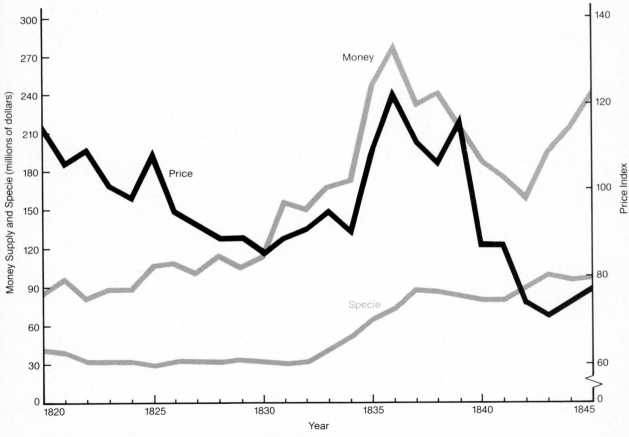

Figure 4-2. Prices and the Money Supply, 1820–1845.

Source: Hugh Rockoff, "Money, Prices, and Banks in the Jacksonian Era," in R. W. Fogel and S. L. Engerman, eds., *The Reinterpretation of American Economic History* (New York: Harper & Row, 1971), Table 1, p. 451.

The Rise of a National Economy

cause the Second Bank helped maintain sound banking practices. This confidence led to a sharp reduction in the proportion of specie people held as money. Paper money would serve just as well, people believed, as long as the banks were sound. But after the demise of the Second Bank people's confidence declined. The proportion of their money that they wanted in specie form went up. Also the Specie Circular 1836, requiring that most federal land sales be paid in gold also increased specie holdings by individuals. People went to the banks for specie and, when some of the banks could not convert bank notes into specie, banking panics occurred. Then everyone wanted to convert, which put great strains on the banking system. The end result was the worst depression of the century, lasting from 1839 to 1843.

By this time, the effects of a depression, especially one as wide and as deep as that from 1839 to 1843, was felt much more severely by the general population. To some degree, this economic contraction was international in scope, like the one to follow nearly a century later. Particularly hard hit was the new class of workers, those tied to the mills and factories. The process of mechanization and systematic production controls were just arriving on the American economic landscape. To these new pressures was now added sharp declines in employment and real wages throughout the business downturn. To the hardships of labor was added the hardship of forced idleness.

Transportation

One of the main deterrents to interregional trade in colonial times was the lack of cheap transportation among the colonies, except along the coast. This had to change if the United States was to become an integrated and ever-expanding market in which specialization could continuously occur. At first we turned to the development of the most obvious methods of transportation: waterways and roads. There was rarely any federal assistance for the development of highways in those days because of constitutional objections. Nevertheless, private companies did build a number of turnpikes. By 1810, there were 180 turnpike companies in New England alone. By 1813, there were about 1,400 miles of privately built roads in New York, and by 1832 Pennsylvania had over 2,000 miles.

The Rivers

By far the most important part of the early transportation network was the natural waterways, especially the great Mississippi, Ohio, and Missouri rivers, as well as the Great Lakes. First flatboats and barges (keelboats) carried all of the freight and passengers on these arteries. By 1815, however, the steamboat was successfully introduced on the western rivers, and keelboating, which had made most of its revenues on the laborious trek upriver, was quickly eclipsed. Comparatively, steamboats were much more efficient on the upstream run. Flatboats did not disappear, however, and these downstream craft remained active throughout the period. Actually the steamboat helped flatboating by lowering the costs of the crew's return upriver.

The steamboat was a vital force in early westward expansion, and a stream of improvements between 1815 and 1860 greatly increased its efficiency and safety. Steamboat boiler explosions, which brought Americans the first hazards of industrialization, were fairly uncommon after 1850, and various changes in the hull and design greatly increased the steamboats' carrying capacity and length of useful service in shallow water seasons (and areas). As a result freight costs on the rivers tumbled between 1815 and 1860, and as late as 1845 the rivers still carried more traffic than all of the other transportation mediums combined.

Most of the gains in efficiency in steamboating resulted from many minor modifications and improvements in the design and structure of the vessel and in the handling and operating of the vessel. The sum of these many small improvements was more significant in reducing the cost of river transport than was the major but single technological advance of introducing steam power.

Canals

Canals, like the natural waterways, had disadvantages, such as freezing in the winter, but they also had many advantages. Mainly, they allowed for relatively cheap transportation among fixed points. The greatest canal-building activity occurred between the late 1820s and the Panic of 1837. The most famous canal, of course, was the Erie, which ran from the Hudson River near Albany, New York, to Buffalo on Lake Erie. Completed in 1825, it extended some 360 miles and could accommodate thirty-ton barges. There were many other canals, as well, such as those built in Pennsylvania, Delaware, Maryland, Ohio, Illinois, and Michigan.

The Railroads

By tapping the interior, New York's successful Erie Canal posed a threat to other eastern cities and their commercial interests. To counter this, Baltimore emphasized the railroad, because canals were not completely practical, due to engineering difficulties, terrain, and high costs of construction there. Of course, there were to be many mistakes with the use of this new transportation mechanism. For example, Baltimore tried to build its railroad over a mountain pass in a period when steam locomotives were not completely worked out in their design and application. Railroads did have advantages, though, and they were soon to be realized. They were speedier than canal transportation, they could be used in almost all weather, and they certainly had advantages for overland routes. These features were particularly advantageous in the provision of passenger services, when the railroads first were built.

For a variety of reasons, then, railroads became the predominant means of transportation in the United States. In the following Issue, we examine whether government action on their behalf was important for their development and the development of the United States. We also analyze the impact of government promotion in general. For example, were government investments a key stimulus to growth? □

Definitions of New Terms

Quantity theory of money and prices: The quantity theory of money and prices is a theory that can be used to predict changes in the price level. Basically, if the economy is fully employed and if we assume that people's habits concerning the use of cash (and the number of transactions) remain unchanged, then an increase in the quantity of money in circulation will lead to a proportionate increase in the price level.

Devaluation: Devaluation is a reduction in the exchange value of money.

Deflation: Deflation is a continuing fall in the price level.

Dumping: Dumping is selling goods abroad lower than costs.

Capital Market: A capital market is one in which loans can be obtained or in which shares in companies can be bought and sold.

Capital equipment: The term capital equipment applies to machines, buildings, and other productive goods.

PUBLIC vs. PRIVATE

Government Was Small

Today, when almost 26 percent of national output is consumed by government at the federal, state, and local levels, it seems almost unthinkable to question whether or not government has any direct impact on the economy. However, this relatively high percentage of government involvement was unheard of in earlier days. In the nineteenth century, for example, no more than 5 percent of **gross national product** (GNP) was accounted for by government expenditures. Most of government activity was much more decentralized than it is today. In particular, the state governments were much more active than the federal government. Nevertheless, government intervention in economic affairs was not in-

significant, and from the very beginning government was active at all levels. In particular, it was responsible in one way or another for much of the development of the transportation system and the manufacturing sector where important changes were occurring. How important it was is, to be sure, another matter, one that is the key to this issue.

Cleaning up the Rivers

The backbone of the transportation system before the Civil War was the natural waterways. The main hazards of the rivers were "snags," trees that fell from the shore and became lodged in the river bed. Pointing downstream and largely submerged, they endangered many steamboats coming upstream.

Between 1811 and 1849, 830 steamboats were lost on the western rivers of the Mississippi, the Missouri, the Ohio, and their tributaries. Fifty were lost by collision, 150 by burning, 184 by explosion, and 446 by snags.

Of course, it did not pay private individuals to clean up the rivers. Had they done so, they would have borne all of the costs, while most of the benefits would have gone to other steamboaters. Similarly, since most river transport was interstate, state and local governments had little incentive to spend money for snag removals. There again the benefits from cleaning up the rivers were widely dispersed and tolls could not be charged by the states on interstate traffic. The rallying cry was "Let the federal government do it!" But for most of the period the federal government did little. Sporadic expenditures to clean up the rivers occurred but the government contribution was less than 1 percent of total resources expended in river transportation. The development of the western river transportation system as a whole stemmed almost entirely from private enterprise.

Helping Out the Canals

Overland travel was a relatively expensive form of transportation for shipping goods across country. Therefore, the idea of a network of canals was thought of very early in American history. One of the earliest and the most successful of the canals, the Erie, connected the Hudson River with Lake Erie, a distance of 363 miles. New York state did indeed intervene in this particular venture— 100 percent. The Governor, DeWitt Clinton, was an early advocate of the Erie Canal. In 1817 the state legislature set up a fund to build that famous waterway. They estimated the cost then would be a little bit under $6 million. "Clinton's Ditch" was finally completed in 1825, costing closer to $8.5 million. Even before the canal was completed—that is, while only sections of it were being used—the tolls exceeded the interest costs on the debt used to pay for its construction. In the first nine years of its existence, the tolls summed to almost $17 million.

The effect of the canal on the movement of goods was dramatic. Much of the produce of Illinois, Indiana, Ohio, and western New York could have an easy route to the Atlantic Coast. Freight rates from Buffalo to New York fell by almost 85 percent and the shipping time was cut to one-half of what it had been previously. By 1853 tolls reached a cumulative value of $94 million on the great Erie Canal.

In the beginning of the canal era, state intervention was great. Between 1815 and the start of the Civil War, almost $140 million was provided by state governments. This amounted to almost three-fourths of the total investment in canals during that period. Some states used indirect financial aid. For example, instead of giving money directly, New Jersey provided a banking privilege to get some of its canals started. After an auspicious beginning, however, direct state intervention in canal efforts dwindled, and there was a tendency to have a mixed government-private system.

Helping the Railroads

Just as with the canal system, state aid was greater at the beginning of the development of railroads than at the end. In fact, toward the latter part of the nineteenth century, there was almost no government help for railroad systems.

In the 1830s, however, the government engaged in some less ambitious and less successful railroad schemes that may have set the foundation for further development of the Iron Horse. In the South, for example, during the period before the Civil War, state financing accounted for 55 percent of total railroad expenditures, of which 75 percent was directly in cash. By the 1850s, private financing of the railroads had taken over most of what the states had done in the beginning (although after the Civil War land grants altered the picture). In this early period, the only assistance from government was at the state and local level. When a state financed a railroad, it provided entrepreneurial aid. When local governments helped finance a railroad, it did no such thing.

The plethora of local aid in the South and the North during this time seemed to induce some weird configurations of railroad lines. One historian, commenting on a railroad in the state of New York, said that it zigzagged across the countryside "in search of municipal bonds."

Comparing Government Investments

If we look at Table IV−1, we find that government expenditures accounted for very different proportions of total expenditures among the different modes. Most of this activity was undertaken by state and local governments, especially in canals and railroads. By these expenditures, they hoped to stimulate regional development. Land values and business activity jumped with the advent of railroads and canals. So it paid state and local governments to become involved. The benefits were internalized by the community to a large degree, unlike benefits from snag removal on the rivers. One noted historian, Harry Scheiber, has termed such involvement "local mercantilism."

The period of greatest involvement was before the Civil War, especially by the state and local governments. Overall, this intervention created an atmosphere that induced private investors to risk their capital in these ventures. For canals, the government stimulus was highly significant; for railroads, it was important; for river transport, it was minor.

Land Grants in Aid

States and the federal government did allow a few land grants to help the railroads. Before the Civil War they were not very important. During that period, only two railroads were completed with the assistance of land grants. However, a total of 130 million acres was eventually given to railroads by the federal government and over 50 million by state governments.

Are There Any Answers Yet?

An answer to whether or not state intervention spurred the growth of the American economy still eludes us. Many historians have labeled the system of mixed government-private enterprise building of canals and railroads "The American System." One historian maintains that during this period the government "everywhere undertook the role put on it by the people, that of planner, promoter, investor, and regulator."[1] But this in fact was only the case in certain very specific examples, such as the Erie Canal. At any rate, the government's role in the transportation system declined as we approached the Civil War. However, this still does not answer the question, "Would the rate of growth of the United States have been lower if the government had not participated even to the limited extent it did?" Using economic data, historians have yet to come up with a definitive conclusion. Certain very obvious examples suggest that this intervention did yield positive benefits. Some have said, for example, that the Erie Canal had effects

---

[1] Robert A. Lively, "The American System," *The Business History Review*, *39*, 1 (March 1955): 81.

Table IV—1. Government Investment as a Percentage of Total Investment in Transportation.

Activity	Time Span	Percentage of Total Investment
River Transport	1815—1860	1 %
Canals	1815—1860	73
Railroads	To 1862	25—30 (plus modest public land grants
	1862—1872	10—12 (plus sizable public land grants)
	1873—1890	1

Source: Erik F. Haites, James Mak, and Gary M. Walton, *Western River Transportation* (Baltimore, Md.: Johns Hopkins University Press, 1975), Chap. 7; Goodrich Carter, "Internal Improvements Reconsidered," *The Journal of Economic History*, 30, 2 (June 1970): 297, Table 1.

on the development of the United States that "ramify almost into infinity." But we can just as easily find some spectacular failures of government intervention, such as occurred with the Pennsylvania Canal System. In fact, on the whole canals were financial failures and a considerable misuse of resources, because technological obsolescence occurred so quickly. One prominent investigator has concluded that perhaps as much as 85 percent of canal investments was a social waste.[2] Ironically, most of these financial failures were due to the arrival of the railroad, which diverted canal traffic to overland routes.

With regard to transportation improvements, the case for a critical growth stimulus via government involvement is shaky at best. In river transport, there was no significant involvement. In canals, the influence was probably negative. In rails, it was positive. Overall, perhaps it was neutral.

What About Manufacturing?

From the very beginning, the government did not car-

ry through Alexander Hamilton's suggestions listed in his "Report on Manufactures." There he suggested that the state undertake a number of promotional activities, such as subsidizing important industries. Up until the Civil War, however, there was very little subsidy of manufacturing. There was also not an overwhelming amount of "protection" in the form of relatively high tariffs, although for a short period we did have rising tariff rates.

The first tariff was put into effect on July 4, 1789, with an average rate of only 8.5 percent. It grew steadily larger, reaching a peak in the late 1820s and then falling thereafter as can be seen in Figure IV—1.

The United States during this period had a system of no quotas, no currency regulations, very little allocation of scarce resources by the government, and few subsidies paid to manufacturing. We had a more or less freely functioning market mechanism in which changes in relative prices and relative rates of return induced resources to flow in directions that would yield the highest rates of return, both to the individual and to the nation. Where the state did have some effect, probably the

most important effect of all, on the growth of the economy was in its Constitutional provisions that generated an atmosphere conducive to the development of large and well-functioning markets.

Establishing the Atmosphere

The key articles in the Constitution—giving power to Congress to tax, provide for a common currency, regulate tariffs, and so on—were of vital importance in providing a framework for a large market system. The Constitution also provided an atmosphere of political stability in which the states would not be imposing restrictive duties on each other's goods. On the other hand, powers left to the states, such as the power to incorporate, often proved beneficial. Certainly the flexibility of state chartered corporations was conducive to industrial expansion in the United States.

It was perhaps in the development of an atmosphere in which everybody knew what the ground rules were, who owned what, and how well it would be protected that the growth of the nation could continue for years to come.□

---

[2] Roger Ransom, "Canals and Development: A Discussion of the Issues," *American Economic Review, 54,* (May 1964): 375.

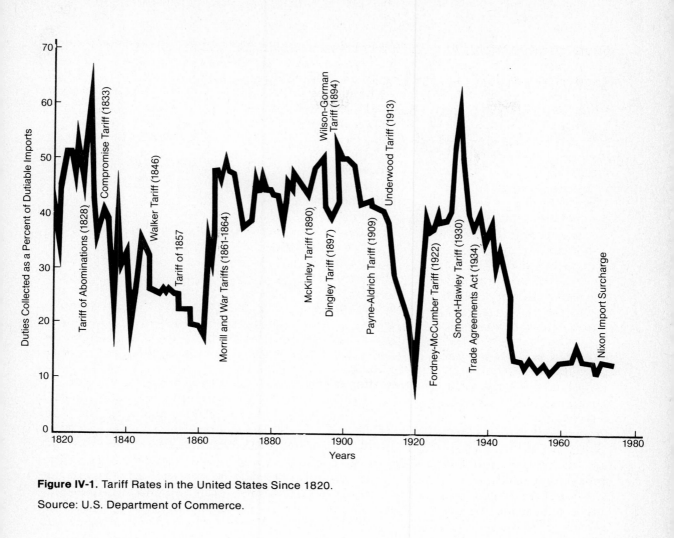

Figure IV-1. Tariff Rates in the United States Since 1820.

Source: U.S. Department of Commerce.

Definition of New Term

Gross national product (GNP): The gross national product is the market value of all final goods and services. When GNP is corrected for price level changes, it is called *real* GNP.

Did Government Intervention Spur the Growth of the Economy?

5. Agriculture, Cotton, and National Growth

From the very beginning, the staple crops from the South accounted for a large percentage of the total exports from America. In the colonial era, rice, tobacco, and indigo accounted for more than one-half of the exports of all the colonies combined. However, a new staple crop was soon to take the place of all the others and to become the leading source of national export income for many years to follow.

King Cotton

Back in 1793, cotton was an insignificant feature of the southern landscape. In fact, since the importance of southern exports had fallen after the Revolution, there was little southern furor when the Constitution stipulated that slave imports would be stopped after twenty years. This was all to change, partially because Eli Whitney invented the cotton ginning machine. The cotton gin removed the bottleneck in the preparation of short-staple cotton and enabled one worker to remove the seeds from more than fifty pounds of raw cotton a day. By hand, a worker could clean only one pound a day. This lowered the cost of American cotton at the same time that England's textile industry was growing by leaps and bounds. King Cotton was on the rise.

Jumps in Cotton Production

The South increased its production of cotton at a phenomenal rate, doubling almost every decade until 1840, after which it still continued to grow, but at a slower rate. We see in Figure 5–1 that by the start of the Civil War, cotton production was up to four million bales a year.

A New Source of Export Income

Cotton quickly became the major export not only for the South but also for all of the United States. Figure 5–2 shows that cotton exports as a percentage of all U.S. exports rose from 38 percent during the period from 1815 to 1819, to 65 percent just before 1840. Although the volume continued to rise, relatively it fell to 51 percent by the start of the Civil War.

There are numerous reasons why the South became so highly specialized in cotton production. First, the southern climate and terrain were particularly well suited for such a crop. This was especially true in the New South, the cotton states of Alabama, Mississippi, Arkansas, Louisiana, and eastern Texas. These new lands were highly fertile and easily cultivated. Moreover, the land policy of the federal government was becoming increasingly liberal over this period. Western lands were becoming easier to obtain, for small and large farmers alike, as feder-

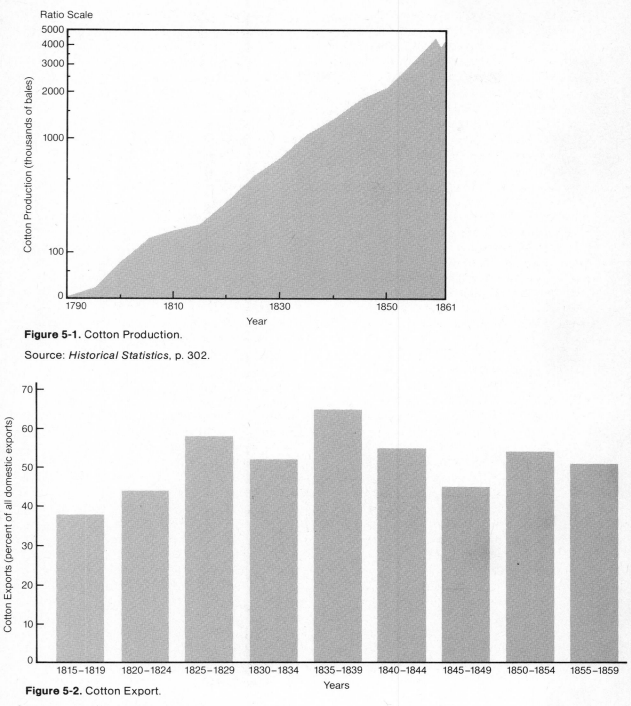

Figure 5-1. Cotton Production.

Source: *Historical Statistics*, p. 302.

Figure 5-2. Cotton Export.

Source: *Historical Statistics*, pp. 538-547.

Agriculture, Cotton, and National Growth

59

ally set minimum land prices fell and credit availability increased. Second, from the plantation system inherited from colonial times, the South had the necessary know-how and entrepreneurial skills. Third, it also had a large pool of unskilled labor, in bondage, to pick and carry cotton. Finally, inexpensive transportation was another important reason why cotton became king in the South. There was a vast network of waterways that could carry the cotton to ocean ports—the main port, of course, being New Orleans. This well-established transportation system allowed cotton farmers merely to cart their bales of cotton to a nearby river and to have them shipped down to large vessels waiting at the dock in New Orleans, Savannah, Charleston, or Mobile.

It is fairly obvious that cotton was what the South would produce best. Since there was the possibility of both interregional and international trade, the South was able to specialize in its comparative advantage: cotton production .

The Antebellum South

Although cotton was king and there were numerous plantations around the southern countryside, the vast majority of people were engaged in yeoman farming that was either subsistence or that left a slight surplus that could be sold to the plantation owners for their own consumption and that of the slaves.

There was very little urbanization in the South, with the obvious exception of New Orleans and perhaps Charleston and Richmond. This meant that there were few local industries, but that did not mean that the South was stagnating, as some historians have said. In fact, in 1840 and even in 1860, the per capita income of free people in the West South Central area was higher than the national average. Moreover, the per capita income was growing all the time, at a rate equal to those of other parts of the nation. The South was far from being an undeveloped region.

Cotton was not the only crop that was grown in the pre-Civil War era. Corn accounted for the most acreage, but it was not a commercial crop; and there was rice in South Carolina and sugar in Louisiana and Texas, as well as tobacco in Virginia. In fact, sugar was one of the staples that was grown on the new lands of the westward migration, which we will talk about in the following section. Lastly, there was abundant livestock for consumption in the South.

The South was not a well-diversified economy. It was quite clear to Southern plantation owners that their comparative advantage lay in cotton production or, to a lesser extent, the production of sugar, rice, or tobacco. We find, for example, that in the Old South, the states along the Atlantic coast, where the costs of producing cotton were much higher than in the New South, there was almost no shift to other types of production. Cotton was still the best thing that a landowner could produce, even when the cost of producing went up. So during the pre-Civil War era, there was little tendency for industry to grow up in the South.

Diversity of Incomes

Although the average income of free people in the South was, in fact, as high as or higher than that of most other regions of the country before the Civil War, there was probably more diversity or inequality in income and wealth than in other sections of the country. To be sure, one of the main reasons for this great inequality was the large number of slaves in the southern economy. For an average slave, more than one-half of his or her income went to the owner, rather than to the slave.

In the period just before the Civil War, almost one-half of southern personal income went to just 1,000 families. There were some egregious examples of concentrated wealth. The Hairstons had 1,700 slaves on all of their plantations. In Georgia, a Mr. Howell Cobb had over 1,000 slaves on his lands. In rural Louisiana, the top 10 percent of families held 96 percent of all wealth!

Little Investment in Education

One aspect of the southern economy that was not favorable to its further development was the limited amount of investment in education. This was partly because much of the population consisted of slaves. It was not generally worthwhile for a slave owner to provide education for those in bondage. In some states, it was even illegal! Most were bought specifically to do tasks that required very few skills. However, it is not certain why the free white population in the South lagged so far behind the rest of the country in obtaining educational resources. In the post-Civil War era, even up to the present, this had grave consequences, because **investment in human capital**, as it is called, is important for increasing the productivity of individuals, regions, and the nation as a whole.

Schools available for each white person in the South averaged almost 20 percent fewer than in the North. And there were almost 50 percent fewer students (per person) going to school in the South than in the North. So small an investment in education is perhaps understandable if most southerners felt that cotton would remain king. After all, there was little need for a highly educated population if the only productive activities would involve growing staple crops.

Cotton and Interregional Trade

The Southwest

The issue of whether or not the cotton economy helped increase the growth of the national economy is an important one. First, how did cotton affect the West? Whether or not the movement west increased national growth is, of course, a debatable issue. But it is clear that cotton caused westward migration on a scale that far exceeded what would have happened in its absence.

As already mentioned, cotton required fertile lands; and cotton, like most crops cultivated for a long time, takes fertility out of the land. Once the natural fertility of the soil has been depleted, it is necessary either to fertilize and/or rest the land or to move on to new lands. Moreover, in the quest for profits, southern cotton growers moved on to new, fertile lands as the price of cotton rose relative to other crops. There was a lag of one or two years between increases in the price of cotton and a new thrust in westward migration. The main surges to the West occurred during the periods from 1816 to 1819, from 1833 to 1837, and, to a lesser extent, in the 1850s. This corresponds fairly closely to the information on cotton prices presented in Figure 5–3.

When the relative price of cotton rose in the American economy, a common scenario generally followed.

1. The relative price of cotton goes up.
2. New plantations are started, taking three to four years to clear the land.
3. The supply of cotton rises.
4. The relative price of cotton falls.
5. Some of these plantations shift to growing corn, but whenever the price of cotton goes up, they shift back to cotton.
6. The demand for cotton rises so much again that most of the cultivated land is being used for cotton production.
7. The relative price of cotton goes up again as demand outstrips supply.
8. A new cycle starts again; more thrust into the West.

There is little doubt that the cotton economy did propel the growth of population into the new Southwest. It also had some effect on the development of manufacturing in the North, but to a decreasing extent, as the North branched out into industries other than textile manufacturing.

The Northeast

That the availability of relatively inexpensive cotton was vital for the development of the New England textile industry is, of course, a well-known his-

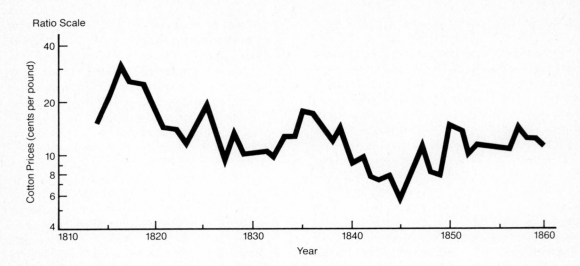

Figure 5-3. Cotton Prices Per Pound Prior to the Civil War.

Source: *Historical Statistics*, p. 124.

torical fact. Moreover, each fall in the price of cotton in the South was an additional stimulus to the North, because cotton was a major input into its manufacturing sector. So to some extent the cotton economy did encourage the growth of industry in New England. Also, southern demand for shoes and cheap textiles to clothe slaves further spurred northern industry, and northern shipping and commercial activities were stimulated as well.

The Northeast and Interregional Trade

Many historians, most notably the renowned economic historian Douglass C. North,[1] have maintained that the demand for foodstuffs by the South spurred the development of the western regions by providing a ready market for products such as wheat. North's argument goes as follows: As the demand for cotton increased, the South would export cotton to New England and foreign ports and buy imports from New England and the West; the West would

[1] See Douglass C. North, *The Economic Growth of the United States 1790-1860*. Englewood Cliffs, N.J.: Prentice-Hall, 1961.

sell foodstuffs to the South and the North and buy certain products from the North. This allowed for a very complete and ever-increasing trade among all parts of the nation. In the process, each region became more specialized and more efficient.

However, when closely examined, the data indicate that even prior to the Civil War the South was almost entirely self-sufficient in foodstuffs. The trade link between the agricultural West (today it is the Midwest) and the Cotton South was minimal. For example, in 1840 the importation of western corn into the South added a grand total of 1 percent to the Southern corn supply. Even the large specialized plantations raised most of their own corn and pork. Most of what the West sent to the South in 1839 was reexported. By 1850 only about 14 percent of the West's exports were consumed in the South. The key to growing interregional trade, then, contrary to North's assertion was not the link between South and West.

The main element of growing regional interdependence was the East-West connection spurred by the westward expansion in the 1850s of the railroad and other transportation improvements. It was the industrializing East that was short on food, and

The Rise of a National Economy

western shipments paralleled the rise of eastern demands. By 1860, the West-North trade flows were more than ten times greater than those between the West and the South. With the railroad tying the West to the North, it is no surprise that the West threw its political support to the North after the South seceded and the Civil War commenced. By 1860, nearly 40 percent of the nation's population resided west of the great Appalachian barrier. Increasingly, as the decades passed, the West took on greater significance, both politically and economically. It was unrivaled in grain production, but it was also well diversified in numerous manufactures—mainly in processing agricultural products. And the difficult question of slavery in the new western territories and status was a critical political issue that added dimension to the rising North-South, slave versus free, conflict. □

Definition of New Term

Investment in human capital: Investment in human capital means the training, schooling, and medical attention given to human beings that yields higher incomes in the future. Investment may be formal, such as going to school, or informal, such as on-the-job training.

issue V: ECONOMIC ASPECTS OF THE "PECULIAR INSTITUTION"

HOW NECESSARY WAS THE CIVIL WAR?

Common Views of Slavery

Some historians have argued that on the eve of the Civil War slavery not only was unprofitable but was moribund as an institution. In other words, the Civil War was apparently unnecessary to eradicate the last vestiges of coercive control over individual freedom in the United States. However, recent evidence indicates that this was not true. This is not to say, of course, that slavery should have been allowed to continue. Nevertheless, it is important that we set our history and our economics straight.

The Rise of Slavery

Slavery was relatively unimportant for almost the first century of settlement in mainland North America. Over 90 percent of all blacks taken as slaves from Africa went to South America (mainly Brazil) and the Caribbean islands. Most of these were engaged in sugar production. In contrast, few slaves went to North America. Before 1730, there were fewer than 100,000 slaves in all of the thirteen American colonies. However, between 1730 and the time of the Revolution, that number doubled and more than doubled again. As in the sugar islands, America's interest in slavery was, of course, economic. The discovery that tobacco could be grown cheaply in Maryland and Virginia encouraged the use of large numbers of unskilled workers to cultivate many acres of land. The same held true for growing rice and indigo in South Carolina.

The Dutch were the first to develop the slave trade with the American colonies, but soon England entered this profitable venture. Slave investments simply returned higher profits than their next best substitute—indentured servants.

While the southern contribution to total exports remained high until the Revolution, there was a reversal in the trend immediately thereafter until cotton became king in the South. At the time the Constitution was written, the forefathers of the nation agreed not to import slaves. As part of one of the great compromises of the Constitution, therefore, slave imports became illegal after 1808. The demand for slaves, which temporarily stagnated, soon expanded however, as the demand for cotton expanded. While slavery declined in the North, it was being intensified in the South.

Northern Emancipation

As we see from Table V—1, various northern states eman-

The Rise of a National Economy

cipated slaves between 1780 and 1804. But the living population of slaves were not freed. Emancipation would have been very costly to their owners. Even the abolitionists recognized the substantial wealth loses that owners would incur if slaves were freed. As part of a political compromise, "gradual emancipation" policies were adopted. Newborn babies would be freed at adulthood (unless they were sold South). Table V—2 shows the ages at which the newborns were freed. Of course, child rearing imposed costs on owners, but by working slaves until their mid-twenties owners were able

to recover (with interest) those costs. In this way, slave owners escaped almost all of the "costs of emancipation."[1]

Emancipation in the northern states was less concerned with the slaves themselves

[1] There was a small possible loss to owners of female slaves since newborns would eventually be freed and would not be the property of the white master. About 10 percent of the value of female slaves was due to the economic value of their offspring. Females were about 37 percent of the total value of slaves. Hence, the maximum loss to owners was 10 percent of 37 percent, or 3.7 percent. The loopholes of selling South, working slaves harder, or reducing maintenance costs probably erased this small amount, however.

than with the political burden of the issue of slavery. Living slaves were not freed. Newborns were freed when they reached adulthood, at an age old enough for them to have paid back their owners for the cost of rearing them. In this way, slave owners escaped almost all of the economic costs of emancipation.

Not Everyone Was a Slave Owner

Although there were many more slave owners in the South than in the North, it was far from true that everyone in the South had slaves.

Table V—1. Northern Emancipation for the "Free-Born.

		Age of Emancipation	
State	Date of Enactment	Male	Female
Pennsylvania	1780[1]	28	28
Rhode Island	1784[2]	21	18
Connecticut	1784[3]	25	25
New York	1799[4]	28	25
New Jersey	1804[5]	25	21

[1] The last census that enumerated any slaves in Pennsylvania was that of 1840.
[2] All slavery was abolished in 1842.
[3] The age of emancipation was changed, in 1797, to age 21. In 1848 all slavery was abolished.
[4] In 1817 a law was passed freeing all slaves as of July 4, 1827.
[5] In 1846 all slaves were emancipated, but apprenticeships continued for the children of slave mothers and were introduced for freed slaves.

Several northern states freed their slaves, but not those alive at the time the emancipation laws were passed. Newborns were freed at an adult age, thus permitting the owner to recover the costs of rearing young slaves to adulthood. In this way, owners of slaves avoided almost all of the costs of emancipation.

Source: Robert W. Fogel and Stanley L. Engerman "Philanthropy at Bargain Prices: Notes on the Economics of Gradual Emancipation." The Journal of Legal Studies, 3, 2 (June 1974): 341.

Table V—2. Per Capita Income Before the Civil War.

	Total Population		Free Population	
	1840	1860	1840	1860
National Average	$ 96	$128	$109	$144
North	109	141	110	142
Northeast	129	181	130	183
North Central	65	89	66	90
South	74	103	105	150
South Atlantic	66	84	96	124
East South Central	69	89	92	124
West South Central	151	184	238	274

We see that the South was far from stagnating before the Civil War. In fact, its per capita income was higher in some of its subregions, such as the West South Central, than the national average. (All expressed in 1860 prices.)

Source: Robert W. Fogel and Stanley L. Engerman, "The Economics of Slavery," in *The Reinterpretation of American Economic History* New York: Harper & Row, 1971, p. 335, Table 8.

By the start of the Civil War, there were 1.4 million free families in the southern states. Only 380,000 of them owned slaves, which meant that only about one-fourth of all southern families were slaveholders. Of this particular group, however, less than one-fourth held ten or more slaves, which means that not even 4 percent of the southern white population had ten or more slaves on their farms. This 4 percent held over three-fourths of the total number of slaves at that time. Hence, slavery was not the all-pervasive institution that one usually thinks it was in the pre-Civil War South. However, those who held power in the southern states were more likely than not to be the owners of slaves, for

slaves were a significant part of the southern wealth. It is therefore understandable that they would object to any threats by the North to emancipate the blacks.

Was Slavery Dying Out?

It is sometimes believed that the South was stagnating before the Civil War and that, since slaves seemed to be unprofitable and less productive than free workers, the institution of slavery would have died of its own accord. But if we examine what was actually happening in the South, slavery does not appear to have been moribund, for the South itself was far

from stagnating. A look at Table V—2 shows that per capita income in the South, although more unequally distributed, was certainly not much lower than the national average, and in some cases, such as in the West South Central area, it was much higher. It was also higher in all cases as compared with the North Central region of the United States, a region that historians have customarily indicated as having a high level of living at that time. If we consider the per capita income of only the free population in the South we see that in 1840 and 1860 it exceeded the national average.

Moreover, the South certainly was not stagnating in

The Rise of a National Economy

terms of its growth rate. Per capita income grew at an average rate of 1.7 percent a year, which exceeded the national average of 1.3 percent a year. It also exceeded the growth rate of the North Central states. The South was a growing economy, one in which its inhabitants anticipated that things would continue to improve, not worsen. Table V—3 shows that the price of slaves was rising generally throughout this period. Clearly slave values were increasing, not decreasing. This increasing price indicated that slaves had rising economic value to southern plantation owners. Farm and household slaves also provided leisure time for owners— another reason, then, why they were desired.

Were Slave Owners Losing Money?

Until quite recently, some historians hypothesized that by the end of the 1850s, slave owners were losing money on their investment in slaves. To understand how the price of slaves was determined, we have to view slaves as a **capital investment**. That is, the potential owner would decide how much to pay for the slave by determining what the *current* value of the slave's *future* net income was.

Table V—3. Slave Prices in the Upper and Lower South.

Period	Upper South Price	Lower South Price
1830—1835	$ 521	$ 948
1836—1840	957	
1841—1845	529	722
1846—1850	709	926
1851—1855	935	1,240
1856—1860	1,294	1,658

There was a gradual increase in the price of slaves for the period from 1830 to the Civil War, reaching a peak, just prior to the Civil War, in the lower South of $1658.

Source: R. Evans, Jr., "The Economics of American Negro Slavery," *Aspects of Labor Economics.* Princeton, N.J.: Princeton University Press, 1962, p. 216.

Profitabiliity Computations

Slaves provided owners with a stream of income. That income was the value of the product that the slave produced for the owner minus the cost of the slave's maintenance. For example, a slave could help the owner increase his cotton production by, say, three bales of cotton. Let's say that those bales could be sold in the open market for 10 cents a pound, or $50 a bale. That would mean that the total revenues of the plantation owner would go up by $150 if he hired this additional slave. We cannot accept that as the first year's *net* revenues on the slave purchase, because we have to subtract out the cost of maintaining the slave, say $25 per year. That meant that the net profits to the owner from having the slave would be $125 per year. This stretched over the expected lifetime of the slave. Let us add all this up and properly account for the fact that some of it occurred in later years. Having done this, assume our answer for the current value of the future streams of net profit from hiring the additional slave would be equal to $1,250. $1,250, then, would be the maximum price that a slave owner would pay for an additional slave. This is indeed how the price of slaves was determined in the open slave market. It was a function mainly of the price of cotton and the productivity of slaves. Ignoring the latter, we find that the price of cotton was, for the most part, either stable or rising. Slave owners anticipated that the price of cotton would continue to be high for many years in the future. So on the eve of the Civil War, they were far from pessimistic about the profitability of slavery.

Cotton Prices Not Falling

Look at Figure V–1. It shows the price of raw cotton in cents per pound, corrected for general changes in the price level. It grew from 7.4 cents in 1840 to 12.4 cents in 1850, then fell again during the first few years of that decade, but started to rise again in 1857. Any drop in the price of cotton was viewed as temporary by plantation owners. They anticipated continuing high revenues from having slaves on their plantation. The price of slaves reflected the slave owners' anticipations of future prices for cotton. The price of slaves in the upper South, for example, was only $521 during the period 1830 to 1835. But by 1856 it had risen to over $1,200. In the lower South in 1860, a prime slave could have fetched $1,800. In Table V–3 the various prices of slaves as five-year averages are shown.

Slaves a Profitable Investment

What did all this have to do with the profitability of slavery? A correct investigation of the data shows that the average rate of return on slaves was as high as or higher than on any other capital investment that was available to southerners during that period. In the lower South, for example, it was 12 percent during the period 1830–1835, falling to about 10 percent on the eve of the Civil War. This was at least as high as rates of return that prevailed elsewhere in the economy. So long as the rate of return on

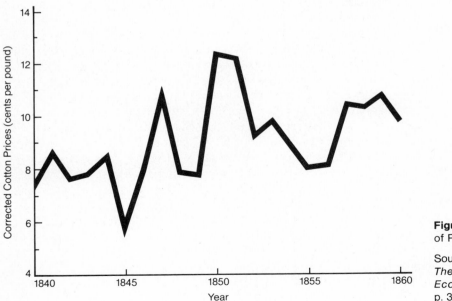

Figure V-1. Corrected Price of Raw Cotton.

Source: Fogle and Engerman, *The Reinterpretation of Economic History*, Table 1, p. 316.

The Rise of a National Economy

investment in slavery was as good as or better than the rates of return that existed in other capital investments, we would expect that the institution of slavery would expand. And that is exactly what happened.

The Viability of Slavery

Slavery was indeed profitable and, at least for the foreseeable future, clearly viable. A slave was economically viable when the value of the slave's output exceeded the costs of the slave's reproduction. This was certainly so if slavery was still profitable and could be so even if it were not. However, some important facts tend to counter this position. At that time, new competition in the world cotton market from India and Egypt was appearing. Moreover, there were the beginnings of a worldwide emancipation movement that was certain to reach the United States sooner or later. Perhaps slavery would have died out of its own accord at some time in the late nineteenth century. Was some type of strong coercive measure necessary to abruptly terminate the existence of this institution? The Civil War did not begin as a war to end slavery, but emancipation was one favorable outcome of that bitter, costly conflict.   □

Definition of New Term

Capital investment: Capital investment is investment in a productive asset—that is, an asset that will yield a stream of income in the future. The purchase of a slave was a capital investment.

6. Secession, War, and Economic Change

During the decades just prior to the Civil War, incomes per free person were higher in the South than in the North, and per capita incomes in the South were rising faster than the national average. Investments in slaves continued to be profitable, and the "peculiar institution" remained viable. No natural forces were leading to the collapse of slavery in the United States, and it could end only by political or military means.

It seems clear in retrospect that secession after the election of President Lincoln was not entirely without cause. The politically dominant slaveholders feared the northern abolitionists and the uncertainty of a newly elected president opposed to slavery. Except for these anxieties, slaveholders were optimistic on the eve of the Civil War. They anticipated a continuation of their social order and also a new era of increased prosperity. In short, the South seceded out of economic strength, not weakness.

The Outbreak of War

The outbreak of hostilities brought with it the usual problems of obtaining labor and paying for that labor, ammunition, and all the items neceessary for war. Because the north was fighting to hold the union together, it was forced to attack. In contrast, the military goal of the South was much more modest: Obtain a draw or a stalemate.

What Happened in the South?

At one time or another, almost one million soldiers served in the Confederate Army. At the height of the war, there were perhaps over one-half million engaged in combat. This represented an impressive 50 percent of the white male population between the ages of fifteen and fifty. As can be expected, the economy suffered from a scarcity of food, clothing, and war materials. The North had quickly set up a naval blockade—a disaster for the South, which had engaged in extensive trade with the East and with foreign ports. At the beginning of the war, only one-tenth of the total value of manufactured products used in the South were made there. Self-sufficiency would indeed be difficult; trade was important. Despite these and myriad other problems, the southern economy supported a large army for four years of extremely heavy fighting.

Shifting Productive Capacities

Among the South's greatest problems was the shifting of productive resources out of cotton—which was no longer a useful industry because the output could not be traded for needed manufactured goods and foodstuffs—into providing increased food-stuffs and supplies for the armies, as well as other manufactured goods for the civilian population. To this end, cotton production was cut back sharply in

1862. The government did not need to enforce this cutback. After all, the southern cotton growers were not going to continue increasing production if they could not sell it. They quickly shifted their capital into areas where relative rates of return were higher. Reduction of the crop continued: In 1863, it was well below one million bales, as compared to four million a few years earlier, and in the following years the output was halved again. Tobacco production also was reduced, again because the surplus over what was consumed in the South could not be sold.

Entrepreneurs made a valiant effort to produce substitutes for the manufactured goods that the South had previously imported. A noteworthy achievement was the development of homespun cloth.

Urbanization

The rise in the manufacturing industry in the South dramatically increased urbanization. Before the Civil War, the South had remained overwhelmingly rural, with only one major city, New Orleans. After the war started, Charleston, Atlanta, Richmond, and Wilmington all became increasingly crowded, for there industrial and administrative employment were available. Southerners were seeking out areas where they could earn the most income, and that no longer was on the farm.

Were the Southern Forces Defeated from Within?

Many observers of the defeat of the Confederacy maintain that the government policy of inflationary finance and inept foreign trade policy caused the downfall of the South during the Civil War. However, the evidence in support of this view is mixed.

Trade Policies

The Confederacy did make a number of mistakes in trade policy, at least in retrospect. The northern blockade really did not take effect until 1863 and 1864, so before that time—that is, during the first two years of the war—the South could have continued exporting cotton to obtain needed munitions, manufactured items, and foodstuffs. However, the Confederate government discouraged any export during this period, so out of a four-million-bale crop from 1861 to 1862, only 13,000 bales were reported to have left the South. The government was so sure that cotton was king that by withholding it from the North and foreign countries (especially Britain), the South hoped to obtain support for the Confederacy by all the industrialists who would be hurt. Obviously, the South would have been better off had they exported as much cotton as possible in order to obtain supplies for the army and the civilian population.

Inflationary Finance

The Confederate government, of course, somehow had to obtain part of the civilian output for use in fighting the war. Foreigners were unwilling to lend very large sums to the Confederacy and, certainly after the northern blockade on trade came into effect, there were very few import duties that could be used to support the war effort. The South did obtain a certain amount of federal government property and that of Union citizens when the war broke out. The most noteworthy acquisitions were the Harpers Ferry arsenal and the naval shipyard at Norfolk. There was a certain amount of confiscation of privately produced goods in addition to internal taxes and loans. But that accounted for less than one-half of the total outlays of the Confederate government during the war. These outlays were valued then at about $3 billion. How was the rest made up? By **inflationary finance**. That is, the Confederacy issued large amounts of paper notes (printed money). Figure 6-1 shows an index of commodity prices in the South that rose from 100 in January 1861 to 9,210 in April 1865. An index of the stock of money grew from 100 in January of 1861 to 2,000 in April of 1865. This displays a typical situation of **hyperinflation**—that is, a dra-

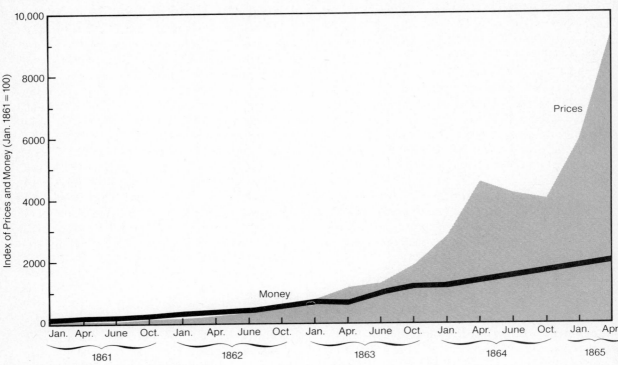

Figure 6-1. Infltion in the Confederacy.

Source: E. M. Lerner, "Money, Prices, and Wages in the Confederacy, 1861-65," *Journal of Political Economy, 63 (February 1955): 29.*

matic, overwhelming increase in the price level over a short period of time. As prices begin to rise very rapidly, consumers start anticipating this rise: They realize that the dollars—in this case, Confederate notes—are going to lose purchasing power because of inflation. That means that it becomes more expensive to hold cash, and so people attempted to spend their dollars before they lost value.

In this way, people bid up prices even faster than would occur otherwise. During these periods, some people think there is a scarcity of money. In fact, it is just the other way around. The reason that prices are going up so fast is because there is *too much* money in circulation, and it is turning over too fast.

The Confederacy also faced a problem not encountered by most countries during hyperinflations: Toward the end of the war, it was assumed that Confederate notes would have a zero exchange value

if there was a Union victory. Clearly. a Confederate dollar would be worth little or nothing if the South lost the war.

That is the main reason that the inflation reached astronomical proportions by the end of 1864.

The Collapse

Valiant as the Confederate forces were, their ultimate collapse was inevitable given the steady drain on southern resources. The physical base on which the southern economy rested was slowly but surely whittled away by the military efforts of the Union. Union forces were continuously making inroads into the western and coastal fronts of the South. By 1861, there were almost no Confederate forces in

The Rise of a National Economy

Missouri; Kentucky and West Virginia were held by the Union. One of the key southern disasters of the war was the loss of New Orleans to federal amphibious forces in the spring of 1862. During that same year, western Tennessee was captured. This event closed off much of the South's access to the Mississippi. Many of the ports that could have been used during the war were unavailable, such as Savannah and Jacksonville. Then, in 1863, the Union conquered Mississippi. The Confederacy was cut in two. In 1864, Sherman marched through Georgia, breaking up the Confederacy into fourths. Atlanta fell. This continuous loss of territory prevented a Confedrate military stalemate. The Union would be preserved, but at great cost to both the North and the South.

The Federal War Economy

The outbreak of the Civil War meant immediate losses to northern merchants, as all of the $300 million in debts owed by southerners were never to be repaid. Most of the cotton textile factories soon became idle. In 1861, over 6,000 business failures were reported by Dun, a forerunner of Dun & Bradstreet. Banks started to fail; for example, 80 percent of the 110 banks in Illinois closed their doors. But by 1863, there was a minor war-related boom underway in the northern states.

Military Labor

About 15 percent of the labor force was involved in the Union effort. There had to be some way to procure these men. In 1863, the North passed the Enrollment Bill for troop conscription. However, this system of draft was quite different from our recently defunct system of conscription. It allowed those who were drafted to pay someone to go in their stead. Thus, even though the method of conscription was somewhat arbitrary; the final determination of who would go to war was quite a bit more flexible.

Obviously those whose civilian incomes were relatively high found it useful—indeed, advantageous—to hire replacements whose civilian incomes were relatively low. And apparently many of the less well-to-do found the "bribes" advantageous, since they accepted them.

This method of conscription tended to trade off equity for efficiency, and some may view the scheme as unfair or unjust. Nevertheless, it is clear that those whose incomes are high suffer a greater dollar cost if they are drafted than those whose incomes are low. From society's economic point of view, then, it is more efficient to allow high-income earners to pay low-income earners to fight the war, because income is generally (though not always) a reflection of a person's productivity in society. As such, if high-income people are left to do their jobs and low-income people fight the war, the total output of the economy will be higher than otherwise. In a situation like this, fairness and efficiency conflict. The North's means of manpower procurement emphasized the latter.

Financing the Northern Effort

With the declaration of war, in 1861, there was an immediate financial panic as banks suspended specie payments, and business failures occurred. The federal treasury was almost empty; federal credit was at a low point, as the government itself suspended specie payment. The Union had to finance the war somehow, and it did it by increased loans, taxation, and paper money.

Loans. With respect to the first form of war finance, J. Cooke, a Philadelphia banker, floated many loans for the government. He popularized bond issues by emphasizing the advantages of the investment and the patriotic duty of the citizens of the North. Over $2 billion were raised in this manner. Cooke's fee was 1 percent on sales up to $10 million and three-eights of 1 percent on sales that exceeded that figure. He made a mint.

Taxes. The North probably used taxation to raise funds more than did the South. Excise taxes were raised in 1862 and extended to numerous goods and services. They produced almost $300 million. The Morrill Tariff, passed in 1861, raised another $300 million. And then there was the income tax, which produced about $55 million.

Money Creation. As in the South, large amounts of paper money were created. Almost half a billion dollars in United States Notes, otherwise called **greenbacks**, were issued. These bills were not backed by gold or silver; they were merely promises on the part of the government to redeem them. Their value fluctuated wildly in terms of gold. By 1864, the rate of exchange was one greenback for 40 cents of gold. By 1864, the price index had risen to two times its pre-1860 level.

Northern Industry During the War

While it is true that some new manufacturing occurred during the war that would not have occurred otherwise, it is not obvious that total output in the North was any greater during the Civil War than it was before, or than it would have been without the war. There are no extensive data for that particular period, for the censuses then were taken in ten-year intervals. However, New York and Massachusetts did take censuses for 1865, and these show that in both states there were declines in real output between 1860 and 1865, and also between 1855 and 1865. It appears that these two key manufacturing states, which accounted for over one-third of total manufacturing value added in 1860 and a little over 30 percent in 1870, did not have a rapidly expanding manufacturing sector during the war years.

Little Capital Investment

Estimates of residential construction during this period indicate that after the war there was twice as much residential building as during the war. Moreover, sales of McCormick reapers showed a boom after the war, not during it. And there was certainly not a large surge in what we normally call *war in-*

dustries. Generally, the Civil War was not one of intensive capital investment. For example, the iron needed for the small-arms production during the war was only 1 percent of total U.S. iron output during the four years starting in 1861—one small factory could have done that. At the same time, the iron used in laying railroad track *decreased* by seven times this figure. Another often-cited war industry was the manufacturing of boots for servicemen. However, at the same time that more boots were needed for federal soldiers, fewer boots were sold to the South. For example, in Massachusetts employment in the boot and shoe industry fell from almost 80,000 to 55,000 during the Civil War. Output fell from forty-five million pairs to thirty-two million.

The Northern Business Atmosphere

It is true that northern business was booming after the first few disorganized months of the war. However, good business does not necessarily imply economic development. Many profits may be derived merely from speculation, and this is just a transfer from one sector of the economy to another. Also, with all the good business, there was just as much poor business in some sectors. In fact, there was more poor business than good in the northern cotton textile industry because it suffered after the blockade of imports from the South. Numerous mills closed down and others were forced into the production of wool, which, as can be expected, grew as an industry to replace the cotton textiles that could no longer be spun. However, there were costs involved in shifting over, and these costs contributed to the reduced productivity in that sector. Moreover, even during the Civil War there were in the North severe pockets of unemployment. To be sure, the conscription at that time did ameliorate to some extent this problem of unemployment, but not completely.

Government Expenditures

There is also the idea that large amounts of government expenditures caused a rapid increase in the manufacturing sector, especially in the North. This, however, was not true. Government expenditures went mainly for bounties, salaries, and food—especially beef—and for various types of unsophisticated weapons. In any event, the total amount of northern government expenditures during the Civil War represented a minor part of total output, and these expenditures were generally substitutes for what the private sector would have spent anyway. In other words, the private sector did not spend as much of its income because the government obtained part of it through loans, increased excise taxes, a new income tax, and inflationary finance.

Postwar Recovery in the South

After the war, the southern economy recovered faster in manufacturing than in agriculture. By 1870, manufacturing production approached the prewar level and transportation and railroads also had recovered. Manufacturing could recover faster than agriculture because the whole makeup of the agricultural society had been altered by the Emancipation Proclamation, while in manufacturing, there had been predominantly a free white labor force before the war anyway.

There is no doubt that in the postwar years the South was burdened by large material and human losses, as well as by an incalculable amount of social disorganization caused by the unquestionably changed status of slaves. Although the full cost of the war can, of course, not be seen in the statistics, Table 6—1 shows the commodity output per capita by region from 1860 to 1880. Whereas outside the South, per capita income increased almost 9 percent, southern per capita output in 1870 was only about 60 percent of what it had been in 1860. Clearly, the South was hurt badly and took many years to recover.

Of course, much of the South's productive capacity had been destroyed—not only its capital, but also its labor. Nearly 259,000 Confederate soldiers had been killed and another 261,000 wounded.

Table 6—1. Real Commodity Output Per Capita (1879 dollars)

	Outside the South	South
1860	$ 74.8	$77.7
1870	81.5	47.6
1880	105.8	61.5

Here we present commodity output per capita by region from 1860 to 1880 in 1879 prices. The South, even after 15 years of recovery from the Civil War, still had a per capita commodity output which was less than before the start of the Civil War.

Source: R. A. Easterlin, "Regional Economic Trends, 1840—1950," in S. Harris, ed., *American Economic History.* New York: McGraw-Hill, 1961, pp. 525—547.

These were almost all men of working age and were a direct loss to the southern labor force. Many were planters or sons of planters, and the loss in entrepreneurial skills and human capital, as well as raw labor, was very high.

In addition, there was the great problem of how to reorganize the entire agricultural system and contend with the social disorganization of a large, politically free, but still economically dependent, black population. With the new rights of freedom, many blacks, especially the women and children, retreated from the fields. And males also typically chose to work fewer hours. In the cotton belt, the overall reduction in labor effort was about 30 percent. No wonder output fell. And, of course, the highly efficient plantations were a thing of the past.

In the North, there were no such problems of economic reorganization. Nevertheless, 360,000 Union men had lost their lives, and 365,000 had been wounded. The Civil War was more costly in blood and human suffering than any other war we have ever fought.

The National View in Long-Term Perspective

The growth rate of total commodity output from 1859 to 1869 was only 2.0 percent per year, the lowest it had been in decades. In fact, if we examine the long-term trends, we see that total commodity output rose at an average annual rate of 4.6 percent between 1840 and 1860, dropping to an average annual rate of 4.4 percent between 1870 and 1900. With respect to industrialization, the shift out of agriculture into manufacturing was as rapid during the two decades before the war as it was during the two decades after the war. If we look at how much manufacturing contributed to the increases in output, we find that while value added in manufacturing grew at about 7.0 percent per annum from 1840 to 1860, it grew at only 6 percent per annum from 1870 to 1900. There was also a relatively large decline in the productivity of labor in the manufacturing sector from 1860 to 1870.

Rather than being a decade of tremendously increased production and industrialization, the Civil War decade marked a departure from the general output, productivity, and income trends that had existed prior to it. At least in part, this should not be surprising, given the fact that out of a labor force of 7.5 million, 1 million men were involved in the fighting. This is a reduction of about 15 percent. How could the economy have experienced an industrial renaissance with that kind of depletion of the working force?

Although the evidence presented strongly suggests that rapid economic expansion did not stem from the war, some historians have argued that the Civil War was a type of second political revolution. It supposedly removed the "backward South" as a political force and allowed the northern Republicans to pass legislation favorable to economic growth. To assess this proposition, we must carefully assess the economic consequences of the legislation passed by the Republican Congresses. ☐

Definitions of New Terms

Inflationary finance: Inflationary finance involves the issuance of large amounts of money to help finance government expenditures, usually during wartime.

Hyperinflation: Hyperinflation is a consistent rise in the price level that attains astronomical rates, such as a 1,000 percent increase a month!

Greenbacks: Greenbacks were U.S. Bank Notes that were not backed by gold or silver; they got their name from their color.

The Rise of a National Economy

THE WAR AND GOVERNMENT LEGISLATION

Perhaps because of faulty data, or perhaps because of the general notion that war is sometimes good for the economy, early students of the Civil War were convinced that it spurred economic growth and industrialization. From Chapter 6 it appears that the Civil War did not itself stimulate growth. In fact, it appears to have retarded the growth rates in the North and reversed them sharply in the South. But this would provide too facile a view of the potential impact of the Civil War on future U.S. economic development. During the war period, several innovative pieces of government legislation were passed that may have influenced the future course of the economy. Some historians have argued that the Civil War was necessary to rid the Congress (especially the Senate) of the southern voting block, which fought legislation allegedly essential to economic development. After their removal, the all-Republican Congress had a free hand, and a series of economic measures were passed. One of the most significant pieces was the National Banking Act.

Enactment of the National Banking Act

Prior to federal legislation in 1863 and 1864, which established a national banking system, the banking atmosphere was one of considerable freedom throughout all of the states. In this era of free banking, state bank charters were easily obtained in just about any state. The main intent of the National Banking Act—at least that which was aired in public—was to establish a national system that would unify all of the banks in the entire United States. However, the original legislation which provided for the chartering of national banks was based on the free banking charters of that day—in almost all respects. The several exceptions made all the difference in the world, as will be explained below. The result was *not* a national banking system and in general *not* the creation of a national institution that would foster further development by greatly expanding credit markets and credit availability.

The War and the Need for More Money

Congress enacted the banking legislation primarily, although not exclusively, in order to increase the government's borrowing power during the war. It did this by requiring all national banks to invest a portion of their capital in government bonds. And the capital that was necessary to open a national bank was, it turned out, substantially higher than most banks actually had, especially in the rural areas. As a result, the system of national banks did not in fact become established as the one and only institution for banking throughout the United States. In the agricultural areas of the country, the average capital of nonnational banks was less than the *minimum* required to open or be transformed into a national bank, and national banks were forbidden to make real estate loans. Moreover, state-chartered banks had their note issues taxed by the federal government. Taken together, these conditions hindered the growth of rural banks. The consequence was higher rural interest rates in the South and West.

No National System Created

Even by 1900, there were still about 9,000 nonnational banks, as opposed to about 4,000 national banks. Obviously, the Civil War legislation did not give the United States a single, unified banking system. Because of the differential treatment of nonnational banks, which slowed their growth, it seems likely that there was actually a restraint on the number of banks that were started after enactment of the legislation, as compared to what would have happened had it never been passed.

A Unified Reserve System

On the plus side of the national banking legislation was the fact that the country's banks were linked together through a reserve system that provided a legally sanctioned formal mechanism for transferring funds between banks. This tended to promote an efficient allocation of loanable funds throughout the country. In other words, it was easier for funds to go to areas where they could yield the highest social product—that is, to areas where the rate of return would be highest. This generally meant the transfer of bank funds from agricultural to industrial uses, which helped funnel credit to areas that required large amounts of capital, such as railroad investment and large-scale industry. Taking the positive and negative effects together, the net effects of the National Banking Act are unclear. It seems highly doubtful that the act was critical to the economic development of the United States.

Giving Away Land

In 1862, the Union Congress passed the Homestead Act. This provided that 160 acres of land hitherto owned by the federal government could be acquired by a settler if he agreed to live on it or cultivate it for at least five consecutive years. What effect did this magnanimous Act have on the distribution of land holdings in the United States and, consequently, on the development of our open spaces? It turns out that the amount of new land put into cultivation after the Civil War that was attributable to homesteading was less than 20 percent of the total new acres taken up until then. The rest was either purchased from federal, state, or local governments, or was given away in the form of land grants to railroads.

Many historians maintain that the Homestead Act caused a reduced growth of national product during this period because it caused farmers to use inefficient amounts of capital and labor on tracts of land that turned out to be too small. Remember that the Homestead Act provided for only 160 acres. By the time it was passed, in 1862, the frontier and most of the land available was pretty far west. Although there was some good land left, most of it was prairie land and good for little more than grazing sheep or cattle. As any rancher will attest, 160 acres of grassland is not much for grazing purposes and in fact will supply only about fifteen or twenty cattle with forage.

The Rise of a National Economy

Helping Out the Railroads

Land grants to railroads were another possible way of disposing of land in the public domain. Other railroad subsidies were also given out during this period, and again we must ask the question: Did federal land grants sharply affect the growth rate?

Remember that during the war years there was almost a total stop to the construction of new railroad mileage. But the federal government had established a policy of subsidizing the railroads by giving them land grants along their rights-of-way. Five railroad systems accounted for 75 percent of all of these subsidies: Central Pacific; Union Pacific; Atchison, Topeka and Santa Fe; Northern Pacific; and the Texas and Pacific railroad systems. The subsidy to the Union Pacific Railroad, which obtained land grants by the Acts of 1862 and 1864, did indeed turn out favorably. The social rate of return—that is, the returns to the investors plus the spillover benefits to society—on that investment was relatively high. So the government subsidies were indeed justified from a social point of view. However, the increase in national income made possible by the Union Pacific was only 0.01 of 1 percent. Similar computations have been made for the Central Pacific Rail-

road, with similar results. Although all of these numbers certainly leave some room for doubt, nonetheless, it appears that legislation allowing subsidies to a few railroads provided positive but very minor impetus to growth. It seems likely that the railroads in question would have been built eventually even without the land grants. Such an alteration in the timing of construction due to the subsidies would have had negligible effects on national income.

Protecting Infant Industries

Even before the days of Alexander Hamilton, the first prominent American leader to advocate high protective tariffs to stimulate U.S. manufacturing, it was well known that certain industries would gain from tariff protection. Under special circumstances, it is alleged, society as a whole may also gain.

By this argument, if certain industries are to be able to start up and become technologically efficient so that they can eventually compete in the world market, they must be "protected" in their infancy. That is, a tariff wall must be erected around that "infant industry." The tariff wall causes the price of imports to rise high enough so

that the less efficient "infant" producer can compete. Later, by learning through doing and by developing better technology, the infant will eventually become a full-grown adult. Then the tariff walls can be lowered.

However, the usual case is that when the infant has grown up the tariffs are not taken off. Nonetheless, the argument is often used when discussing the economic impact of legislation during the Civil War.

It should be remembered that the two decades prior to the Civil War saw the rise of manufacturing and economic growth under a low tariff policy. The Republicans, however, came into power in 1861 committed to making sure that there were higher duties to "protect" American manufacturers. Since there were no southern congressmen to fight them, the Republicans raised the tariff even before Lincoln took office. Then, using the excuse that they needed to raise more war revenues, they raised the tariff even higher. By 1867, the average duty on imports reached a whopping 47 percent. It was not clear at that time which industries benefited and who was hurt.

Distortions Caused by Tariffs

What is clear is that in almost all cases a tariff causes a distortion and a misallocation of resources. After all, the highest economic value from scarce resources is obtained by using them where they have the highest comparative advantage. If other countries can produce goods at a lower price than U.S. producers, consumers can take advantage of that if they want to maximize their economic welfare. Of course, certain industries may be hurt in the short run, but others end up producing goods for which other nations do not have a comparative advantage. We export the latter and import the former. The results are gains from trade, and that is why so many economists (and consumers) are against setting up tariff walls.

Even though the tariff was raised substantially during the Civil War, it is not at all obvious that the northerners benefited and that economic growth in general was increased. No doubt some of the manufacturers benefited; and no doubt the economy as a whole suffered.

This is just another instance where there is no positive evidence to show that legislative actions during the Civil War helped promote the growth of the United States. Considering the package of Civil War legislation as a whole, it also appears that the growth stimulus was very weak, especially from the national perspective.

Technological Advance

Finally, it should be emphasized that this was a period when technological advance and diffusion was increasing sharply. The loss of labor from the farms (for the war effort) encouraged the substitution of capital for labor, such as McCormick's reaper. In addition, the 1860s and 1870s were decades of sharp increases in animal power—often in place of human energy.

Not only the spread of advanced technologies but also the development of new ones in ever-widening scales of application added to the growth impetus of the period. Increasingly, technological changes and innovation (or technical diffusion) became commonplace in transportation, manufacturing, mining, and construction. And the development of more perfect capital markets, in conjunction with higher overall levels of investment, readily channeled these advances in technology into the production process. Technological change was increasingly becoming a vital part of the story of U.S. economic growth, especially by the last half of the nineteenth century. □

Definitions of New Terms

Social rate of return: The social rate of return is the rate of return on an investment that takes account of not only the benefits to the private investor but also any other benefits that society obtains.

Infant industry argument: The infant industry argument is used in support of high tariffs: Presumably an industry, if protected by a high tariff, can improve its technology and efficiency so much that later on when it is full-grown, the tariff can be removed, but it will still be able to compete in the world market with other full-grown competitors.

The Rise of a National Economy

Part IV
New Strides
Toward Economic
Prominence,
1865—1919

The Ruthless Businessman Par Excellence

Jay Gould

(1836-1892)

Railroads and Gold Manipulations

Can you imagine that one man caused a major panic on what Wall Street called Black Friday (September 24, 1869)? It may sound impossible; still, it actually happened. That one man was Jay Gould, who with the help of his flamboyant sidekick, Jim Fisk, cornered the market in gold, sold out, and watched it fall. Gold was a very precious commodity after the Civil War, for the issuance of greenbacks, which could not be redeemed at par in specie, brought great speculation in all precious metals. However, the growth of confidence in the government, improvement in the U.S. trade balance, and perhaps the postwar prosperity brought the price of gold down again in terms of greenbacks. By 1869, $131 in greenbacks bought $100 of gold. Gould bought $7 million worth, helping send the price up to $140. Since Jim Fisk seemed to have similar ideas, they banded together and started to buy all the gold they could, with as much money as they were able to get out of a Tammany Hall-controlled bank called the Tenth National. At the same time, however, they were worried about the $80 million in gold that the U.S. Treasury held, part of which could be thrown on the market at any time, causing them great financial loss.

To forestall that day, Gould befriended the man who had married President Ulysses Grant's middle-aged sister. To make sure this man used his influence correctly, Gould bought him $2 million in gold bonds on margin, so if the price of gold continued to rise, Grant's brother-in-law could reap sizable profits. When Major Dan Butterfield was named Assistant U.S. Treasurer at New York, he, too, suddenly had somewhere around $2 million in gold bonds in his account, purchased, of course, by Gould.

By September of that year, Gould and Fisk really did have a corner on the entire gold market, when the price of gold was at $141 in greenbacks for $100 in gold. When Gould got wind that the president was going to force the U.S. Treasury to unload its holdings of yellow metal, he quietly started selling out, as did all of his associates, while simultaneously acting and talking like a bull. The price of gold first went up to $150, then to $164 in greenbacks, for $100 of gold.

Finally the president ordered the U.S. Treasury to sell $5 million in gold immediately. In fifteen minutes, the price fell twenty-five points. Gould and Fisk were already in their headquarters, guarded by police and their own men. Gould alone made $11 million. But, kindheartedly, he announced his regret over the Black Friday panic. And Assistant Treasurer Butterfield sanctimoniously pointed out that only speculators had lost money.

No one had ever dreamed that little Jason Gould, who was born in Roxbury, New York, the son of poor hill farmers, would become a great American financier. He first started working for a blacksmith, then became a clerk in a country store. He learned the rudiments of surveying and obtained enough education before his twentieth birthday to write the *History of Delaware County and Border Wars of New York.* Before he was twenty-one, he had $5,000 in capital, with which he joined hands with a New York politician and opened a large tannery in northern Pennsylvania. He abandoned the tannery, became a leather merchant, and finally found where he had a special genius—speculating in small railroads.

His notoriety became immense during his battle with Cornelius Vanderbilt over the Erie Railroad. While they were attempting to bring the price of Erie stock down, Fisk and Gould found a printing press in the cellars of the Erie offices and turned out phony stock certificates. Eventually, they did get control of the Erie, the stock of which they successfully "watered."[1] The money he made on the Erie and other speculative ruthless adventures was Gould's starting capital for cornering the gold market. The public scandal was so great that Gould was finally ejected from his control of the Erie on March 10, 1872. At that time his fortune was estimated to exceed $25 million.

Furthermore, he went on to still greener pastures. He took over the Union Pacific Railroad, became its director, and remained in virtual control until 1878, while at the same time buying control of the Kansas Pacific. Then in 1879 he bought control of the Denver Pacific, Central Pacific, and Missouri Pacific. In another seemingly unscrupulous deal with the Union Pacific and Kansas Pacific, he made a stock deal that supposedly netted him $10 million. Gould was the epitome of the ruthless American businessman. He apparently had few friends, but some observers point out that he was a warm and kindly family man, enjoying the diversions of books and gardening. He died of tuberculosis at age fifty-seven with an estate of $70 million. □

---

[1] The term *watering* comes from the practice of salting cattle just before they go en route to market and not allowing them to drink until just before being weighed.

The Great
Steel Maker

Andrew Carnegie
(1835-1919)

Industrialist and Scientific Philanthropist

"A messenger boy of the name of Andrew Carnegie, employed by the O'Reily Telegraph Company, yesterday found a draft for the amount of $500. Like an honest little fellow, he promptly made known the facts, and deposited the paper in good hands where it awaits identification" (news clipping from the *Pittsburgh Dispatch*, November 2, 1849).

Five hundred dollars was indeed a lot of money for the son of a Scottish weaver—it represented ten years' wages. Later in life, it would represent merely what Andrew would earn every ten minutes of every day. The saga of Andrew Carnegie has indeed inspired generations of schoolchildren. At age twelve, the young immigrant worked in a cotton mill for $1.20 a week. Then he moved into the telegraph department of the Pennsylvania Railroad, where he quickly became the private secretary of its head. He started investing, first in a small oil company, and then in the Woodruff Palace Sleeping Car Company. Soon the young man was building railroad bridges, iron rails, and the like. Carnegie also made a small fortune in oil and took several trips to Europe selling railroad securities. His operations in bond selling, oil dealing, bridge building, and the like were so dashing and successful that conserva-

tive Pittsburgh businessmen regarded him as somewhat of a Young Turk. By 1873, however, Carnegie thought that steel was the new American industry. He began his famous policy, which he described as "putting all my eggs in one basket and then watching the basket." He was then thirty-eight years old. His business life for the next three decades was to some extent a microcosm of the industrial history of the United States for the same period. During this time, he was a staunch advocate of tariffs for infant industries, but he considered them wicked "when used merely to swell the profits of an established business." Even before he retired, he advocated the removal of tariff duties on imported steel. (As well he might, since his firms could produce at lower cost than the British!)

Industrialist Andrew Carnegie rose to power in the steel industry during the period after the Civil War that has been characterized as one of uninhibited exploitation and cutthroat competition. Even Calvinist attitudes were insufficient to excuse what was happening. Carnegie found his philosophical underpinnings in the English writer Herbert Spencer, who applied the fundamental principles of Darwinian evolution to society. His thesis was that of social Darwinism—in the struggle for existence, survival went to the fittest, whether it be in business or economics. And the fittest had to become the wealthiest. When Carnegie read Spencer, he found an idol. The industrialist said that when he read Spencer's *First Principles* in 1862, "light came as in a flood and all was clear." Carnegie and other businessmen of the day used Spencer as an argument against government intervention and also against the rise of unions. However, during this period big business, in conjunction with the government, was active in attempting to throttle free competition.

In 1868, the steel maker wrote a memo to himself: "Thirty-three and an income of $50,000 per annum! Beyond this never earn—make no effort to increase fortune, but spend the surplus each year for benevolent purposes. Cast aside business forever, except for others." He did not follow his advice until he was sixty-six, but then he engaged in what he called *scientific philanthropy.* The major projects worth giving money to were universities, free libraries, hospitals, and parks, in that order, in addition to swimming baths and churches, which ranked low on his list.

Carnegie retired after the sale of his steel company to the new United States Steel Company in 1901.

Of the $250 million he got, he left a $5 million pension and benefit fund for his trustworthy employees. He did not stop giving from that moment. Over $60 million of his money went into almost 3,000 free public libraries around the world. The size of Carnegie's gift depended on the town's population; it averaged $2 per person. (This formula left some small towns with an uneconomical library that had to be closed down; nobody ever thought of pooling the funds for regional libraries.)

Giving away money seemed to be as hard as making it. "Pity the poor millionaire, for the way of the philanthropist is hard," he wrote to a newspaper in 1913. After working for ten years at giving away $350 million, he realized that no one man could do such a big job; the Carnegie Corporation in New York started with an endowment of $125 million. It was the first modern philanthropic foundation administered by trustees who were skilled in their different areas. Carnegie chose only trustees who had been good businessmen.

He died in 1919 after fulfilling his personal pledge of giving away just about everything he had accumulated. □

7. ◆ Peace and Renewed Progress

Once the Civil War was over, the nation returned with renewed vigor to its primary economic task—raising its standard of living. The railroads expanded far into the West, investment banking became big business, and the health standards and educational attainment of the population rose. The period from 1865 to 1890 has been considered the epoch of unbridled freedom for business. Fortunes were made. Wealth was accumulated. This was the era of large trusts and monopolies, the development of which prompted the passage of our first antitrust act in 1890. This was also an era of tremendous increase in the communications capacity of the nation. The harnessing of electricity for communications by Samuel F. B. Morse was only a beginning. Thomas Edison and Alexander Bell continued Morse's pioneering work, giving the nation an intricate telephone network. In 1908, another great achievement had been heralded by the introduction of the first Model T. Mass production techniques had become available for a mass market created by continuing population growth and unprecedented immigration rates.

Increases in Living Standards

While per capita income had been increasing rather steadily through the 1840s and 1850s, the Civil War brought an abrupt pause to this upward march. In 1870, average income in the North was slightly above its prewar level; in the South, it was dramatically below the prewar level. However, as portrayed in Figure 7−1, the standard of living after 1870 began to rise at an unusually, but only temporarily, high rate. This rate of advance was about the same for both the North and the South, but recall that the South was now at a much lower level relative to the North. The 1870s' growth spurt for both regions was in part a catching up (or making up for lost ground) phenomenon, a counterpart to the pause of the 1860s. The growth rate remained high in the 1880s, but was lower than in the 1870s; finally, it slowed again and resumed its long-run normal trend by the turn of the century, about 1.6 percent per year. In addition, there were large amounts of immigration during that period, and population grew at a fairly rapid rate. Hence, total output expanded even more than per capita income. Its average rate of growth was around 4 percent a year. The eightfold increase in total output is shown in Figure 7-2.

The Growing American Citizenry and Territory

During this half century between the two wars, there were expansions both in the number of people who worked and played in the United States and in the extent of territory in which they lived. Population grew at an average rate of 2 percent a year,

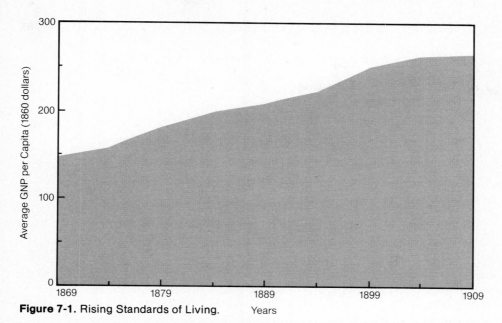

Figure 7-1. Rising Standards of Living.

Source: R. E. Gallman, "Gross National Product in the United States, 1834-1909," in National Bureau of Economic Research, *Output, Employment and Productivity in the United States after 1800* (New York: Columbia University Press, 1966) p. 30.

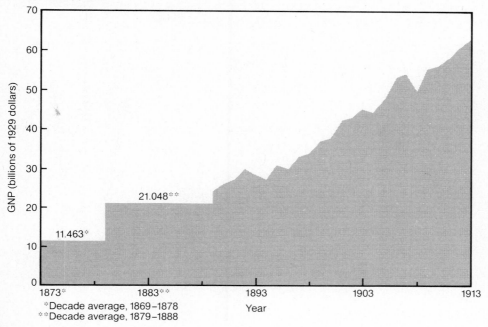

*Decade average, 1869–1878
**Decade average, 1879–1888

Figure 7-2. Growth in Total Output.

Source: J. W. Kendrick, *Productivity Trends in the United States*, National Bureau of Economic Research (Princeton, N.J.: Princeton University Press, 1961).

rising from 36 million at the end of the Civil War to over 100 million by the beginning of World War 1. By the end of the period, however, the growth rate of the population was slower than at the beginning.

Why Population Grew

Population grew for two reasons: (1) there was a large influx of immigrants, and (2) the birth rate exceeded the death rate. The second reason contributed far more to population growth than the first.

Immigration

Nevertheless, immigration was important, and many thousands of immigrants landed on our shores during this period, as shown in Figure 7−3. The bands in Figure 7−3 represent business depressions. It is not merely coincidental that decreases in net immigration coincided with business depressions in the United States. After all, one of the main reasons that people spend the energy and money and pay all the other costs involved in migrating to another country is increased real standards of living. When business recessions and depressions in the United States reduced the possibility of finding employment, there was less economic incentive for immigrants to come.

Fertility

It is perhaps less easy to explain why the fertility of the native population decreased toward the end of this period. But perhaps by addressing the economics of the matter, at least a partial explanation can be found. Urbanization increased during this period as more and more people moved off the farm and into the city. When this happened, children were no longer as productive as they had been on the farm, where they normally began working at very early ages. But in cities they typically worked less. Hence, children were generally less valuable as producers in the city. Also, twentieth-century urban women had greater opportunities to work outside the household. Therefore, if they were forced to stay home to raise children, they bore a cost—lost wages—that they did not bear on the farm. This

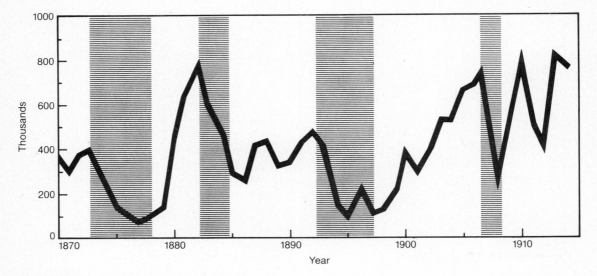

Figure 7-3. Immigration into the United States.

Source: Simon Kuznets and E. Rubin, *Immigration and the Foreign Born* (New York: National Bureau of Economic Research, 1954), p. 95.

New Strides Toward Economic Prominence

was an additional incentive to limit the number of children per family in the city.

Education and the Labor Force

Many activities raised the levels of skills of the working force. Among these were investments in education and other investments in human capital. Strictly speaking, these are investments because they create the possibility of increased production in the future. That is a primary effect of education, whether it be formal or informal. Formal education is, of course, going to school. But informal education is important also. This involves on-the-job training—gaining more experience in one's work and by observing what is happening around oneself.

Together, these investments greatly enhanced the productivity of the labor force. The American nation has always had high literacy rates. In 1870, almost 90 percent of all adult white Americans could read and write. By the beginning of World War I, this figure had risen to 96 percent. The black population, while having only a 20 percent literacy rate in 1870, increased it phenomenally to 70 percent by 1910. In 1860, the total resource cost devoted to education was 1.4 percent of the GNP; by 1900 this proportion had doubled. This figure includes not only the direct but also the indirect costs of education. The direct costs are fairly obvious—books, tuition, and the like. The indirect costs involve current income lost by going to school. Clearly, one of the greatest costs of going to school is the foregone income that could have been earned had a person remained in the labor force. This is the **opportunity cost** involved and these costs are forever present.

Investment in Health

Investing in education was not the only way to raise the productivity of the labor force and of the population at large. Investment in health was another way, a most important one, in the nineteenth century. Compared to today, health standards in those times were abysmal, although they were probably superior to what existed in other countries in the world. There were numerous epidemics: Yellow fever, smallpox, typhoid, diphtheria, typhus, and cholera were common. There were also dysentery, malaria, and the "grippe." Tuberculosis was rampant. Today we know the causes of these diseases, but at the end of the Civil War, medicine could hardly be called a science. During that half century, there were very few improvements in medical care per se; in fact, one was often better off by not going to a doctor. There were only two serious diseases that responded to the black bag of the M.D.: Malaria could be treated by applications of quinine, and smallpox prevented by a vaccination.

It was, rather, the discovery of the need to improve sewage disposal and treatment and to provide pure water that accounts in large part for the vast improvement in health standards at that time. The discoveries of Louis Pasteur and the subsequent pasteurization of milk contributed much. A falling death rate was sure to result, and indeed it did—in 1915, it was about 60 percent of its 1870 level. But more important economically, better health conditions allowed workers to be more productive, to be absent from work less, and to feel generally more like pursuing their individual endeavors.

Improving the Land

Although there were more people than ever before, and more living in cities than ever before, there also was much more land being worked. We acquired tremendous additional acreage in territories before the Civil War: The Republic of Texas joined the states in 1845; the Oregon Territory became ours in 1846; the Mexican Secession gave us even more land in the West and Southwest two years later. These additional lands gave us 70 percent more territory. But land that is idle or in isolation is useless. Only when it is *improved* can it increase the productive capacity of the nation; so improving the land was a vital task, especially for a nation of individuals striving for increased standards of living. At the end of the Civil War, this 70 percent increase in the national domain was virtually uninhabited by whites. During the next fifty years, however, the "frontier" was finally eradicated. There were no longer large areas in the United States that had no white population. This large availability of land allowed Americans to forestall any detrimental effects that crowding or falling output per additional worker (diminishing returns in production) might have had. The specter of a zero increase in output from an additional worker never haunted North America, as it occasionally haunted Europe. We always had new land to ease the population pressure and lower the labor-to-land ratio. Far more important than land availability, however, to the rise of cities, was the rise of productivity in agriculture. Whereas in colonial times nearly 90 percent of the population was engaged in agricultural activities, by 1860 this figure had fallen to 60 percent, by 1880, 50 percent, and by 1900, 38 percent. In spite of this percentage decline of the agricultural labor force, there were tremendous gains in total output. Acreage and productivity per worker increased, as did, in absolute numbers, the population engaged in this activity. So this period was still one of *absolute* growth, both of workers and of output, in the farming sector.

By the end of the nineteenth century, there was little frontier left. The amount of land in cultivation doubled after the Civil War. The expansion in agricultural output was not as rapid as in industry, but it grew faster than before the Civil War. Two different factors accounted for this expansion, the most obvious being the physical extension of cultivated land. But also important was increased productivity, the rise of output relative to the inputs of land, labor, and capital. Although productivity change in agriculture was less rapid than in manufacturing, it accounted for perhaps 40 percent of the increase in total farm output. And the pace of agricultural productivity advance in the last half of the century was several times higher than in the first half. This was the age of the mechanical reaper, the horse-drawn cultivator, and the improved harrow. We saw, therefore, a rapid rise in the agricultural implement industry. The fortunes of Cyrus McCormick can attest to that.

It must not be overlooked, of course, that many of the advances in agriculture were inseparably linked to transportation improvements and, in particular, the coming of the iron horse. It was only with the expansion of the railroad network that farming moved westward to the fertile new lands in Nebraska, Kansas, Texas, Oklahoma, the Dakotas, and the Far West.

The Golden Age of the Iron Horse

At the beginning of the Civil War, there were perhaps 30,000 miles of railroad track in all of the United States. By the end of the nineteenth century, most of today's existing railroad bed and track had been completely laid. There were over 200,000 miles of track, most of it was standard-gauge width, quite unlike the unintegrated system that had existed in 1860. Moreover, whereas in 1860 there were hardly any bridges, in 1900 they dotted the landscape. Locomotives increased in power and grew in number; freight cars multiplied by twenty in only forty years. And the capacity of each car increased 300 percent; hence, the rolling car capacity of the railroads had jumped by a multiple of eighty by the end of the century. Employment on the railroads also jumped, growing from 100,000 to one million individuals. Whereas in 1860, 1 percent of the labor force were engaged in railroad employment, three times that proportion were involved in it by the turn of the century. Passenger miles and ton freight miles increased immensely—500 percent and 6,000 percent, respectively. The railroad had become a freight carrier. But because other means of traveling had been found, the role of the passenger train was relatively diminishing. By the year 1910, the railroad reached its peak years of carrying people.

High Finance

The 1880s saw a wave of competitive construction in the railroad industry. Each system found itself in competition over certain routes with other systems. There were *eleven* lines going from New York to the Midwest!

The monetary debt of all the railroad systems combined began to exceed that of the entire United States government. In floating much of this debt, numerous deals—some of them shady—enriched speculators. These were the days of the Vanderbilts, the Fisks, and the Goulds. Some schemes led to local monopolies. Cornelius Vanderbilt, for example, was busy during and after the Civil War buying all the small railroad lines he could. He controlled the lines running from New York City to Albany. Then he started buying New York Central stock in 1865. Not content with the rate at which he was acquiring that company, he devised a scheme to cause the price of Central's stock to drop. Part of this scheme involved stopping his trains short of a bridge at Albany, thus forcing the Central's passengers to cross by themselves to make the connection (even in the rain). There were other underhanded deals and ultimately capitulation of the Central Railroad and the combination of the Central line with Vanderbilt's Hudson line, with Vanderbilt, of course, as president.

There were also scandals with the construction of the railroads to the West, the most famous involving Crédit Mobilier, an ephemeral construction company. It was rumored that the Mobilier made direct profits for building the Union Pacific at between $33 and $50 million. And this scandal involved congressmen as well as business people.

Rate Wars and Price Fixing

Whenever possible, the railroad systems tried to get together to fix rates so that they would not compete and could therefore avoid price competition. All parties to an agreement could feel they would be better off. But these associations (cartels) were usually only temporary. The incentive for cheating on such agreements is tremendous, particularly if one is not caught. If one railroad cheated on a rate-fixing agreement, it could obtain lots of business, thereby increasing its profits, since the other railroads would not lower their prices if they were still abiding by the agreement. There were continuous pools and internal regulating committees for railroads, but none of them seemed to work; none of them seemed to ensure a continuous system of rate fixing. This was a time, then, of secret rebates. This was also a time of **price discrimination**. Most railroads ended up charging more for short hauls than for long hauls because there was generally no competition in short-haul routes. It was only in the long-haul routes that more than one railroad would build competing lines.

Finally, in 1887, the Interstate Commerce Act created the Interstate Commerce Commission (ICC) and with it a set of rules to create "fair" business practices by railroads. In reality, however, many economists and historians believe that the ICC was created at the behest of the railroad lines so that they could have government supervision of their rate fixing.

Structural Changes

Accompanying these many important changes in the economy, the rising standard of living, the increasing pace of life associated with the railroad, high finance, communications, and increased city dwelling, were basic changes in the structure of the economy. We can view these distinct changes in the structure of the economy by looking at Table 7–1. There we see that the percentage of commodity output attributable to agricultural production fell from 53 percent in 1870 to 33 percent by the end of the century (although there was still an *absolute* increase in farm output). The opposite was the case for manufacturing, whereas in the areas of mining and construction combined there was no change.

During these decades, the U.S. economy had transformed and had become primarily a manufacturing instead of an agrarian economy. At the same time,

Table 7—1. The Changing Composition of Commodity Output.

Year	Agriculture	Manufacturing	Mining and Construction
1869	53	33	14
1874	46	39	14
1879	49	37	14
1884	41	44	15
1889	37	48	15
1894	32	53	15
1899	33	53	14

At the beginning of the period, agriculture accounted for 53 percent of total commodity output, whereas manufacturing, only a third. These proportions reversed themselves by the turn of the century.

Source: R. E. Gallman, "Commodity Output, 1839–1899," in *Trends in the American Economy in the Nineteenth Century*, National Bureau of Economic Research (Princeton, N.J.: Princeton University Press, 1960), p. 26.

the percentage distribution of the labor force was changing accordingly. Farming, fishing, and mining engaged more than half the working population in 1870, but barely a third by 1910. This trend was to continue even until today, when a little more than 4 percent of our population is in these fields. What happened, of course, was that the labor force became more active in the manufacturing, trade, and construction sectors.

There was also a distinct movement to the West. This was understandable, since migration usually responds to economic opportunity, and that is where the opportunities were. People moved in an attempt to improve their economic standard of living, and Americans have always been highly mobile.

Money and Prices

Curiously enough, these changes came primarily during decades of falling prices. In Figure 7–4, we see that the period after the Civil War was gener-

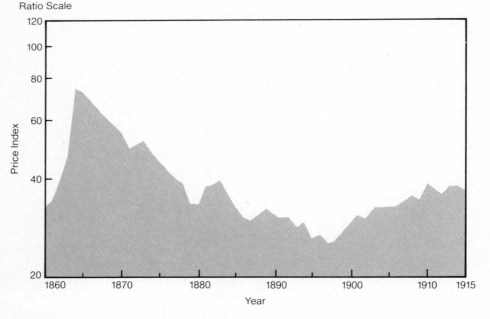

Figure 7-4. The Price Level, 1860–1915.

Source: Bureau of Labor Statistics.

New Strides Toward Economic Prominence

ally one of a drop in the price level, that is, of deflation. Notice, however, that when the price index in Figure 7−4 is compared with the graph of average GNP per capita in Figure 7−1, there is a slight negative correlation. In other words, falling prices or deflation did not mean depression, or declining real incomes in the long-run.

Reduced Supply of Greenbacks

There was, however, a distinct relationship between changes in the price level and changes in the stock of money during that period. Right after the Civil War, the federal government deliberately reduced the quantity of greenbacks in circulation in order to raise the value of a greenback to a dollar in gold. This exchange, "at par," finally happened in 1879. Meanwhile, there were some—primarily farmers—who wanted more, not fewer greenbacks. In particular, the Greenback Labor Party associated a rising price level with a higher price of products and hence higher incomes and a higher standard of living.

On a Gold Standard

After the year 1878, we were on a *de facto* gold standard. That is, gold served as a medium of exchange and also as the backing for reserves in the banking system. Hence, the entire money stock was tied to the production of gold, which did not increase rapidly enough to keep up with the need of money for the nation's transactions. Consequently, the economy experienced deflation for three decades. It was only after discoveries of gold in South Africa and the Yukon, plus development of the relatively inexpensive cyanide reduction process, which allowed the gold stock—and, hence, the money stock—to increase faster than the increased rate of output, that the deflation was stopped. Lastly, notice that in the latter period under study (1898−1915) a rise in prices finally occurred. □

Definitions of New Terms

Price discrimination: Price discrimination is charging some people higher prices than other people when these higher prices do not reflect higher costs. Price discrimination is usually illegal, although often practiced. (Every time you go to a movie and there are special student prices, you are the beneficiary or victim of price discrimination.)

Opportunity cost: Opportunity cost is the alternative cost of doing something. Opportunity costs can be explicit, as in the case of a clearly marked price of a good or service, or implicit, as in the case of a value of a person's leisure time.

THE FARM PROBLEM

The late nineteenth century was a period of dramatic change for the country. Because of emancipation, it was a period of severe adjustment for blacks and many whites as well. Because of impending industrialization, new situations and hazards caused rising concerns for decency, security, and fairness. For many reasons, farmers (and others) complained that the fruits of economic growth were passing them by. It was an era of agrarian discontent.

The Agrarian Movement

The plight of the farmer was vocally expressed through a number of novel political movements in rural America (mainly the Midwest), shortly after the Civil War. These movements flourished all through the 1870s and in the latter part of the 1880s and early 1890s. Their peak of effectiveness coincided with two periods of falling prices.

Agrarian discontent was also based on hatred of capitalist creditors, whom the western farmers thought were gouging them with usurious interest rates. Another complaint was discrimination in railroad rates that were not consistent with the differences in costs for different types of railroad transportation. There was a hatred for the common practice of charging more for short hauls than for long hauls.

The most influential force was the Populist Movement, but in addition to the Populists, there were several other groups—the Grangers, the Farmer Alliances, and the Greenback Movement.

To make higher profits for the farmer, some Grangers tried to eliminate the middleman. In addition, they attempted cooperative mass marketing schemes to eliminate the profits of distributors and encouraged state laws in the 1870s to regulate railroads. They also had important educational and social functions. By and large, the Grangers were organized most effectively in the farming states of the upper Mississippi Valley.

The Farmer's Alliances and the Greenback Movement focused primarily on the issue of falling prices and what to do about it. They wanted an increased circulation of paper money. The Alliances, which were eventually absorbed into the Populist Party, pressed for the free coinage of silver (as well as more gold, which was then in use).

As noted, one of the purposes of the agrarian movement was to stop falling prices. Farmers were convinced that the price of manufactured goods was rising relative to the price of agricultural goods. As John F. Kennedy once said, the "farmer is the only man who sells everything at wholesale, buys everything at retail, and pays transportation both ways." While it is true that farm prices were falling during this period, so were the prices of manufactured goods. In fact, it looks as if the average **terms of trade** for farmers—the average prices of farm products relative to other prices—stayed about the same, overall, between 1865 and 1900. During this period, the relative amounts of goods and services that the farmer could buy with a unit of his or her crop (their terms of trade) did not decline. By their actions and discussions, however, it is clear that many of them apparently believed otherwise.

The Credit Question

Farmers were convinced they were being ruthlessly exploited by large creditors from the East. They complained about the high interest rates they had to pay, particularly about the conditions under which they were able to obtain credit. It is true that prices fell over this period and hence debtors were hurt in the process—at least until people adjusted their expectations to these conditions of deflation. But before this adjustment, debtors paid off their loans in dollar amounts greater than they anticipated.

As people became accustomed to the fall in prices, however, the price of credit, like all other prices, fell accordingly. In any event, since most mortgages held by farmers were of relatively short duration—three or four years—they could not have been hurt for very long (unless they were foreclosed or renewed their loans with the conditions prevailing). And at the same time, the largest debtor group in the nation was the railroads, not the farmers, so the unexpected falling price level affected the profits of the railroads and the manufacturers as much as or more than farmers.

It is quite true that credit was somewhat limited, particularly in the western and southern agricultural regions. We stated, however, in Issue VI that one of the reasons for the restriction in credit was the National Banking Act, since it prevented the growth of smaller banks in less-populated regions and allowed those which did exist to have a monopoly on money lending. In this instance, the farmers did have a legitimate gripe. But consider also that farmers often were not very good credit risks at that time. A tremendous number of mortgage companies failed during this period because of the poor credit risks they had taken with farmers.

Railroad Rates

The farmers were rightly concerned and annoyed about the discriminatory railroad rates. But it is not clear that a large percentage of farmers were really victimized by actual price discrimination against them. For example, rates west of the Mississippi were higher than those east of Mississipi, but this was a function of the actual costs of providing railroad transportation in these two different regions. The real factor was that western railroads had lower loading ratios. That is, because of major seasonal fluctuations in the demand for their services, their cars were not loaded as much as were those in the East. Essentially, then, during certain times of the year there had to be empty freight cars shipped from the East to the West to take account of seasonal peaks. This increased costs for railroads operating in the West, and one would expect them to charge a higher price. In fact, the rate of return to western railroads was less than to eastern ones.

Credit Again, and Commercialization, Too

The discontent among farmers was real enough, however, and there was just too much smoke for there to be no fire. But the many issues farmers raised and causes they damned were not central to the real problems underlying agricultural conditions in America in the last half of the nineteenth century.

In earlier times, most farmers were relatively isolated from the market and were involved in commercial agriculture only on the periphery. Basic essential tools and equipment, which were not generally too costly, and various luxury items were obtained by sporadic selling of crops or livestock. But after the Civil War, agricultural productivity soared and so did the degree to which farmers were engaged in commercial agriculture—production for market. This brought forth a host of new problems. For instance, farmers were often forced into debt because after the Civil War one could not be a farmer without also being a capitalist. Farmers had to buy equipment — reapers, planters, harrows, and the like. They also had to buy chemical fertilizers and large amounts of land and sometimes irrigation facilities. Beside depending on banks, farmers had to depend on grain elevators and railroads to market their crops.

Often this required an extension of credit, and when prices fell for their crops foreclosures on their farms sometimes resulted. It was a time when farmers seemed forced to take risks that earlier generations of farmers had not encountered. It was a time when the stakes were higher than ever before. And to make matters worse, it was a time when U.S. agriculture became heavily involved in the international economy. As well as approaching industrial dominance in the world, we were becoming the most modern and productive agriculture economy. The welfare of American farmers became increasingly dependent on conditions remote from them and little understood by them. For them, it was an impersonal world where a bumper wheat crop elsewhere could cause world (and U.S.) wheat prices to drop sharply. Whose fault was it? Many thought it was the person at the railroad, or at the grain elevator, or the creditor at the bank. ☐

Definition of New Term

Terms of trade: Terms of trade are the terms on which a specific sector trades with another sector. In agriculture, for example, the terms of trade can be found by seeing what a unit of agricultural product will buy in terms of units of manufactured products.

8. Increasing the Tempo of Economic Life

The half century after the Civil War was a period not only of rapid economic growth and of large increases in population and westward movement, but also of tremendous structural change—that is, change in the basic makeup of the entire U.S. economy. We were able to allude only briefly to some of these changes in the last chapter. It is time now to deal with them more thoroughly. The years between the Civil War and World War I was a period of the rise of cities, with all the accompanying gains and costs; a period of increasing industrial power and concentration; and finally, a period of massive changes in the agricultural sector. These trends continue even into the present, and we are still faced with finding solutions to the multitude of complex problems of modern society.

Urbanization

As Figure 8−1 shows, at the end of the Civl War decade, about one-fourth of the population lived in cities of 2,500 or more. Fifty years later, almost one-half the entire population was crowded into cities. In fact, by the end of World War I there were more city dwellers than country folks. Of course, this does not mean that everybody lived in big cities. In fact, it was not until more recently that the population concentrated itself into what we consider the major cities in the nation. In 1870, for example, out of the 663 extant cities, almost 500 had a popu-lation of less than 10,000. This proportion was to fall somewhat, but not drastically; even by 1910, 1,665 cities of the extant 2,262 still had populations of less than 10,000. Before assessing the problems that the city dweller of the past faced, let us examine some of the reasons why cities exist in the first place.

The Economics of Why Cities Exist

It is not accidental that many major cities are located near areas of significant mineral deposits or natural resources, or in areas that can be easily serviced by natural transportation networks. In other words, there are many *natural* reasons why cities are located where they are. Cities serve as focal points for commerce and in some cases extractive industry (mining). Also, concentration of industry within a fairly constrained area allows for decreased costs of production. This is because there are many interactions between firms; if the firms are spread out, they have to engage in extensive long-distance communication and transportation in order to trade. When they concentrate in one region, they save on many of these costs. Furthermore, a concentration of production will generally lead to what are called *economies of scale*. That is, firms that can obtain sufficient levels of production will find that their average costs fall. This may be due to factors often associated with the techniques of **mass production**, such as assembly-line means of production.

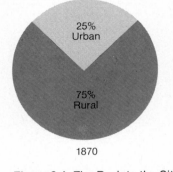

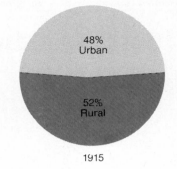

Figure 8-1. The Rush to the Cities.

Source: U.S. Bureau of Census.

In addition, the concentration of people and resources in the city allows for more efficient provision of such public services as education, fire and police protection, potable water, improved sewer systems, and the like.

A Hierarchy of Cities

Prior to the Civil War, most cities were retail trade centers. It was only after the war that many of them became oriented toward manufacturing. As manufacturing grew from barely one-third of commodity output in 1860 to over one-half in 1900, we would expect certain concentrations to occur in very physically constrained areas, and indeed they did.

A regular hierarchy of cities grew up that remains with us even today. The most basic characteristics of this hierarchy are as follows:

City Size	Characteristics
2,500 to 10,000	Mainly trading centers; the reduction in costs are enough to get people to drive short distances in from the countryside; total demand not high enough for the provision of specialized services.
10,000 to 50,000	Still mainly trading centers, but provision of certain specialized services, such as stock brokers and the like.
50,000 to 250,000	Still commercial trading, plus increasing specialized services: stock brokers, insurance salesmen, more specialized doctors, and so on.
250,000 and more (Major Urban Centers)	Commercial trading, many specialized services, operas, orchestras, brain surgeons, gourmet food, and so on.

By 1890, we had indeed reached the era of big cities. New York, Chicago, Philadelphia, Boston—they all had their special characteristics and their special brands of vice and social disamenities: tuberculosis, slum housing, crimes, pollution, and corruption. At that time, the top ten cities were also the big manufacturing centers. They accounted for more than 40 percent of all manufacturing output and were the focal points of commerce, finance, and communications.

Value of Land

Despite their bad effects cities certainly provided ample rewards to thousands of businesses that located in them. For example, in Chicago, from 1873 to 1910, the value of inner-city property rose by more than 700 percent. Land and other property was immensely valuable in the centers of crowded cities.

A Struggle for Life

Urbanization may have allowed for more profitable business opportunities; it may have resulted in economies of scale; it may have resulted in increased specialization and higher real living standards for the nation at large; but it also meant, particularly at the beginning of the period we are talking about, increased mortality and morbidity among the urban populations. In 1860, it was far safer to live on the farm than to reside in the city: The death rate per 1,000 in the countryside was about twenty, as compared to about thirty in the large city. What did people die of in the city? Mainly communicable diseases: diphtheria, tuberculosis, and the like. They drank foul water from wells that were polluted by improper and unsafe sewage systems, and, hence, they contracted typhoid and dysentery. Because they were unable to obtain as much fresh food as people who lived in rural areas, their diet was not as healthy.

This was all to change with passing decades. Rising real incomes enabled people to demand better health conditions. For example, they were willing and able to pay for better diets, which lowered morbidity rates. They also could afford more spacious housing. In addition, purification of water, improved sewage disposal, regular garbage collection, and swamp draining became more common. So, in spite of the numerous unhealthful aspects of congested urban living, people had obtained distinct improvements in health in the city by the eve of World War I. There still remained numerous problems for the urban dweller, as there are today. Nevertheless, the benefits from living in the city apparently outweighed the costs, and progress was made.

For instance, the difficulties of movement within the cities eased as technological changes in intra-urban transport occurred, such as trolley lines. And, of course, one of the most obvious benefits from living in the city was higher income: Uncorrected for the higher skill level of the workers in cities, real wages were twice those in the countryside. Also, and perhaps no less important, there were many more things to do in the city, just as there are today. Farm life must have been quite dreary in the good old days compared to the numerous possibilities for diversified life-styles in New York, Chicago, New Orleans, Miami, San Francisco, and, to a lesser degree, in places such as Austin, Sacramento, Kokomo, and Pullman.

Monopoly Capitalism

The structure of American business was changing throughout this period. There was a shift away from **proprietorships** and **partnerships** to a form of business organization called the **corporation**. The corporation was not really new, but it emerged rapidly during this period for several reasons. A corporation is a legal entity owned by stockholders, who usually all have limited liability; that is, the most they can lose is the value of their stocks. They cannot be assessed any further liability even if the corporation goes bankrupt. Another appealing aspect of the corporation is that it is essentially eternal: The death of shareholders does not terminate the legal existence of the corporation, whereas it does for proprietorships and partnerships. A corporation has another advantage, its enhanced ability to obtain large amounts of capital. A corporation can sell shares in itself, and it can float large amounts of debt capital. This is generally more difficult for partnerships and proprietorships because of their uncertain longevity. Because this was a period of industrial expansion and because, as never before, it was an era of large-scale manufacturing, the corporation became a common feature of business enterprise.

Steel was certainly one of the most preeminent of the industries that required large amounts of capital. The Bessemer and open hearth processes for making steel allowed the rapid development of this industry. Moreover, these two processes are most efficient when used to produce large amounts of steel. It is not hard to imagine, then, that large companies were soon to spring up in this industry, the most famous being the one founded by Andrew Carnegie in 1872. Eventually his properties were consolidated with others by J. P. Morgan. Here we had the first billion-dollar company in the world—United States Steel.

The petroleum industry also saw rapid development. Many people know that John D. Rockefeller made his fortune providing such petroleum products as kerosene for heating and manufacturing. In the twentieth century, the automobile became a most conspicuous consumer of Rockefeller's oil. Henry Ford's application of assembly-line mass production techniques, using interchangeable parts to produce the Model T, gave a tremendous boost to this industry. By 1919, annual automobile sales were a billion-dollar affair.

All of this rapid industrialization was merely an extension of what had occurred in England, and was similar to what was occurring in France and other European countries. This was the era of America's industrial revolution. This industrial revolution was paralleled by a scientific revolution and the beginning of a technological elite, or technocracy. M.I.T. (Massachusetts Institute of Technology) was founded. Engineers were universally recognized as necessary and desirable in an industrial society. The age of Taylorism was upon us. Frederick W. Taylor, while working at Bethlehem Steel Company, discovered that worker efficiency could be improved by analyzing in detail the movements required to perform a job and then carrying on experiments to determine just the right size and weight of tools. Thus, time and motion studies became fads. It was realized that industry could profit through advances in scientific knowledge, and it did. It was also realized that higher profits could be made by creating monopolies and many attempts to erect monopolies occurred at that time. That is why we call this the age of monopoly capitalism.

The Growth of Business Consolidation

In 1890, there were twelve important trusts, or combinations, worth a total of $1 billion. By 1903, such combinations had a capital of $3 billion, and by 1904, $7.2 billion. This represented 40 percent of all American industry. One of the reasons businesses consolidated was to gain greater market control. Another was to reap the benefits from economies of scale. When one is able to cater to a national market—which was the case during this period—why not take advantage of falling average costs per unit by expanding production? And what easier way to expand production than to merge with similar companies?

There were basically two types of consolidations. One was **vertical mergers**, and the other **horizontal**. These descriptions have nothing to do with geometry, but merely with what aspect of the production process is acquired by merger.

Vertical Integration

When firms vertically integrate by merger, the various production processes are brought under one name; for example, a coal mine is consolidated with an electric utility plant. Mergers of this type were not so feared in those days; but the other kind was.

Horizontal Integration

In horizontal integration, one company buys up similar companies, the most famous example being Rockefeller's Standard Oil, which acquired or forced many competitors into the Standard Oil Trust.

Antitrust Legislation

Of course, people naturally feared monopolies and even the possibility that giant companies might take over the country. Therefore, Congress passed the Sherman Antitrust Act in 1890. However, the Sherman Antitrust Act unexpectedly contributed to a wave of consolidations, which peaked between 1897 and 1903. This is because one way around the illegality of conspiring in restraint of trade was to merge. Mergers at that time were not against the law, even if they resulted in reduced competitiveness in an industry. Eventually, in 1910 and 1911 Standard Oil and American Tobacco were prosecuted under the Sherman Antitrust Act, but until then this was generally a period of a government hands-off policy. As Jefferson once said, the best government is "that government which governs least." And many congressmen, senators, and presidents felt it best to leave business alone. Did this hands-off policy diminish the welfare of workers, both on the farm and in the city? The next Issue addresses this question. □

Definitions of New Terms

Mass production: Mass production is a production technique involving many units of a product. Mass production techniques are generally associated with a conveyor belt and large-scale assembly factories. When the techniques of mass production are used, the fixed or sunk costs are distributed to an ever-increasing number of units, thus reducing the average per unit cost of production.

Proprietorship: A single-owner business is called a *proprietorship.*

Partnership: A partnership is a business entity involving two or more individuals joined together for business purposes but who have not incorporated. Their liability is generally limited to their personal assets.

Corporation: A corporation is a legal entity owned by stockholders in the company. Normally the stockholders are only liable for the amount of money they have invested in that company.

Vertical mergers or integration: Vertical mergers or integration involves the joining together of businesses that engage in the various stages of producing a final product. For example, the merging of a coal company with an electric utility would be a vertical merger.

Horizontal integration: Horizontal integration involves the merging of businesses in the same activity, such as the merger of several gasoline companies, or several shoe-manufacturing companies.

THE PLIGHT OF THE WORKERS

period? Were they becoming worse off than they had been used to or than they could have expected to become? Was a large percentage of the population feeling the pinch of industrialization?

The Plight of Workers

During the first half of the nineteenth century, the pace of economic change accelerated. The Civil War was a costly interruption to a trend of industrial expansion that would lead the United States to a position of industrial dominance throughout the world. Considered in terms of the broad span of history, there is little doubt indeed that an industrial revolution was unfolding in America between the Civil War and World War I.

Emphasizing an alternative perspective, many social commentators and historians have noted that during this era of monopoly capitalism, the little person—the factory worker and others—suffered greatly. There is little question about the sordidness in the slums and factory lives of many workers in America. There is little question that many people lived an existence that by present standards was almost unthinkable.

Making Correct Comparisons

But we cannot properly apply today's standards to the kind of life that existed before World War I. Instead, we should cautiously compare the circumstances of the past in its proper historical context and in terms of the hopes, the expectations, and the conditions of yesterday. And most importantly, we need to find out what really took place.

What was actually happening to workers during this

Blue-Collar Discontent

For many years, the available scattered evidence on wages confirmed some historians' claims that workers suffered losses in real wages during the era of unbridled monopoly capitalism. Because of monopoly elements in the economy it was believed that the standard of living of workers fell from the time of the passage of the Sherman Antitrust Act until the days of World War I. However, the most recent and more complete estimates of real wages of manufacturing workers, shown in Figure VIII-1, counter those beliefs. Real wages did fall in several short periods, but over the entire quarter century, from 1890-1914, they rose considerably, being about 30 percent higher at the end of the period than at the start.

It is also instructive to consider alternative income distributions. For instance, what would have happened if monopoly capitalists had been unable to extract any monopoly profits during this period? In the first decade of the twentieth century—a decade near the supposed zenith of monopoly in the economy—corporate profits *totaled* about $1.4 billion per year, on an average. Not all corporations were monopolies, but for the sake of exaggeration we may assume they were. Of course, some of this profit was attributable to monopoly practices, but actually most of it was a normal return to capital, like interest on your bank savings—say 5 or 6 percent. If the President or the courts could have taken the amount in excess of the normal rate of return and redistributed it to everyone (except for the stockholders and company managers), individual incomes would have increased by about 1 or 2 percent, on an average.

Monopoly certainly was more visible than ever before in the late nineteenth century. This was largely due to the tremendous growth in the size of firms and also to the growth of trusts and mergers of firms. But it is not actually clear that the economy was becoming more monopolistic. As transportation costs fell and com-

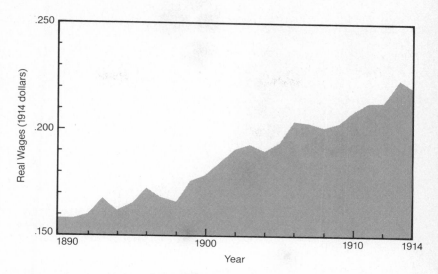

Figure VIII-1. Hourly Earnings in Manufacturing.

Source: A. Rees, *Real Wages in Manufacturing*, 1890-1914 (Princeton, N.J.: Princeton University Press, 1961), p. 4.

munications improved, isolated regional monopolies came under increasing competitive pressure. For the average American consumer, the unfolding of the nineteenth century may have actually brought on less monopoly rather than more. In any case, we can be sure that in this era of industrialization workers were earning more and that real incomes were rising.

Some Real Costs

The rise in real wages and the lack of leverage of corporate abnormal (monopoly) profit on average incomes does not indicate, however, that no problems were

caused by industrialization. Certainly the rash of strikes between 1880 and 1914 and the appearance of considerable labor violence in the 1890s (not to mention the "get tough" attitude toward labor of many conservative states and local authorities) amply attest to the tensions of the times. Clearly this was directly related to the process of industrialization. But progress always has a price, and this was a period of significant growth and economic change. Against the benefits of rising material standards of living, we can now compare some of the costs that were brought about by the rapid industrialization in the nineteenth century.

Did the Common Person Gain from Industrialization?   103

Living Environment

One involved the living environment in which many industrial workers found themselves. Life in many factories was dismal, and there was little job security because foremen could discharge workers abruptly if they wished or business conditions warranted it. Moreover, life in the homes near the factories was often less pleasant than in the countryside. There were numerous **external diseconomies** associated with the urban industrial complex that grew up during the age of industrialization. Moreover, workers were subjected to more severe and costly business cycles. Recall that when the United States had mainly an agrarian economy, with many largely self-sufficient farms, the effects of bad business conditions on the vast majority of people were not as great as when the economy became industrialized. By the end of the nineteenth century, however, workers increasingly experienced periods of more severe recession and depression. In fact, the recession and/or depression that began in 1893 was one of the very worst in the history of the United States. We see in Table VIII—1 that the percentage of the labor force unemployed in depression years (starting in 1876) was not insignificant.

Table VIII—1. Unemployment During Recessions and Depressions.

Year	Percentage Unemployed
1876	12—14
1885	6—8
1894	18
1908	8

The unemployment rate during the recessions of the period under study was considerably higher than during the recessions and depressions in prior periods. In fact, the unemployment rate in 1894 is exceeded only by the periods during the Great Depression.

Source: S. Lebergott, *Manpower and Economic Growth* (New York: McGraw-Hill, 1964), pp. 187, 512, 522.

Unemployment Trend Up

To provide a more complete picture of what happened to unemployment, Figure VIII—2 shows that there has been a slight but noticeable upward trend in the average rates of unemployment from 1800 to the present. In the past, unemployment meant hardship for workers. Unemployment is an integral part of an industrialized capitalist society. Mass unemployment rarely exists in any society where everybody is basically self-employed or a slave or serf. To minimize the cost of economic progress, we can attempt, as we have by many government

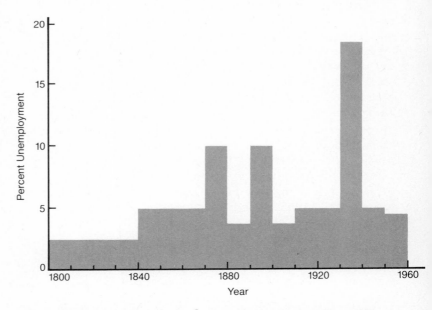

Figure VIII-2. The Long-Term Trend in Unemployment, 1880 to 1960.

Source: S. Lebergott, *Manpower and Economic Growth* (New York: McGraw-Hill, 1964), pp. 181, 512, 522.

New Strides Toward Economic Prominence

programs, to alleviate unemployment and its effects. We have not yet found the magic formula for stopping recessions, but that does not mean that we are worse off as a highly developed industrial society than we would be if we all went back to self-sufficient activities.

This conclusion would also apply to the situation on the eve of World War I. Many people had been hurt by the progress of the last half century, but even more had gained from it. If we take a very broad view of the changes of the period, it would be difficult for us to conclude that the common person was hurt by the industrial revolution. Life for the average worker was difficult at the turn of the century, but it was better than that of the previous generation of workers. □

Definition of New Term

External diseconomies: These are costs associated with an economic activity that are not taken account of by those who create them. In other words, external diseconomies are paid for by the public without any compensation made to them by the responsible parties.

9. The Great War

With the assassination of Austrian Archduke Franz Ferdinand in Sarajevo, in 1914, war began in Europe.

Soon the Great War spread to most of the rest of the world. The Central Powers, Germany and Austria-Hungary, were fighting against the Allies—France, England, and Russia. In 1914, America was in the throes of a recession. Unemployment had reached an uncomfortable one million the year before. From the very beginning, America attempted to stay out of the conflict. In fact, the Democrats used a slogan for President Wilson's reelection that would soon be forgotten: "He kept this country out of war." That was in 1916. In April 1917, the United States declared war on the Central Powers. War production and preparation for war had started earlier, however, and we had started sending war materials and supplies to the belligerents as early as 1914. It was not unlike an earlier time, in 1793, when, as a neutral country, we were able to trade with both parties to the conflict. After the first shock of war, our exports increased by leaps and bounds. The trade surplus for each of the years 1914 and 1916 was over $5.2 billion. Other countries made up for this deficit *vis-à-vis* the United States by liquidating investments, shipping us gold and by borrowing from us. In some cases, we were never repaid, particularly for the loans made to Germany. Nonetheless, most observers have concluded that our preparation for the war and entry into it pulled us out of a serious recession. By 1916, most of our unemployment had vanished.

World War I was the first modern war—one fought with formidable weapons that required large amounts of capital, supplies, and manpower and that involved, at least indirectly, the entire industrial economy of each modern nation involved. War had become expensive. While the Civil War cost the Union $3.5 billion, the Great War cost the United States alone $33.4 billion. This was a period of increased government expenditures and increased government powers. Government spending after World War I was significantly higher than before. Federal revenues, for example, were only $750 million when we entered the war, but rose to almost $5 billion after it.

Manpower and Production

Of course, the war had to be fought with soldiers. Although the United States did not use large amounts of its available labor force for the actual fighting, the total number of Americans who finally served during the conflict numbered almost five million—about 5 percent of the population. In addition, another three million were needed for war production. It is true that during this time unemployment was lowered, but most of the civilian population did not become materially better off. This is because a significant fraction of our labor, capital, and resources was expended for the war effort. Of course, the final victory for the Allied Forces is not to be downgraded, but it must be concluded that the actual standard of living fell during the war period.

New Strides Toward Economic Prominence

Industrial production did not increase very much after an initial spurt when hostilities broke out in Europe. Industry produced about 1 percent more from 1916 to 1917, but in 1918 and 1919, it produced less than it had several years earlier. Since we were using up part of our real output for the war effort, fewer consumer goods and services were available to the private sector, particularly since production did not significantly increase during the height of the hostilities.

Were We Unprepared?

It may seem that we were totally unprepared for the war effort, because the President was relying on his ability to keep us out of the war in order to be re-elected. However, this is not a completely accurate view. The Naval Consulting Board had an Industrial Preparedness Committee as early as 1915. This became a full-fledged Committee on Industrial Preparedness in 1916. This organization was financed soley by private contributions, although it was officially an arm of the federal government. By late 1916, there was a new organization called the Council of National Defense (CND). President Wilson said that the purpose of the CND was to organize "the whole industrial mechanism . . . in the most effective way." Even before we entered the war, the CND set up a Munitions Standards Board, in February 1917. Eventually, the CND was to designate an entire system of food control, censorship of the press, and purchasing war supplies. Finally, a couple of months after we joined the Allies, a War Industries Board was established to take control over much of the economy. Figure 9−1 shows what a complicated control mechanism was brought upon the economy by the rigors of war production and distribution.

Controls

War always creates an atmosphere conducive to expansion of government powers. The Great War was no exception. In fact, we might view World War I as a period that developed much of the administrative machinery that set the stage for many of the government control mechanisms instituted during Roosevelt's New Deal.

To be sure, the War Industries Board took its job seriously. It soon became the coordinator and allocator of commodities and allowed the fixing of prices and the setting of priorities in production. Bernard Baruch became head of this great bureaucratic organization in March 1918. Baruch was an obvious candidate, for he had been an earlier supporter of our entry into the war and he had already presented a scheme for industrial war mobilization to the President in 1915, well before most people thought we might enter the conflict. All of the leaders of the various departments in the control mechanism for war mobilization proved to be from big business. And, as can be expected, they looked out for their own. For example, in the granting of war contracts, there was no competitive bidding. The big business-dominated War Industries Board handed out contracts as seemed appropriate to it, often ignoring costs and efficiency in the process.

Price Fixing

Since wars have generally been associated with inflation, government controllers sought to establish price-fixing mechanisms to control inflation. Despite their attempts however, inflation was inevitable because of the methods of war financing. Nonetheless, the stage was set and so a Price-Fixing Committee of the War Industries Board was formed. Naturally, the public was told that the committee would set maximum prices so the consumer would not be hurt.

Price fixing in the agricultural sector was presided over by none other than Herbert Hoover. Instead of direct control over food, his Food Administration used a vast network of licensing agreements. Every producer, warehouser, and distributor of food had to obtain a federal license from the Food Administration. The licenses were used to

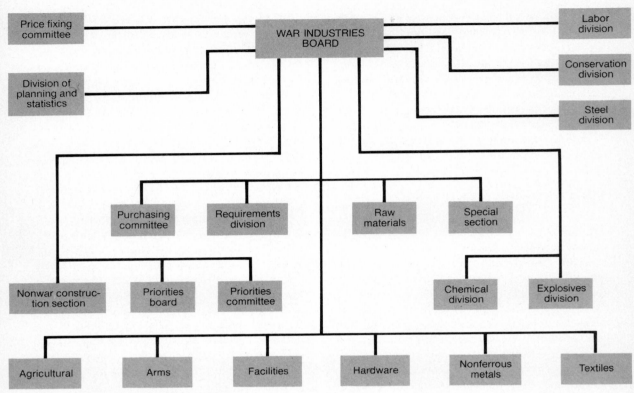

Figure 9-1. The War Industries Board.

control prices, because they were only granted if the licensees set prices to allow "a reasonable margin of profit." The goal, it would seem, was not to lower prices, but rather to stabilize and ensure higher noncompetitive prices. Certainly that was the end result, and any competitor who tried to increase profits above prewar levels by price cutting was threatened with the loss of its license. And when direct price controls were applied, a maximum was not set, but rather a *minimum.* For example, the Food Control Act of 1917 set a minimum price of $2 a bushel on the 1918 wheat crop. This figure was later upped by $.25 in the summer of 1918.

Other Forms of Control

The government completely took over some industries, such as the railroads. At the beginning of

the war, the railroads agreed to form a Railroads War Board and to cease competitive activities. However, the quest for higher profits superseded the railroad managers' patriotic promulgations. Price cutting became common, and more and more overt forms of competition appeared. Finally, President Wilson seized the railroads on December 28, 1917. Hence, railroads were monopolized and given direct government operation. Many important railroad personnel were appointed to leading positions in the Railroad Administration. Soon there were numerous rules for compulsory standardization of locomotive and equipment design and for the elimination of duplicate passenger and coal services. Additionally, no railroads were allowed to solicit business that they did not already have. All of this was done even before the Railroad Administration was legalized by the Federal Control Act of March 1918.

New Strides Toward Economic Prominence

Where It All Led

The entire system of controls was more or less dismantled after the cessation of hostilities. However, the stage had been set for collective action by which government and business joined together in a cooperative atmosphere. This was similar to, but on a vastly different scale than, government involvement in early nineteenth-century transportation mediums. This cooperative atmosphere was to prevail again years later, under Franklin Delano Roosevelt's administration.

Financing the War

As can be seen in Figure 9–2, federal expenditures rose rapidly during the period under study. But federal expenditures do not arise out of thin air. Even the government faces a **budget constraint**, just as you or anyone else does. If expenditures are increased, they must somehow be financed. There are generally only three ways that the government can finance its expenditures: (1) taxation, (2) borrowing from the public, and (3) money creation.

Taxation

Taxation is the most obvious manner in which the government pays for its expenditures, but in looking back it seems clear that none of our major wars have been completely financed by taxation. The Great War was no exception, although Congress continuously increased tax rates in an effort to offset its increased expenditures. Moreover, there was a change in the entire tax structure during the war, emphasizing more direct taxes and more progressive tax rates. For instance, in 1916, the maximum personal income tax rate was raised from 7 percent to 15 percent, and the maximum corporation rate was raised to 14.5 percent. In 1917, there were increases in estate taxes and again in personal and corporate income taxes. The maximum rate went up on the personal taxes 67 percent, and the normal corporation rate rose from 2 percent to 6 percent, with the maximum excess profits rate going up to 60 percent. This still was not enough, so the Revenue Act of 1918 (which was eventually passed in February 1919) increased the maximum personal rate to 77 percent, the normal corporation tax rate to 12 percent, and the maximum excess profits tax rate to 65

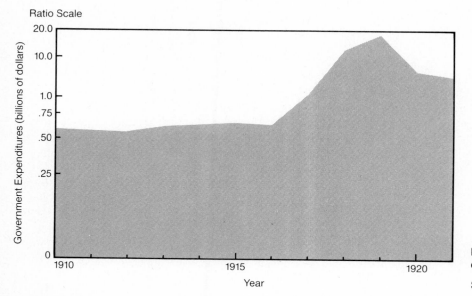

Figure 9-2. Rising Government Expenditures.

Source: U.S. Treasury.

percent. Ultimately, taxes provided about one-third of the revenues needed for the war effort.

Borrowing from the Private Sector

When the government runs a deficit—that is, spends more than it receives—it may borrow by selling government bonds to the public. The federal government took full advantage of this option during World War I. In addition to its regular bond sales, which occur all the time in today's dynamic economy, it instituted four Liberty Loan drives, and one postwar drive, joyously called a Victory Loan. A total of $19.1 billion was raised in this manner. But, in fact, the government's increased bond sales were, and still are, a postponement of the inevitable, a disguised form of increased taxes. After all, when the government sells a bond, it obtains money from people either as individuals, or owners of banks, or corporations. In return, it promises to pay interest for a certain number of years and then pay back the original price of the bond, called the *principal*. But how does the government pay the interest? Out of revenues. Where does it obtain revenues? From taxes. That means that when the government runs a deficit and makes up for it by selling bonds, it is increasing the future tax liabilities of the nation.

Of course, it is obvious that one cannot get something for nothing. If someone gives up part of his or her income to buy bonds so that the government can increase its expenditures, that person has to be paid a reward. And the reward is the interest rate, which we can call a reward for waiting. So we have the options: Either pay taxes today to finance government expenditures, or pay higher taxes in the future to pay for those government expenditures. Lastly, the money used for government finance (bonds) is diverted from elsewhere, leaving less for private investors and consumers.

Money Creation

The last method of government finance is money creation. It happened during the Revolutionary War, when Continentals were printed. It happened during the Civil War when Confederate notes and greenbacks were issued. And it happened again during World War I. But by this time a more formalized machinery for money creation had already been established.

The Federal Reserve System and Money Creation

You will recall that the National Banking System was established by legislation during the Civil War. However, it did not create a national system as originally intended. Moreover, its check clearance system was costly and inefficient. Because there were so many faults in the National Banking System, government officials felt the need to create a new one, so in 1913 the government passed the Federal Reserve Act. The Federal Reserve System was based on twelve district banks; every member commercial bank would belong to one of these. In each of these district banks, the member banks would be required to maintain a certain amount of reserves. That is, if the **reserve requirement** was, for example, 20 percent, a member bank that had a million dollars in checking account deposits and outstanding notes would have to keep $200,000 on reserve in its district's federal bank. The Federal Reserve banks were empowered to issue a new type of paper money called Federal Reserve notes. These were to be secured by **commercial paper** (the promissory notes of businesses) and gold. The district banks were also empowered to lend reserves to member banks who requested them. Note, however, that this function was considered a privilege and not a right of the commercial banks. Finally, a more efficient and less costly check-clearing system was instituted.

The Federal Reserve is governed by the Federal Reserve Board. Originally, this was merely an administrative agency with little control over the system's operations. Today the board of governors of the Federal Reserve essentially take responsibility for the total supply of money in the economy. The various committees decide which monetary policies to pursue and how to effect them. But this was not the case during World War I. Then the system was relatively passive, and it felt obliged to give the United States Treasury its full support. This meant essentially that it was to pursue an easy money policy, to allow a large amount of money—demand deposits and currency—to enter the economy. This helped the bond sales of the federal treasury.

One of the easiest ways for the Federal Reserve Board to create a situation of easy money is to increase the reserves of its member banks. When member banks have more reserves, they can loan out more money. One of the ways that member banks can obtain reserves is to borrow from the Federal Reserve Banks. During the war, the Federal Reserve Board lowered the interest rate charged and also freely granted loans to member banks at that lower interest rate. In this manner, the banks' reserves increased dramatically. This in turn led to a rapid increase in the money supply in circulation. For example, in 1917 money per capita was $225. In 1919, it had risen to $350 per person. Not surprisingly, the wholesale price index jumped by 20 percent and the consumer price index by 35 percent. We have already noted the outcome of massive increases in the amount of money in circulation; obviously, spending is easier when there is excess cash available and so prices rise. This happened in Europe because of the gold and silver flows from the New World in the fifteenth and sixteenth centuries; it happened in the American Revolution; in the Confederacy and the Union during the Civil War; and again in World War I. Figure 9−3 shows both the increases in the stock of money and the increases in the price index.

It is generally thought that government expenditures financed by taxation and borrowing from the private sector are not inflationary because in both cases private purchasing power is reduced therein. If a person pays part of his or her income in taxes, other private expenditures are usually reduced. If an individual or a business firm decides to lend money to the government by buying a bond, then again individual power, or ability to spend in the private sector, will be reduced. Such is not the case when expenditures are financed by money creation.

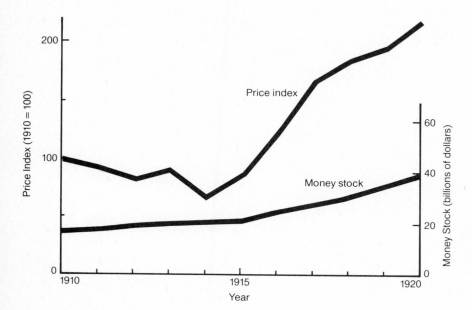

Figure 9-3. Money and Prices During World War I.

Source: Bureau of Labor Statistics.

People who eventually receive this extra cash do not want to reduce expenditures. Indeed, they want to increase them. Notice that inflation is also another form of taxation, but a very special kind. If the price level rises, everybody who holds dollar bills or has a checking account suffers. After all, if one has $100 in the bank and keeps it there for a year while the price of everything goes up 10 percent, that $100 has lost 10 percent of its value. It has depreciated by 10 percent. In effect, then, you have paid a 10 percent tax on holding these dollars. There is no way to avoid this tax unless one converts and trades only in goods, not dollars. But that would be extremely inconvenient. Consequently, governments often resort to this type of tax. It is easy to collect and very difficult to avoid. In addition, government officials can avoid the touchy questions of legislating new taxes and higher rates.

U.S. Involvement

The United States was an active participant in the war for only nineteen months. The American casualty rate was not high compared to that of the Civil War or World War II, but it was significant: 75,000 dead and 225,000 injured; a total of 300,000 casualties. Certainly many Americans had been reminded of the realities of scarcity after World War I, although they really had not paid the kind of price that Germany, France, England, Russia, and other participants in Europe had paid. ☐

Definitions of New Terms

Budget constraint: This is the constraint that an individual, a government, or even the world has on its spending capacity. One is limited in how much one can spend by one's budget constraint. So, too, is the government, except that it has the means of expanding its budget constraint by selling bonds and by creating money.

Reserve requirement: The reserve requirement is the reserves that commercial banks that are members of the Federal Reserve System must keep on account in their district Federal Reserve bank or in currency in their vaults. These reserves are expressed as a percentage of checking and savings account deposits outstanding.

Commercial paper: Commercial paper is the debt issued by individual corporations or by business persons.

IN SEARCH OF FREEDOM

Freeing the Slaves

Abraham Lincoln signed the Emancipation Proclamation on September 22, 1862. It stated:

> That on the 1st day of January, A.D. 1863, all persons held as slaves within any State or designated part of a State the people whereof shall then be in rebellion against the United States shall be then, thenceforward, and forever free; and the executive government of the United States, including the military and naval authority thereof, will recognize and maintain the freedom of such persons and will do no act or acts to repress such persons, or any of them, in any efforts they may make for their actual freedom.

We all know by now that just because legislation goes into effect the world does not necessarily turn upside down (or rightside up). While legislation obviously can have an immediate impact, it generally takes time for the full effect to be felt. Although blacks were freed during the Civil War, their emancipation certainly was not obvious during the next five decades. Blacks generally remained in the South, where their political freedom and economic standing were held in check. Even in 1915 there were still lynchings: Fifty-four blacks were hanged that year.[1]

Moving Out of the South

There had been some migration of blacks from the South to the North ever since the Civil War. However, until the beginning of World War I it was only a trickle. Starting in 1916, there was a mass

---

[1] So, too, did thirteen whites die by the rope.

exodus of blacks to northern cities unprecedented in the history of the nation. And the entire geographical distribution of this minority group in the United States radically changed. Whereas in 1900 only 23 percent of blacks were living in urban areas, the trend toward urbanization picked up so rapidly that barely a half century later 60 percent were urban. Almost all of the migration to the North during World War I was a movement to cities. In fact, the 1920 census revealed that almost three-fourths of northern blacks were found in the ten industrial centers of the nation, such as New York, Chicago, St. Louis, Pittsburgh, and Kansas City. If we look at different cities, we find that by the time of the Great Depression more than 50 percent of the blacks in New York, Chicago, Philadelphia, Washington, Detroit, Memphis, St. Louis, Cleveland, and Pittsburgh had been born in some other state. Detroit, for example, had more blacks from Georgia than did Augusta or Macon. Chicago had as many Mississippi-born blacks as the entire black population in Vicksburg,

Meridian, Greenville, and Natchez.

Why Did It All Happen?

Why did it take fifty years for blacks to start their massive migration to the North? Was it merely fortuitous that the start of World War I signaled the start of black migration? Perhaps, but another explanation may be more plausible. It involves two aspects of the war: the increased demand for workers and the decreased immigration from Europe. Additionally, at this time the boll weevil was ruining cotton cultivation, making it less profitable for rural blacks. In Table IX—1 we see the percent of reduction from full yield per acre of cotton due to the boll weevil. It started out as only 1.3 percent in 1911, but it grew to 13.4 percent in 1916 and increased dramatically until the middle of the Roaring Twenties.

While there were many social and political reasons why blacks would want to go to the North, as there were many such reasons for Germans and Swedes and Italians and Scots to want to come to America, the overriding reason was economic: They went North to achieve a higher material standard of living. In the period just before our entry into World War I, blacks were making 10 to 15 cents an hour in the

Table IX—1. Boll Weevil Destruction (1911—1925).

Year	% Reduction in Yield/Acre of Cotton due to Boll Weevil
1911	1.3
1912	3.3
1913	6.7
1914	5.9
1915	9.9
1916	13.4
1917	9.3
1918	5.8
1919	13.2
1920	19.9
1921	31.0
1922	24.2
1923	19.5
1924	8.0
1925	4.1

The percentage of reduction in full yield per acre of cotton due to the mischievous boll weevil rose dramatically during World War I and a few years thereafter, reducing the profitability of cotton growing for rural blacks (and whites).

Source: U.S. Department of Agriculture, Statistical Bulletin No. 99, Table 52, p. 67.

South. Soon they were hearing stories about northern employers willing to pay 30 or even 40 cents an hour.

A decision to migrate, in purely economic terms, includes not only the potential gain in income but also any costs involved in migration.

Costs of Migration

The most obvious cost of migration is transportation. By World War I, the transportation costs had been drastically reduced, because the railroad had essentially linked all parts of the nation together. Potential black migrants would look at the price of a railroad ticket as the most immediate cost they had to endure. After that would come the cost of searching for a job on arrival in another city. The job search cost could be high if, in fact, the migrant were out of work for a long time. During this period, however, migrants generally felt that job search costs would be minimal since they expected to find work immediately on arrival.

Another cost to consider was the cost of setting up a new household in a different city, and dismantling the one the migrant left behind. The costs here were not only economic but also psychic—losing old friends and trying to make new ones, leaving relatives, and so on. In the economic decision, then, the expected stream of *differences* in wages must be compared with the anticipated migration costs.

Labor Raids

There was a very good reason for many blacks to believe that they could obtain instant work in the North at higher wages, for the South was filled with northern labor contractors, who advanced or covered the cost of transfer North. Whites in the South were becoming increasingly upset at what they called *labor raids* to lure southern blacks to northern jobs. In fact, various state and local governments in the South attempted to prevent the raids by passing ordinances that allowed the fining and imprisonment of anybody convicted of "enticing" a laborer to leave the city for another place of employment. Other states placed heavy license taxes on emigration agents. The demand for labor was high enough in the North, however, that it still paid four licensed agents to put up $1,000 each in Birmingham in order to "entice" blacks to come North.

The Effects of Immigration Laws

Even though the North had been expanding its industrial economy for many years, our liberal immigration laws had made it unnecessary to go South to obtain workers. We see in Figure IX−1 that immigration into the United States each year sometimes reached as many as 1.28 million foreigners. During the first fourteen years of the twentieth century, over 12 million immigrants found their way to the United States. This all came to a screeching halt, however, as we became more involved in the war and more xenophobic. For instance, literacy tests of foreign immigrants were enacted. In

1915, less than a third of the 1914 number of immigrants arrived, and in 1916, only a fourth. By 1918, a mere 110,618 foreigners landed in the United States, while 94,585 left. The flow of relatively cheap foreign workers had stopped. But by 1915 the North still needed more labor. This opened up employment opportunities for blacks and other low-skilled labor on an unprecedented scale. Northern industry was expanding to meet the demands of a war-torn older continent, and eventually we were to enter that struggle and increse the demands for war production even more.

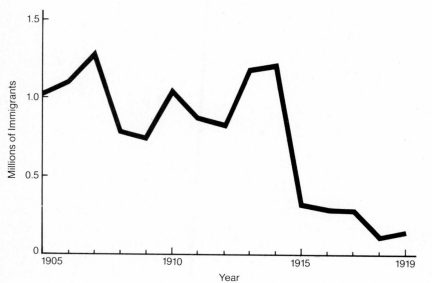

Figure IX-1. Immigration into the United States.

Source: *Historical Statistics*, p. 56.

New Meaning for the Black Franchise

It is generally considered that by 1914 blacks were completely disfranchised in the South. Even the handful of black voters who remained were considered such a challenge that in South Carolina, the General Assembly voted in January 1914 to repeal the Fifteenth Amendment to the United States Constitution! But in the North blacks could vote and even hold office. Civil rights for blacks in the national political arena made a great leap forward during this period of massive migration. The large numbers of blacks who came into northern cities were potential voters. Politicians had to take greater cognizance of this increasingly important subsec-tion of the population. By 1915, the first black, Oscar dePriest, was elected to Chicago's City Council. Blacks were registering and voting in the largest numbers since the turn of the century, and by 1921, the New Jersey House of Representatives had a black president, Assembly-man Walter G. Alexander. Later on, the Democratic Party in New York State made an attempt to win the black vote by taking a strong posi-tion against the Ku Klux Klan.

According to students of black history, the migration caused by our entry into World War I, the increased demand for more labor, and the shutting off of immigra-tion from abroad are respon-sible for laying the ground-work for equal rights for black people.[2] Of course, blacks were still far removed from a status of equal rights and socioeconomic equality, and race riots occasionally marred the landscape of the United States, especially in the north-ern cities. But World War I ushered in a new momentum toward equality, because "in the very process of being transplanted, the Negro was becoming transformed."[3] ☐

---

[2] It is important to note that although the particular statistics would dif-fer, the general forces and trends of this time period also applied to women. The substitution of female for male labor was very evident, just as was the substitution of black for white workers.

[3] Alain Locke, "The New Negro," *The Negro Caravan* (New York: Random House, 1969), p. 950.

New Strides Toward Economic Prominence

Part V
Economic Life
in Modern America,
1920—1980

The Industrial Unionist

John L. Lewis
(1880-1969)

President, United Mine Workers, 1920-1960

"I have never faltered or failed to present the cause or plead the case of the mine workers of this country. I have pleaded your case not in the wavering tones of a mendicant seeking alms, but in the thundering voice of the captain of a mighty host, demanding the rights to which free men are entitled."

These dramatic words from John L. Lewis were a combined program, epitaph, rallying call, and challenge to business management, consumers, and presidents alike. During his forty years as president of the United Mine Workers (UMW) and as the major spokesman for industrial unionism in an era of increasing consolidation between craft and industrial unions, Lewis ran the United Mine Workers with absolute control. He brought the union to prominence in the American Federation of Labor, formed the Congress of Industrial Organizations (CIO) and broke with the American Federation of Labor (AFL), then returned to the AFL and eventually forced the union to stand on its own for the twenty years before his death.

Industrial unionism received its greatest push during the early 1930s. The combined effects of the Depression and the increased numbers of unskilled and semiskilled workers in most American indus-

tries presented a serious challenge to the craft union doctrine of the AFL, founded by Samuel Gompers. It became evident to men such as Lewis that it was no longer valid to base union solidarity and bargaining positions on skills, irrespective of industry; he believed strongly that it was important instead to organize unions within specific industries, drawing the membership from as wide a basis within the industry as possible.

One of the major "advantages" of the tactic is the crippling effects of a strike within the industry. And through the late 1940s and into the early 1950s, Lewis led some of the most economically dangerous and emphatically effective strikes in American history.

Lewis was born to Welsh immigrant parents in Iowa in 1880. His father was a miner and a strong trade unionist. Along with some of his brothers, Lewis entered the mines at the age of fifteen, after leaving the only formal schooling he would receive. Six years later, he traveled in the western United States, working in various mines and learning about the mining industry. Lewis eventually became one of America's foremost experts on the coal mining industry, and almost all of his expertise was the result of his own reading and study. Upon returning

Economic Life in Modern America

to Iowa, he joined the UMW local and began extensive work in the Union leadership.

He came to the attention of Samuel Gompers, and in 1911 was named a field agent of the American Federation of Labor. While traveling widely throughout the United States, he rose in the UMW ranks, becoming president of the Union in 1920.

Lewis had his first of many confrontations with the federal government during World War I, while serving on the National Defense Council; in that position, he opposed government operation of the mines, a controversial question he was to take on again twenty-five years later.

The AFL convention in 1935 was torn by the economic troubles of the country and the internal disagreement between the trade and craft unions. In a dramatic walkout, Lewis joined with several other trade unionists to form the Congress of Industrial Organizations, leaving the AFL to the craft unionists. The momentum behind Lewis' move resulted in several important gains for his union and for labor at large.

In 1933, he had successfully fought for the passage of Section 7a of the National Industrial Recovery Act, which provided workers with almost complete freedom to choose representatives of their own choice for collective bargaining purposes. In addition to its effect on the total strength of the labor movement, the provision weakened the ability of the present union leadership to retain control.

He eventually organized four million workers into the CIO. The early years of the organization, of which the UMW was the core, were marked by violent strikes, one of which drew sharp criticism for both sides from Franklin Roosevelt. Up to that time, FDR had received Lewis' personal and organizational backing. "It ill behooves one who has supped at labor's table and who has been sheltered in labor's house to curse with equal fervor and fine impartiality both labor and its adversaries when they become locked in deadly embrace," declaimed Lewis. After that point Lewis and Roosevelt were on strained terms, culminating in Lewis' support for Wendell Wilkie for president in 1940.

Lewis resigned as president of the CIO in 1942 and pulled the UMW out of the organization. He returned to the AFL for a period of less than two years before taking the United Mine Workers down its own road. In 1955, the AFL and CIO merged without the participation of the man who had had a significant impact on the histories of both organizations.

Lewis' direction of the UMW was based on an "all the wagons in a circle" approach to confrontation with the government. "It is better to have half a million men working at good wages and high standards of living than to have a million working in poverty." (Lewis certainly knew that the law of demand applied to coal miners, too.)

His program to improve the wages and living conditions of his membership was based on his skillful ability to turn potential crises to his advantage. During the 1950s, increases in automation in mining were threatening to cut his membership; but automation was needed if coal was to remain competitive with oil and natural gas. He obtained a contract agreement that placed a royalty on mined coal. The royalty was channeled into the union's pension fund, eventually boosting its value above $170 million.

Probably Lewis' most trying years were those of the Truman administration, as he attempted to lead strikes in both the soft and hard coal industries in the face of court injunctions. Truman seized the mines and had them worked by federal troops, but Lewis eventually received the settlement he wanted. He ran up more than $2.1 million in strike fines, and probably damaged the competitive position of the industry.

One of his major achievements was the 1952 Federal Mine Safety Act, the first of its kind in the United States. His dramatic appearance at the site of a mining disaster in 1951 provided a strong push for the Act in Congress. Also during the 1950s he won extremely favorable settlements, including payment for underground travel time.

After his semiretirement in 1960, the UMW fell on hard times. Under the leadership of Tony Boyle, the union suffered through a membership slowdown, and then was subject to a series of government investigations into corruption and the murder of a candidate for Boyle's office.

Two weeks before he died, Lewis was called on by Ralph Nader and other concerned observers to rescue the union from Boyle's heavy-handed policies. But Lewis was too old, and there was a conflict of interest inherent in the situation; Boyle was a devoted disciple of Lewis and held his position partially through Lewis' influence in the union.

Lewis' tenure as a major influence in American labor was rivaled by few men in its length and probably by no man in its power. His commitment to his union's membership and its needs was single-minded. When he died, the miners closed the mines in memory of him, as they had done many times in response to his call to strike. □

Economic Life in Modern America

The Miracle Man of Wartime Merchant Shipbuilding

Henry J. Kaiser
(1882 - 1967)

An Audacious Industrialist

"A World War II Liberty Ship was big, very big. Nonetheless, Henry J. Kaiser was able to produce one in eight days flat! In his seven shipyards in Oregon and California he produced over 1,500 ships during the war. How did he do it? By introducing prefabrication and assembly-line techniques, along with a new and better welding process. This feat may have seemed a miracle, but should only have been expected from the man who had built up empires in paving and construction before the war. He had done that by submitting lower bids than much larger firms on all the government contracts he could apply for in the 1930s. He went on to help build Bonneville and Grand Coulee dams. Kaiser even had the audacity to bid on providing five million barrels of cement for Shasta Dam even though he did not have a cement company! He got the bid and founded Permanente Cement Company, which had the largest plant in the entire United States, located in Permanente, California. Between 1931 and 1945, he completed seventy major construction projects.

Kaiser was not a boy to stay in school in his native Sproutbrook, New York. He quit at the age of thirteen to become a cash boy, later becoming a salesman for the J. B. Wells Dry Goods Store in Utica. Then he went into the photographic supply business, and while still in his teens became a partner in the firm of Brownwell and Kaiser in Lake Placid, New York. Tiring of the photography business, he sold out in 1906 and moved to Spokane, Washington, where he went into the hardware business as a mere employee. Then the paving industry took his fancy, and he soon became a self-employed contractor, handling numerous highway and street projects in Washington, Idaho, and British Columbia. Then he moved his headquarters to Oakland, California. While still a road builder, he constructed 200 miles of highway in Cuba at a cost of over $18 million. One of the biggest innovations Kaiser introduced while in the road-building business was the substitution of diesel engines for gasoline motors in his tractors and steam shovels, thereby greatly reducing operating costs. When he went into the dam construction business, his prowess as an organizer and innovator did not abate: As head of the contractors building the Boulder Dam, he got it completed two yeares ahead of schedule. Construction of dams led to the building of tunnels, bridges, dry docks, jetties, air bases, troop facilities, and even to the excavation for the third locks in Panama.

Kaiser, perhaps more than any other industrialist of the time, was convinced that vertical integration was the only way to solve supply problems. For building his ships in California, Oregon, and Washington, he needed steel, so he put up an integrated steel plant in Fontana, California. The ships also needed engines, so he and his associates purchased an iron works in Sunnyvale, California, where engines were built for Kaiser and other contractors. He also built a magnesium plant (magnesium was not used only for shipbuilding; in one form it was used as the incendiary material known as "goop").

The list goes on, for Kaiser got himself involved in airplane building during the war, also. He designed his plant in Bristol, Pennsylvania, where he not only built parts, subassemblies, and surfaces for flying fortresses, but also put together experimental Army and Navy planes.

After the war Kaiser saw the possibility of profit in the automobile industry. He formed the Kaiser-Fraser Corporation, which was the first major new U.S. independent auto producer after the war. The future of independent auto producers seemed bright right after the war, but by the early 1950s it was a downhill road. In an attempt to strengthen his market position Kaiser bought up the assets of the bankrupt Willys Motors in 1953. In the end, though, Kaiser Motors failed, and its over $90 million in debts were assumed by Henry J. Kaiser's more profitable enterprises.

Kaiser never stopped expanding his empire. He went into aluminum right after the war, and within five years Kaiser Aluminum and Chemical Company had sales of $150 million. By 1956, this figure had risen to $330 million, with a net profit of over $40 million. Kaiser has left his mark on American economic and social life. There are Kaiser hospitals, and Kaiser housing developments such as on Oahu, Hawaii. There are numerous other less obvious imprints of this audacious industrialist's activities, many of which are based on one man's quest for continued industrial efficiency. □

10. The Roaring Twenties and the Depressed Thirties

The Twenties: Social and Moral Upheavals

The decade of the 1920s was distinctive in many ways. It was ushered in by the 1919 smash hit, "How Ya Gonna Keep 'Em Down on the Farm After They've Seen Paree?" And in fact the twenties was a period when the *absolute* number of farmers in America declined for the first time. Larger portions of incomes, which rose steadily over the decade, were directed away from agricultural products and toward services and other commodities, especially such consumer durables as refrigerators, electric appliances, radios, and above all, automobiles. Technological change continued briskly, not only effectively reducing the costs of production but also vastly widening the array of goods available to consumers. This was the decade of the consumer durables revolution: Many new goods (such as those just listed) were produced, and more and more common items became more readily available.

When the pitch of wartime excitement subsided, renewed sentiments for isolationism appeared. In addition, there were significant political changes when women finally gained the right to vote. It was the decade of the "great experiment," when the strength of a moralistic minority temporarily won over the rights of individuals to sin by the drink of their choice. Prohibition and speakeasies were colorful examples of the social and moral upheavals of that unique decade. So, too, were the Capone mob, the President Harding quip that "the business of America is business," and the collapse of the coal unions as electric power competition undermined the market for coal.

The routine of going to work, paying bills, worrying about this or that occupied the vast majority, much as it always has. Scarcity, the necessity of making hard choices, and other essentials of economic life still prevailed. But the comforts of life were rising and the automobile in particular opened up vast new opportunities for increased leisure, recreation, mobility—in a word, freedom. By the early 1920s, over three million new automobiles were being purchased each year and by 1929, there were twenty-six million cars on the road. Although some did not share in the gains, for many it was indeed a decade of great prosperity.

Over the decade, real incomes per capita marched upward at the record rate of 2 percent per year. The growth of productivity was unusually high throughout most sectors—in manufacturing, construction, agriculture, and elsewhere.

Agriculture Looks to Government

Although output per worker in agriculture increased 26 percent over the decade, largely due to the introduction of the gasoline tractor, which replaced nearly one-third of the horses used on farms, many farmers were discontent. The fall in costs did not seem to help them, and generally, farmers did not fare well in the 1920s. By comparison to the bonanza years of World War I, they were distinctly worse off.

The broad extension of government powers prompted by World War I was sharply curtailed in the twenties. But in one key area, namely agriculture, the pressure of government control and intervention remained.

One of the key figures responsible for this was none other than Herbert Hoover, who headed the Food Administration during World War I. After the war, Hoover became Relief Administrator in Europe; on returning to the United States, he was appointed Secretary of Commerce by President Harding. Immediately, on his appointment, he set out to "reconstruct America." During the recession of 1920–1921, Hoover repeatedly presented his views on how public works could be used to stabilize employment during depressions. Keeping close to the food problem, with which he had been so familiar during World War I, Hoover helped write an act passed in 1921, which expanded the funds allotted to the still-existing War Finance Corporation (WFC). This act permitted the WFC to lend directly to farmers' cooperatives.

Not satisfied, Hoover attempted to create a federal Farm Board that would support farm prices by creating a federal corporation for stabilization. This corporation was to purchase farm products and lend money to cooperatives. For a short time, this worked, and farm prices were supported by government purchasing. But the Farm Board's budget was too limited and there were no attempts to regulate (curtail) supply. Consequently, when farmers began growing more in response to the price supports, excess supplies drove prices down. Nevertheless, Hoover and others learned from these experiences, and they set the stage for subsequent attempts at price supports and supply controls made in the 1930s.

The Great Stock Market Crash

Toward the middle of the Roaring Twenties, the stock market was booming, and stock prices were rising at astounding rates. Barbers, janitors, butlers, and ditch diggers all had money in the stock market and were making money on their money. Increasingly, people wanted to buy and were allowed to buy on margin. That is, they only had to put up a certain percentage of the total price; their brokerage company would furnish the rest. Of course, they paid interest on this loan, but since their stocks were going up so fast, they still made lots of money.

Figure 10–1 shows the stock market from the beginning of the 1920s to the depths of the Depression. By 1929, stock prices were already two and a half times what they had been a mere three or four years earlier. Trading was increasing every day. Something had to give, and it did. In October of 1929, investors started to get jittery. There were new reports that economic activity was falling. With possible threats of a recession, confidence tilted downward, and people began to sell. Of course, nobody ever conceived of what would follow.

On October 1, an average share's price fell $5 to $10. On October 3, the same thing occurred again. The next day was no better. Prices kept declining, although the number of shares traded was actually relatively small. Toward the end of the month, when disaster seemed near, business and political leaders tried to intervene in order to stop the precipitous decline. However, on Monday, October 28, 1929, there was a nationwide stampede to unload stocks. In the last hour of trading, over three million shares were traded. In just one day, the value of all stocks fell by $14 billion. The next day was even worse. Blue Monday was followed by Black Tuesday. Although stock prices rallied for the first few months in 1930, that was the last major rally that a nation of investors was to see for many years to come. By the summer of 1932, the value of stocks had fallen by 83 percent from their September 1929 prices! For every dollar invested, only seventeen cents remained.

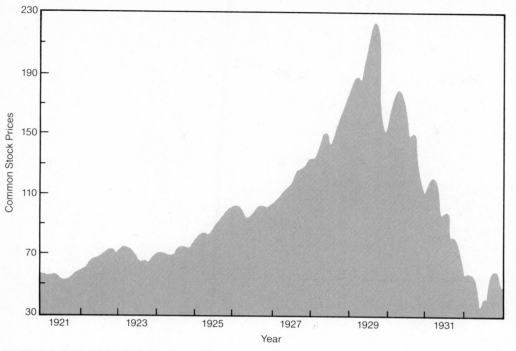

Figure 10-1. The Stock Market.

Source: Standard Statistics Index of Prices of 421 Common Stocks.

The Rest of the Economy

It was not long before the entire nation was well into a serious recession. Of course, no one imagined that this recession would become the greatest depression in the history of the United States. In fact, at the time, the great American economist, Irving Fisher, who was also a leader in the Temperance movement, was busy giving speeches to Rotarians and similar groups. He proclaimed that the economic troubles of the United States were bound to be short-lived because Prohibition had made the American worker more productive!

Despite Prohibition, total real output fell continuously after 1929, a phenomenon that rarely occurs. Because the population continued to grow, real output per capita was falling even more rapidly. Figure 10−2 shows that by 1933 actual output was

at least 35 percent below the nation's productive capacity. In fact, the total output lost during this Great Depression was a little over $350 billion measured in 1929 prices. If the Great Depression had not occurred, America could have built, for example, another 700,000 schools, each costing a half a million dollars, or another thirty-six million homes, each costing $10,000. Never in peacetime was so much output lost.

The Employment Situation

Of course, the employment situation also grew increasingly bleak. As can be seen from Figure 10−3, by 1933 fully one-fourth of the entire labor force was out of work; that is, one out of every four adult members of society who wanted to work could not find a job. And unemployment stayed high for

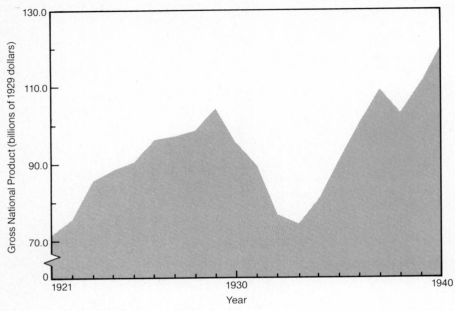

Figure 10-2. Real Gross National Product.

Source: J. W. Kendrick, *Productivity Trends in the United States*, and U.S. Office of Business Economics.

many, many years. The Great Depression was not a short-term event. From 1930 through 1940, an average of ten million people were out of work, in a labor force that was less than one-half of ours today.

Moreover, the labor force may have been understated at that time, thus understating the actual amount of unemployment. There was a consistent "no jobs for married women" policy throughout the entire 1930s, and married women were denied jobs in favor of men. Additionally, many moved their families into rural areas or onto squatters' land. Instead of looking for a job in the city, they attempted to scrape out a bare existence in the countryside.

The Banking System

By March 1933, the entire commercial banking system in the United States had virtually collapsed. This was the end of a third wave of banking panics, which began in 1930. To shore up confidence in banks, one of newly-elected President Franklin D. Roosevelt's first steps was to close every bank in the country and declare a temporary moratorium on debts. Between 1929 and 1932, more than 5,000 banks—one out of every five—had failed and their customer's deposits vanished. When Roosevelt's banking holiday ended, another 2,000 banks permanently did not open their doors for business. Both personal savings and income fell.

By 1932, people were *dis*saving—spending more than they earned—almost three-fourths of a billion dollars, whereas in 1929 they had saved over $4 billion. Not only did banks fail, but so did thousands on thousands of other financial intermediaries—loan companies, credit unions, and the like.

And Farmers, Too

As emphasized earlier, real agricultural incomes did not rise very much during the 1920s, and farmers were considered one of the few groups that had missed out during these years of prosperity. Then the Depression hit, and farm incomes declined tremendously. By 1932, the net income of farm operators was barely 30 percent of what it had been in 1929.

Economic Life in Modern America

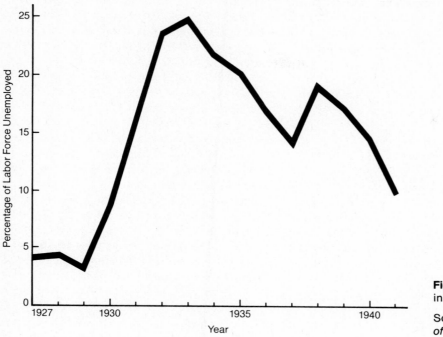

Figure 10-3. Unemployment in The Depression.

Source: *Economic Report of the President.*

This does not mean, however, that total farm output was lower. In fact, it was about 3 percent higher. What had happened was that farm prices had plummeted. Prices received by farmers in 1932 were a little over 40 percent of what they had received in 1929. Of course, the demand for food is relatively price inelastic. When farmers tried to counter their falling incomes during the early years of the Depression by increasing their output, they found they could sell their increasing supplies only by lowering prices even more. After all, it takes a tremendous reduction in the price of corn or wheat to get consumers to buy much more of each. That is always the case when one is dealing with a product whose demand is relatively price-insensitive.

Unsurprisingly, farmers became delinquent in paying their taxes and their debts. In 1929 alone, there were almost 20 forced farm sales per every 1,000 farms because of failure to pay taxes or debts. This figure had risen by 100 percent in 1932. Even this understates what actually happened, because as the Depression wore on, local tax officials became more and more tolerant of farmers who did not pay their taxes. And it usually did not do much good to force a farm sale. Who would buy the farm, and at what price?

The Rest of the World

Although it was little consolation, the United States was not much worse off than the rest of the world. By 1932, the world's total number of unemployed measured at least thirty million. The international monetary system was in chaos. The value of gross trade in the world was falling daily. 1931 was a year of international crisis never again to be matched. It began in May after the failure of the Credit Anstalt, which was the most important bank in Austria. Its failure made many other banks uneasy, both Austrian and foreign. Foreign creditors rushed to Austria to take out deposits. Then Hungary suffered the same problem. Next was Ger-

The Roaring Twenties and the Depressed Thirties

many. The crisis finally hit the center of the international monetary world—London. No country seemed able to maintain the price that its currency was valued at in terms of gold. No country seemed strong; no currency did either. By the time President Roosevelt was inaugurated, the international economy was as much in a shambles as was America's. And Hitler was winning votes in Germany.

Why Did It Happen?

Why did what would otherwise have been a normal recession turn into the greatest depression in modern history? The debate still continues. We have already obliquely referred to some general notions that people had about the Depression. One notion was that Americans were living beyond their means. But there is very little evidence for that; the productive capacity of the nation was not particularly strained in 1929. Others believe that the failure of the agricultural sector to prosper led to the ultimate demise of the rest of the country. But we find little evidence that such a small part of a big economy could bring on a great depression. Perhaps it could cause a recession, but nothing of the magnitude of what happened. That leaves us with two major and, in some sense, competing theories of why it all happened.

The first theory is associated with John Maynard Keynes, founder of **Keynesian economics**. The second is associated with Milton Friedman, the leading proponent of **monetarism**.

The Keynesian Explanation

In 1936, when we were still in the Depression, a rather remarkable book appeared, *The General Theory of Employment, Interest and Money*. It was written by John Maynard Keynes, a respected and eminent economist who lived and worked in England. In his book, Keynes introduced the possibility that unemployment would exist for a long period of time. That is, he introduced the possibility (hitherto un-

thought of) that unemployment on a large scale would not correct itself by natural forces within the economy. He pointed out that what was necessary to keep full employment was *effective* aggregate demand. He also pointed out that one of the key factors driving the economy was investment. To provide for investment, there had to be saving. In other words, consumers would have to be willing to save part of their income in order for investors to have resources for investment. But, noted Keynes, there might be times when there is not enough effective investment demand to use up all of the private sector's savings. When this occurs, there would be unemployment, for saving as such is only useful when it is put back into the economy. And it is put back into the active economy only when investors use it to build houses or machines or buildings.

Proponents of the Keynesian theory of how income and employment are determined point out that during the 1920s the public engaged in an abnormally high level of saving. According to the Keynesian theory, this was dangerous, because unless those savings were put back into the economy by investment a drop in aggregate demand would result. Unemployment would occur. In fact, however, during the twenties there was a very high rate of net investment. But such a situation would eventually mean a reduction in the rate of investment as the stock of private capital reached excessively high levels. When this occurred, the expected profitability of future investment would probably fall. Hence, businessmen would feel less desire to increase investment. Unless consumers decreased saving accordingly, the desired level of saving would exceed the desired level of investment. Reduced demand on the part of the entire public would result, as would unemployment. A recession would begin and could develop into a depression, according to this theory. The government would have to step in to increase effective aggregate demand by appropriate monetary and fiscal policies.

Basically, then, according to Keynesian theory, the Great Depression occurred because of a *collapse in the desire for new capital formation on the part of business people.* That is, there was a *collapse in investment demand.* Investment fell behind saving, reducing output, and thereby causing unemployment. This theory is borne out by all the available statistics. We see in Figure 10−4 that net investment fell precipitously in the years following the stock market crash. But why the stock market crash? Perhaps the reduction in net investment could have been triggered by something else. At least that is what the other major theory contends.

Milton Friedman and Monetary Theory

While not denying the possibility that investment decisions by business people relative to saving decisions by individuals are an important determinant of how the economy moves, the proponents of monetarism, led by Milton Friedman, place considerably more emphasis on what happens to the amount of money in circulation. While our sketch of their theory is simplified, perhaps even oversimplified, we can point out its most obvious aspects and apply it to what happened during the Great Depression.

Monetarists believe that what happens in the short run in the economy can be determined by how the Federal Reserve System alters the amount of money in circulation. Money, remember, is comprised of currency and checking account balances. As noted in the last chapter, the Federal Reserve System was chartered before our entrance into World War I, to establish a sound elastic money supply. According to the monetarists, during the Great Depression, it did just the opposite. Now, why should the amount of money in circulation be important?

The monetarist theory states that people have a certain desire for money because it facilitates transactions. That is, to live in a world without money would be quite costly indeed, for we would have to resort to barter. Therefore, people keep money in their checking accounts and in their pocketbooks in order to facilitate transactions and to have a temporary store of purchasing power. If the number of transactions goes up, therefore, the amount of money desired by the public should increase. In other words, there should be some relationship between the level of income and the level of money desired by the

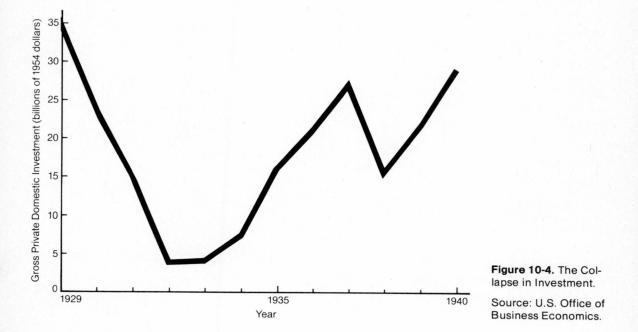

Figure 10-4. The Collapse in Investment.

Source: U.S. Office of Business Economics.

public. And, indeed, according to the monetarists, this relationship not only exists but is fairly stable. Therefore, if the Federal Reserve System increases the total number of dollars and transactions do not increase, some people will find that they have excess money. In order to get rid of their excess money, these people will attempt to spend it or will buy bonds. This will lead to, among other things, an increase in the amount of goods and services demanded. Hence, if full employment prevails, this will lead to a rise in prices. If we are not at full employment, it will lead to, at least in part, a rise in output and employment.

Now, taking the opposite tack, if the Federal Reserve System, sometimes called the *monetary authority,* decides to *decrease* the amount of money in circulation, then some individuals and businesses will find they have less money than they desire, which is, as we have noted, a function of how much income they make. Accordingly, they will spend less. But when lots of people spend less, the total demand in the economy for goods and services falls, and either prices or output will fall. In any case,

money income will be decreased, and so will employment.

The Money Supply

Now, using this very simplified version of monetarist theory, we can assess what happened during the Depression. Although the Federal Reserve made lots of overt attempts to stimulate the economy, the statistics presented in Figure 10−5 show that the money supply in circulation actually decreased by a third from the start of the recession to the depths of the Depression. According to the monetarist theory, this could only mean one thing: a reduction in the total demand for goods and services and, hence, a reduction in output and employment. The monetarists maintain that what would have been just another recession turned into the Great Depression because of the contractionary efforts that the Federal Reserve engaged in during this period. Whether or not the Federal Reserve was aware of what was happening is irrelevant. Figure 10−5 shows

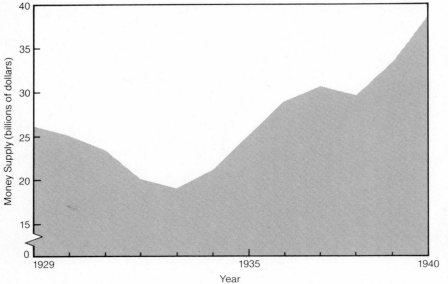

Figure 10-5. The Money Supply.

Source: Board of Governors of the Federal Reserve System.

Economic Life in Modern America

that the money supply decreased rather than increased. The monetary authorities dealt a crippling blow to an already weak economy and, hence, the depression deepened.

Possible Reverse Causation

At this point, we should mention the possibility of the reverse causal link between the money supply and income. We find that, as incomes fall, banks are less inclined to loan out money. Hence, not all of the reduction in the money supply is necessarily to be blamed on the Federal Reserve. In fact, some observers maintain that the Federal Reserve has the power to pull on the string, but it cannot push. Banks at this time were very unwilling to loan out any of their increased reserves. But, of course, that just means that the Federal Reserve would have had to increase reserves even more to reverse the decline in the money supply during this period. Moreover, much, if not most, of the decline in the money supply was created by runs on banks (bank panics). These failures were caused to a very significant degree by drastic declines in the value of their capital assets, mainly bonds. The Federal Reserve certainly had the power to strengthen these asset holdings by bond purchases. This would have made banks solvent, reduced the sense of alarm, and stemmed the tide of bank failures. Sadly, however, the Federal Reserve often sold rather than bought bonds. This action was unfortunately characteristic of many countercyclical measures that were misused during the 1930s. □

Definitions of New Terms

Keynesian economics: Keynesian economics recommends controlling the levels of economic activity (employment and inflation) by changing aggregate demand through taxes and government spending.
Monetarism: Monetarists believe that unexpected changes in the money supply cause fluctuations in real output and employment in the short run.

THE GREAT WATERSHED: THE 1930s

Before the New Deal

There are lots of myths concerning what happened before the election of President Franklin D. Roosevelt and what happened after. In the main, many observers contend that Hoover was a complete *laissez-faire* president who was unwilling to attempt any government intervention to pull the economy out of a deepening recession. On the other hand, many contend that President Roosevelt took Keynesian economics to heart and attempted, by every means necessary, to stimulate the economy through federal programs designed to increase aggregate demand. Both of these common notions are misleading. We have already made reference to the interventionist attitude that Hoover had ex-

hibited during World War I. That attitude was to continue during his time as Secretary of Commerce and, more importantly, during his first three years as President.

Hoover, the Government Advocate

Hoover was both a mobilizer and an economic planner during World War I. During the 1920s, he was a persistent advocate of government-business partnership in stabilizing industry. In fact, Hoover campaigned for reelection in 1932 on a platform of past government intervention into the private business affairs of the nation. He said, "We might have done nothing. That would have been utter ruin. Instead, we met the situ-

ation with proposals to private business and to Congress of the most gigantic proportion of economic defense and counterattack ever evolved in the history of the Republic."

He was not exaggerating much, for as soon as the stock market crashed in 1929, he started putting his program into operation. He called a series of White House conferences with the leading financiers and industrialists of the day. He got them to pledge, for example, that they would not reduce wage rates and that they would expand their investments. His theory was that the way to prevent recession was to maintain the purchasing power of the working people. How better to do that than by not reducing their wages?

Keeping Wages Up

What Hoover ignored during this period was that if prices are falling and wages stay the same, then the *real* wages are rising. Just as with any other good or service, the demand for labor is negatively related to its price. If labor's price—the real wage rate—goes up, a lower quantity will be demanded. If there is unemployment, an explicit program to keep real wages up will lead not to more employment, but rather to less. And that is exactly what happened. It was only in 1932, after several years of extremely severe depression and extensive unemployment, that money wages began to fall.

Hoover had been quite active in trying to prevent that decline and, indeed, was outraged by the United States Steel Corporation's first attempt at lowering wages in the fall of 1931. Overall, real wages actually rose from 1929 to 1933. In an economy that is growing, this is normal. But on the other hand, in an economy that is declining, we would not expect this. It could only lead to a decrease in the number of workers demanded because just like the demand for everything else, the demand for workers falls as the price rises, other things being the same.

Expansion of Public Works

In December of 1929, Hoover proposed to expand public works by some $600 million. In 1931, Hoover was instrumental in pushing through the Employment Stabilization Act, which establishd an Employment Stabilization Board. This Board expanded public works during the Depression and was allo-

cated $150 million to do so. Hoover was not content to stop there. He instituted the start of the Boulder, Grand Coulee, and Central California dams and also signed a treaty with Canada in order to build the St. Lawrence Seaway. Hoover was the first President to actively engage in large amounts of public works.

Finally, in January of 1932, Hoover created the Reconstruction Finance Corporation (RFC). It was modeled after the old World War I Finance Corporation, which extended emergency loans to business. The U.S. Treasury furnished the RFC with half a billion dollars, and it was allowed to issue bonds up to another $1.5 billion.

Also, even prior to the Depression, Hoover had established a Federal Farm Board, which was ready to take action as soon as the Depression arrived. Its first big operation was to cartelize wheat farmers into cooperative marketing units in order to withhold wheat stocks, thereby causing a rise in prices. But this did not work well. Persuasion was not adequate to keep wheat farmers voluntarily from producing more wheat. Then the Grain Stabilization Corporation was set up. It was supposed to purchase enough wheat to prevent the price of wheat from falling. However, opposing economic forces were too great.

A Change of Heart

Finally, in the last year of his administration, Hoover changed course. Many advisors had encouraged him to continue his efforts to increase the scope of government intervention in the marketplace and to increase the amount of cartelization among industry leaders. When he declined, he was labeled a *laissez-faire* President. Although that label is somewhat out of line with what actually happened during the first three years of Hoover's administration, Franklin Roosevelt was nonetheless able to capitalize on it and become President for the remainder of his life.

The First Hundred Days

Roosevelt's sweep into office allowed him to push through Congress a massive amount of legislation in the first 100 days of his administration. Space limitations prevent us from giving the details of every program that America's thirty-second president instituted. We can, however, look at the major ones.

It must be noted that Roosevent did not enter the presidency with the idea that government deficit spending was a necessary stimulus to economic recovery. In fact, it was only later in his administration that he appears to have believed deficit spending was indeed the way to prosperity for an economy in a gravely depressed state. We find in many of the utterances of the President that he was convinced that a balanced federal budget should be maintained. Nonetheless, he wanted to start numerous programs to put the country back on the road to recovery.

Using Hoover's Ideas

Many of Roosevelt's ideas were merely extensions of Hoover's. Roosevelt felt that it was necessary to increase workers' wages in order to increase purchasing power in the economy simultaneously and reduce "cutthroat" competition. Therefore, he was convinced that a new system of cooperation among workers, businessmen, and the government was necessary. Hence, the National Industrial Recovery Act (NIRA) was passed, and the National Recovery Administration (NRA) was formed. Its basic purpose was to allow collusion among businessmen to prevent price cutting. Those businessmen who joined in the national recovery effort were allowed to post the Blue Eagle emblem to identify themselves.

For labor, Section 7a of the National Industrial Recovery Act allowed for collective bar-

gaining by employees. This was a great impetus to the union movement, which had started many years before.

From the very beginning, a considerable portion of the population was against the National Recovery Administration and its obvious monopolizing tendencies. Finally, on May 27, 1935, the Supreme Court, in the *Schechter* case, declared that the NIRA was unconstitutional.

Farm Programs

Remember that the Federal Farm Board had already been set up with an appropriation of half a billion dollars to be used to stabilize the prices of the three major commodities in the program: wheat, cotton, and wool. The Farm Board soon ran out of money, though, in attempting to keep the price of these commodities high. The major replacement for the Farm Board was brought about by the Agricultural Adjustment Act of 1933. It established within the Department of Agriculture the Agricultural Adjustment Administration (AAA). Its stated goal was to support farm prices and to control the production of farm products. These were further supported by the Bankhead Cotton Control Act, passed in 1934, as well as the Curr-Smith Tobacco Control Act. Both of these Acts levied fines

on farmers who produced in exess of their quotas. Many farmers who signed agreements to limit their production were given benefit payments from the government. From the very beginning, there were scandals over the programs of the AAA. One was called "The Murder of Six Million Little Pigs."

What happened was that a survey at that time showed young pigs to be extremely numerous, indicating that in the near future there would be such a large quantity of pork supplied that prices would have to plummet in order to sell it all. So the Farm Bureau, the National Corn Hog Committee, and the Farmers Union recommended that six million pigs be killed. They were, and the baby pork was bought by the Federal Surplus Relief Corporation. In another incident, people were enraged that the AAA had farmers plow under eleven million acres of cotton already growing.

At this time, the Commodity Credit Corporation was formed. It was allowed to make what are called **nonrecourse loans** to farmers with cotton used as collateral. In other words, the farmers would pay the Commodity Credit Corporation cotton in exchange for a stipulated price that was above the market price. Farmers never had to repay the loan, but if they

Economic Life in Modern America

decided to, they could get their cotton back. The Commodity Credit Corporation is still in operation.

Effects of Price Supports

Finally, the original AAA was declared unconstitutional in 1936. Undaunted, Roosevelt revised the legislation and the AAA of 1938 was passed. It contained a soil conservation program, production allotments, Commodity Credit Corporation nonrecourse loans, payments to farmers who kept their production within quotas, and federal purchase of so-called surpluses. All of these programs had essentially been in effect earlier, but the AAA of 1938 made them slightly more flexible. These programs were destined to have perverse effects on the farming sector of the economy from their very inception. After all, if a farmer is paid a price support, then the benefits he receives are directly proportional to the amount of production he has. The bigger the farmer, the bigger the payment from the government. What happens is that the richest farmers have received the most money from the U.S. Treasury and the poorest have obtained the least. In 1973, for example, it was estimated that the top 7 percent of farmers were receiving 42 percent of the benefits under the various farm subsidy programs. Additionally, consumers were paying prices considerably in excess of what they would have paid without a farm program, and, of course, the world had less food and paid higher prices.

Unions and the Wagner Act

Soon after the NIRA was declared unconstitutional by the Supreme Court, the Wagner Act was passed. Using a slightly different wording from that used for establishing Section 7a of the NIRA, Roosevelt argued that the inequality in bargaining power between individual workers and large businesses depressed" the purchasing power of wage earners in industry" and prevented "stabilization of competitive wage rates and working conditions." To remedy all this, the Wagner Act guaranteed the workers the right to form labor unions, and engage in collective bargaining. This Act was declared constitutional by the Supreme Court in 1937, after which the strength of organized labor grew rapidly in the economy.

Union Membership

Of course, it was not in the 1930s that unions were first started. The concept of unions goes back as far as the Middle Ages, when journeymen's associations were formed.

Craft Unions. The American labor union movement started, however, with what are called local **craft unions**. These were groups of workers in individual trades, such as baking, shoemaking, and printing. Many of the earlier craft unions were curtailed by unfavorable court judgments. We see in Figure X—1 that the percent of the labor force organized into unions was still extremely small in 1930. At the beginning of the Depression, labor union membership fell drastically, from 12.2 percent to 7.4 percent of the labor force. However, within a few years after the passage of the NIRA and then the Wagner Act, membership jumped by more than 100 percent. By this time, many national unions had been formed.

Industrial Unions. To take the place of the Knights of Labor, the American Federation of Labor was started in 1886 under the leadership of Samuel Gompers. By 1900 the AFL boasted a membership of over one million workers. These federations were basically composed of numerous craft unions. **Industrial unions**, on the other hand, seek to organize the workers in an entire industry, regardless of the individual jobs these workers are doing.

In any event, during World War I an increasingly favorable climate of opinion toward unions developed. By 1920 membership had reached five million. Then there was a great decline until the New Deal. After the Wagner Act was passed, several other great unions were organized, one being the United Mine Workers Union under the presidency of John L. Lewis. He became head of the Congress of Industrial Organizations, a group of industrial unions. As can be seen in Figure X—1, the combined efforts of the AFL and the CIO increased the percentage of workers unionized by leaps and bounds from the Great Depression until the end of World War II.

Other Programs: Relief and Social Security

Numerous other programs were instituted during the New Deal. Many of them were aimed at providing employment for the impoverished. There were the CCC and the NYA and the CWA and the WPA.[1] None of these

---

[1] Civilian Conservation Corps, National Youth Administration, Civil Works Administration, Works Progress Administration.

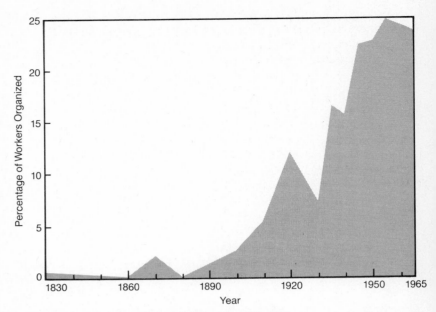

Figure X-1. Growing Union Membership, 1830-1965.

Source: L. Davis, et al., *American Economic Growth* (New York: Harper & Row, 1972), p. 220, and U.S. Department of Labor, Bureau of Labor Statistics.

particular programs lasted, but they did provide jobs for a certain number of people during the Depression years, and similarly designed programs are being implemented today. One program that did last was Social Security.

Social Security

The Social Security Act was signed by Roosevelt on August 14, 1935. It provided one of the most important social insurance programs in the history of the United States. The major aspects of it were unemployment and old age insurance plus survivors' ben-

efits. It started out small, enabling the federal government to provide grants to states to help them meet their old age assistance programs. There were also grants for aid to dependent children and to the blind.

The Social Security Act levied a basic payroll tax on payrolls of all employers, which was initially 1 percent but which rose to 3 percent after 1937. While it is not clear how effective the Social Security provisions were during its early years, today we have ample evidence how the Social Security system works. All workers who are covered start paying Social Security the

Economic Life in Modern America

minute they start making money, no matter how little. The basic rate in 1978 was 6.05 percent for the employer and the employee alike, applied to the first $17,700 of earned income; these figures are scheduled to climb steadily in the future.

However, employers do not actually pay their 6.05 percent. Since the employers' payments are part of their costs of hiring, they accordingly offer lower money wages to workers than if there were no Social Security payments. The employee indirectly pays the Social Security tax because the Social Security payment is ultimately a tax on labor income. Of course, it is redistributed to older, retired workers, but those who are paying view it simply as a payroll tax. After all, it does reduce their spendable income. It is not, strictly speaking, a guaranteed insurance program. Death benefits can be small or even zero unless the deceased leaves a long-lived widow or minor children. Furthermore, Social Security payments are voted on by Congress. One can never be certain that Congress in the future will be as generous as Congress has been in the past. Nevertheless, it remains very visible, and it is one of the major social insurance programs in existence today.

The New Deal and Aggregate Demand

Despite all of the fanfare about the first 100 days of Roosevelt's campaign for programs against the Depression, it is not really clear that they had much effect on aggregate demand. After all, besides considering what programs were instituted, we also have to look at how they were paid and at what other programs were dropped.

In Roosevelt's campaign, he criticized Hoover for large budget deficits that had been marked up after the Crash of 1929. In fact, Hoover's administration had the largest federal deficit in the history of the United States prior to Roosevelt's election. Once elected, Roosevelt told Congress that he did not want the country to be "wrecked on the rocks of loose fiscal policy." Apparently he took his warning seriously. Deficits during the Depression years were indeed small. In fact, in 1937 the total government budget, including federal, state, and local levels, had a surplus of $0.3 billion. During this time, taxes were repeatedly raised. The Revenue Act of 1932, passed during the depths of the Depression, brought the largest percentage increase of federal taxes in the history of the United States except for periods of war.

Fiscal policies, then, were in fact extremely weak, and even perverse. At the same time that the federal government was increasing expenditures, local and state governments were decreasing them. If we measure the total of state, federal, and local fiscal policies, we find that they were truly expansive only in 1931 and 1936, as compared to what the government was doing prior to the Depression. And these two years were expansive only because of large veterans' payments, passed by Congress in both years—by the way, over the vigorous opposition of both Hoover and Roosevelt. In both 1933 and 1937, and, to a lesser degree, in 1938, fiscal policy was quite a bit less expansionary than in 1939.

Roosevelt's administration has often been characterized as expansionary. In fact, however, it was not; the New Deal's primary effects were reform and the establishment of pronounced government controls over wider spheres of American economic life. □

Definitions of New Terms

Nonrecourse loans: Nonrecourse loans are loans that farmers obtain from the Commodity Credit Corporatioin in exchange for their crops as collateral. These loans need not be repaid, and in such cases the government keeps the crops.

Craft unions: Craft unions consist of workers who have one particular skill, such as printers, bakers, or shoemakers.

Industrial unions: Industrial unions, such as the United Auto Workers, are organizations of workers in an entire industry irrespective of their particular job classification.

11. Facing Another World War

The decade of the 1930s was dismal indeed. Workers and business people were concerned with little other than pulling themselves out of a deep, dark depression. The publication in Germany of Adolph Hitler's book *Mein Kampf* stirred little excitement in America. Even the outbreak of European hostilities in 1939 did not concern many Americans. Little did they know that they were soon to enter into the most devastating war in the history of the world. On the eve of World War II, in September 1939, 9.5 million men and women were out of work. This accounted for 17 percent of the entire labor force. At that time we were spending 1 percent of GNP on war production.

The Situation Worsens

By and large, the 1930s were a period of relative isolationism; it seemed all too clear to the average American, or even to congressmen and senators, that our major problems were at home. Few Americans were sympathetic to a military preparedness program even after fighting broke out in Europe. Although Roosevelt succeeded in appointing a War Resource Board in August of 1939, it quietly closed its doors a mere five months later. And yet things continued to worsen in Europe. France fell in 1940; the so-called invulnerable Maginot Line did not even hold against the first effective German attack. In May 1940, the office of Emergency Management was appointed, to be succeeded a few days later by the Council of National Defense.

Finally, the Selective Service Act was passed in September 1940 and war production started to increase. We entered into lend-lease agreements with the Allies, thereby increasing demands even further for war production. Figure 11−1 shows the impressive efforts made to help supply the Allies and to supply the United States itself with war materials once we got involved. From an index of 100 in 1939, it had risen to 5,600 by 1943. In 1943 American war production was as great as the combined war production of Italy, Japan, and Germany.

Managing War Production

Although still quite unsure of our course in 1941, an Office of Production Management was established that January. It was to provide for emergency plant facilities in case we entered the war. There was no doubt by the summer of 1941 that we were in trouble with respect to our defense capabilities. The Japanese sneak attack on Pearl Harbor on December 7, 1941, caught us totally by surprise and found us shockingly unprepared. Nobody had anticipated that the war would reach us so soon. The War Productions Board was immediately set up to oversee industrial output. Agencies multiplied rapidly; a number of them are listed in Table 11−1. Because this rapid multiplication of war agencies cried out

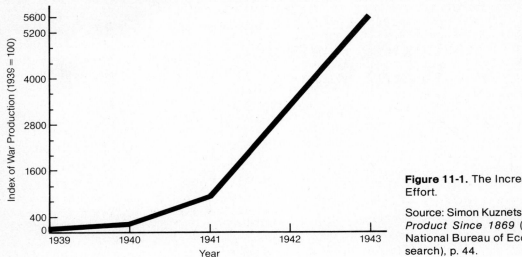

Figure 11-1. The Increased War Effort.

Source: Simon Kuznets, in *National Product Since 1869* (New York: National Bureau of Economic Research), p. 44.

for overall management, the Office of War Mobilization was created in May 1943, at the height of hostilities. But by then it was literally impossible to oversee all of the war activities in which the industrial sector of the economy was engaged. The next year this office had a new word tacked on—Reconversion—for by 1944, we were convinced that the war would end shortly and that we would have to face the arduous task of reconverting the economy back to peacetime endeavors.

Table 11—1. The Proliferation of Government Agencies During World War II.

Office of Emergency Management
    Committee of Fair Employment Practice
    Foreign Economic Administration
    National War Labor Board
    Office of Defense Transportation
    Office of Inter-American Affairs
    Office of War Information
    Office of Scientific Research and Development
    War Production Board
    War Shipping Administration
National Housing Agency
    Federal Home Loan Bank Administration
    Federal Housing Administration
Board of War Communications
Office of Censorship
Office of Price Administration
Office of War Mobilization and Reconversion
    Surplus Property Board
    Retraining and Reemployment Administration

President's War Relief Control Board
Selective Service System
Joint Chiefs of Staff
    Office of Strategic Services
Joint War Production Committee—United States and Canada
Permanent Joint Board of Defense—United States and Canada
Combined Chiefs of Staff—United States, United Kingdom, and Canada
Combined Shipping Adjustment Board—United States and Great Britain
British-American Joint Patent Interchange Committee
Munitions Assignments Board—United States and and Great Britain
Joint Mexican-United States Defense Commission
Pacific War Council
United Nations Relief and Rehabilitation Administration
United Nations Information Organization

Economic Life in Modern America

Labor Procurement

We had a problem of providing sufficient manpower not only to fight the war on several fronts but also to generate war production in the factories. A War Manpower Commission was established in April 1942. Its task was to provide an adequate supply of labor to all sectors of the military and the civilian economy. The draft, of course, solved the military labor problem. In 1944 and 1945, 11.5 million men and women served in the Armed Services. As can be seen in Figure 11–2, the employed civilian labor force first grew quite rapidly and then leveled off toward the peak of the war. What happened was that members of the economy who were formerly not in the labor force decided to join. These included women, retired people, and teen-agers who had quit their schooling early. That is, the labor force **participation rates** of various groups in the economy increased. A participation rate is the percentage of the total number of people in any given subsector of the economy who are engaged in the labor force. The participation rate of women over age fourteen, for example, was about 25 percent at the end of the 1930s; by 1944, it had risen to 36.5 percent. Overall, the participation rate in the population over fourteen years old jumped from less than 55 percent before the war to about 62.4 percent in 1944. Many of these changes were permanent, particularly with respect to female participation rates.

Paying for the War

As pointed out time and again, the government must somehow finance its war expenditures. It has three ways to do so: by taxation, by borrowing from the private sector, or by money creation. All three were used in World War II as federal expenditures grew by leaps and bounds from 1939 to 1945. So, too, did the federal government's deficit—that is, the difference between federal expenditures and federal tax receipts. The deficit reached an astounding $53.9 billion in 1945. This was more than one-half of federal expenditures in that year!

Taxation

Of course, the President did attempt to raise taxes. As early as January 1940 Roosevelt asked for addi-

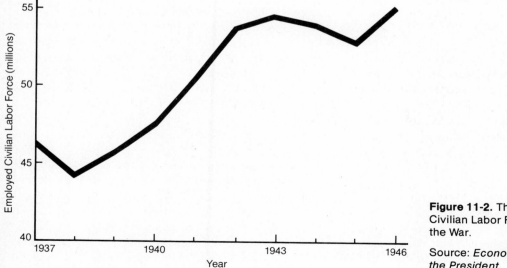

Figure 11-2. The Employed Civilian Labor Force During the War.

Source: *Economic Report of the President.*

tional taxes to pay for anticipated war expenditures. How did Congress respond? In June 1940, it merely lowered personal income tax exemptions and added slightly to the personal income tax surtax rate. In addition, it charged a little more to corporations, and there were some nominal increases in gift, excise, estate, and other assorted taxes. Nevertheless, tax receipts quickly fell behind expenditures. In October 1940, when it was obvious that the fighting was intensifying rather than subsiding, an excess profits tax was passed, with rates ranging from 25 percent to 50 percent. The corporate profit rate was raised to a maximum of 24 percent. About a year later, the maximum personal income tax rate went up to 77 percent and the corporate rate to 31 percent. The next year taxes were raised again, the personal tax to a maximum of 88 percent and the corporate to 40 percent. In addition, the maximum excess profits rate on corporation profits was now 90 percent. When the President asked Congress the following year, 1943, for even more taxes, they refused. However, a year after his request they were amenable to increasing the maximum marginal tax rate on individuals to 94 percent.

None of these measures was enough. Only 61 percent of the entire war effort was financed by taxation.

Selling Bonds

Because of the growing government deficit, bonds had to be sold. Just as there were Liberty Loans in World War I, there were Liberty Loans in World War II. In fact, the U.S. Treasury conducted seven of them, plus one Victory Loan. All told, during this period loans from the private sector accounted for 28 percent of government expenditures. That left 11 percent to be made up by money creation.

Money Creation

During these years, government expenditures increased more than the increases in taxes and bond sales taken together. Therefore the Federal Reserve System was coerced into helping the Treasury. Its primary objective was to ensure the Treasury adequate funds to meet all government expenditures. In March 1942, a special committee in the Federal Reserve System asserted its desire to prevent a rise in the interest rates of government bonds. So from that date until 1951, the Federal Reserve either "pegged" or supported the interest rate at a very low level: 2.5 percent on long-term bonds, and 3/8 of a percent on ninety-day Treasury bills. To maintain such low rates of interest, the Federal Reserve had to stand ready to buy all the government bonds offered when interest rates started to rise above the support level. At that time anybody could exchange cash for government bonds. But every time the Federal Reserve bought a bond, it increased the base on which the money supply rested. It is not surprising, then, that the money supply grew 12.1 pecent a year from 1939 to 1948 as a result of the Federal Reserve's bond purchases. The Federal Reserve had essentially abandoned control over the monetary system during this period of bond support. This is clearly seen in Figure 11−3, which shows what happened to the money supply from the latter part of the 1930s through 1950.

Price Controls

Whether from an excessive demand by the government for war production or from the increased amount of money that the Federal Reserve was putting in circulation, mounting pressure on prices soon resulted. Many knew this was going to happen, but nobody wanted it. Hence, the Price Control Act of January 1942 established the Office of Price Administration. By mid-1943, fully 95 percent of the nation's foodstuffs were rationed, and maximum prices and rents had been established. The Anti-Inflation Act of October 1942 then established the Office of Economic Stabilization. Its purpose was to limit wages and salaries and to curb prices and rents not yet controlled. At the height of price controls, these two offices, along with the Office of War Mobilization, created in 1943, were aided and abetted by almost 400,000 volunteer "price-watchers" scat-

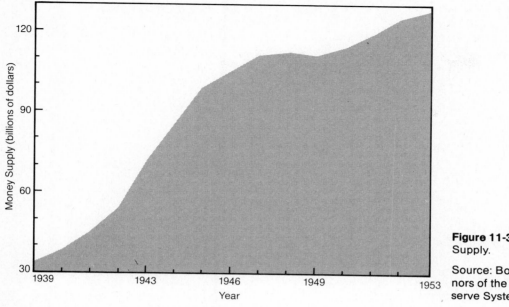

Figure 11-3. The Money Supply.

Source: Board of Governors of the Federal Reserve System.

tered throughout the country. Through this enormous nationwide effort, wholesale prices rose only 14 percent from November 1941 to August 1945. Figure 11−4 shows what happened to prices before, during, and after World War II.

Controls and Repressed Inflation

Price controls were not new to Americans of course. But the effects of controls were little understood. Instead of inflation, the shortage of goods relative to money came in another way. During World War II, we had what is known as **repressed inflation**. That is, the inflation did not actually show up in the price statistics because of rationing and price controls. Obviously, during World War II workers and business people had extra cash to spend. Hence there was a situation of pent-up demand, and yet the amount of resources for consumer goods production was limited, since so much was needed for war production. Normally, when there is an excess demand for goods or services, prices rise.

But price controls held prices down. Queuing and rationing became common practices.

Black Markets

In addition, in many situations black markets sprang up. A **black market** is an illegal market where goods and services are sold at higher than controlled prices. There were also numerous other ways that individuals obtained goods and services, such as favors for the supplier of a rationed good or service, or special arrangements for under-the-counter payments in addition to the stated price. There are many ways in which individuals can circumvent price controls. It is not clear how much of this actually happened during the war, but many accounts indicate that illegal or semilegal wheeling and dealing was rampant. Price controls were finally lifted after the end of hostilities in 1945 and then prices really soared, as Figure 11−4 clearly reveals.

This lends further support to the contention that repressed inflation existed during World War II. When prices were allowed to rise, they did, indicating

Facing Another World War

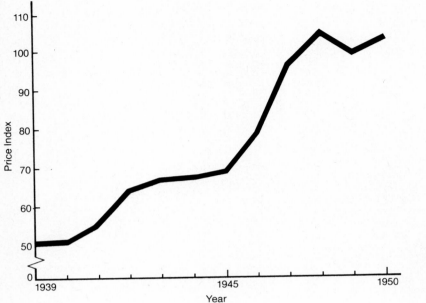

Figure 11-4. Inflation During the War.

Source: Bureau of Labor Statistics.

that they would have risen all along in the absence of controls. Note that it took a large amount of bureaucratic effort to police controls effectively during the war, even during this period of active patriotism. Although it was modestly successful for a short while, it is very unlikely that such measures would be effective in normal times or over longer periods.

The War Ends Without a Depression

Even before the war ended, government officials and other concerned individuals worried about the possibility of a postwar recession. They remembered what had happened after World War I, and they also were well aware of the new Keynesian ideas that had become popular in those days (and still are). As presented by Keynes during the depths of the Depression, demand must remain high for unemployment to stay low. It appeared that when the war ended there would be a serious drop in

demand, because government expenditures would fall drastically. This would lead to a multiple contraction in the level of income, thus leading to high levels of unemployment. Everybody wanted to prevent this but nobody quite knew how. What actually happened was just the opposite: Many individuals had high levels of **liquid assets**. That is, they had large amounts of government bonds and cash on hand when victory came. They wanted to spend them once the many restrictions on the production and sale of consumer durables such as automobiles, refrigerators, and washing machines were lifted. This happy opportunity to purchase new durable goods whose production had been greatly curtailed led to booms in these industries right after the war.

There was also unprecedented activity in the construction industry. Housing units were being speedily built. And lastly, government services contracted somewhat, but not back to their prewar levels. While the unemployment rate did jump from about 1.9 percent in 1945 to 3.9 percent in 1946, this latter figure was a more normal peacetime level of unemployment. In fact, it is what is generally called

Economic Life in Modern America

normal or *frictional* unemployment in a dynamic economy. It was not until several years later, in 1949, that we actually experienced what could be considered a recession. Just in case, though, the Congress passed the Employment Act of 1946, sometimes referred to as the Full Employment Act. It reads as follows:

> The Congress hereby declares that it is the continuing policy and responsibility of the federal government to use all practicable means consistent with its needs and obligations and other essential considerations of national policy, with assistance and cooperation of industry, agriculture, labor and state and local governments, to coordinate and utilize all its plans, functions, and resources for the purpose of creating and maintaining, in a manner calculated to foster and promote free competitive enterprise and the general welfare, conditions under which there will be afforded useful employment opportunities, including self-employment, for those able, willing, and seeking to work and to promote maximum employment, production, and purchasing power.

In addition, the Council of Economic Advisors was set up to make a continuing study of the American economy and to assist the president in preparing a report on the state of the nation every year. That council still exists today, and the government is continuously engaged in smoothing out economic activity in the United States.

World War II as a total war was unprecedented in scale for the United States and the rest of the world. During that time, government expenditures grew by leaps and bounds. In the process, some people feel, the most serious depression in our history was erased. However, others feel that it is not at all obvious that in fact the war pulled us out of the Great Depression. We examine these alternative views in the next issue. □

Definitions of New Terms

Participation rate: The participation rate is the proportion of the total population working, or the percentage of the total subpopulation working. We can find participation rates, then, for the entire economy and for various subclasses, such as men, women, married men, married women, etc.

Repressed inflation: Repressed inflation is inflation that is not allowed to manifest itself in rising prices. The symptoms of repressed inflation are shortages, black markets, under-the-counter "deals," and discrimination against certain classes of consumers.

Black market: The black market is an illegal market where goods and services are exchanged at prices that exceed legally controlled maxima or where national goods are transferred illegally.

Liquid assets: Liquid assets are assets that are easily exchangeable for cash without a change in their value. The most liquid asset is, of course, cash itself. The next most liquid asset might be a savings account, and then a U.S. government short-term bill.

issue XI: DID WORLD WAR II PULL US OUT OF THE DEPRESSION?

WERE INDIVIDUALS REALLY BETTER OFF DURING THE WAR?

Unemployment Drops

Many people assume that World War II pulled us out of the Great Depression. As the story goes, our tremendous unemployment was eradicated by the stimulus of a war economy. And the low levels of per capita real income at the end of the 1930s also changed during wartime.

First let us consider what happened to unemployment. Figure XI-1 shows that unemployment was in excess of 17 percent when hostilities began in Europe. This figure was still almost 15 percent in 1940. It then dropped to an incredible 1.2 percent by 1944. Overall, then, it seems

clear that the war effort nearly eliminated unemployment. But something else was happening at the same time, namely, conscription. The Selective Service Act was passed in 1940, and soon thereafter large numbers of men and women joined or were drafted into the armed services. These represented a significant fraction of the labor force, as we see in Figure XI-2. Is it accurate, then, to say that the war economy erased the prewar 17 pecent unemployment rate, when 17 percent of the labor force was in the armed forces at the height of the war? Clearly, a very significant and increasing fraction of the labor force

was conscripted. Of course, this is one way to eliminate unemployment, but it is rather a drastic procedure for generating unemployment reductions. Generally, it is assumed that high production rates create increasing demand for more and more workers, thus eliminating any residue of unemployment. Moreover, this is what most students of World War II believe happened during that period. In fact, however, it appears that conscription had much to do with eliminating the unemployment of the Great Depression.

Nevertheless, the fact remains that the output of the economy expanded rapidly during wartime.

Increasing Output

Increases in war demand during the early 1940s definitely stimulated aggregate demand. The output of the economy increased at a tremendous rate. As Figure XI-3 shows, total real GNP grew by leaps and bounds from the beginning of the war to its end. But were individuals really becoming materially

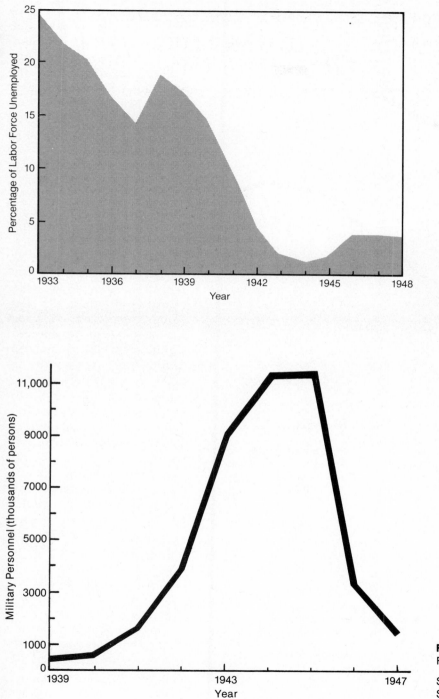

Figure XI-1. Percentage of Labor Force Unemployed.

Source: Bureau of Labor Statistics.

Figure XI-2. Our Fighting Forces During World War II.

Source: Bureau of Labor Statistics.

Did World War II Pull Us Out of the Depression?

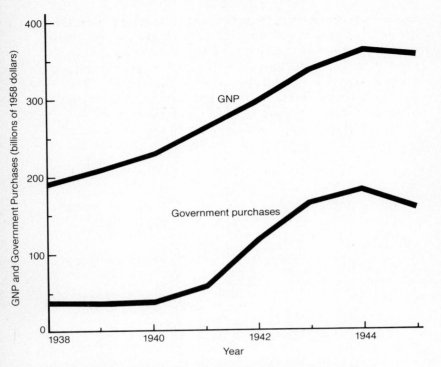

Figure XI-3. Growth of Real GNP and Government Expenditures.

Source: U.S. Department of Commerce

Table XI−1. Personal Consumption During World War II.

Year	Total Personal Consumption Expenditures in Billions (1958 Dollars)	Per Capita Personal Consumption Expenditures in Billions (1958 Dollars)
1940	$155.7	$1,178
1941	165.4	1,240
1942	161.4	1,197
1943	165.8	1,213
1944	171.4	1,238
1945	183.0	1,308

This table shows total personal consumption expenditures in billions of 1958 dollars. There was little rise during this period, and if we look at per capita personal consumption expenditures in 1958 dollars in column 3, we see that in 1942, 1943, and 1944, per capita personal consumption was less than in 1941.

Source: U.S. Department of Commerce.

better off during this period? Figure XI−3 shows that the total amount of government purchases of goods and services skyrocketed during the war. Much of the increase in output actually went to war production, not to enrich the personal lives of Americans. For example, the trend of per capita personal consumption expenditures for the period 1940 through 1945, as indicated in Table XI−1, is negative. In 1942, 1943, and 1944, per capita personal consumption expenditures were *less* than in 1941. Moreover, those figures include people in the armed services, a full 5.5 percent of the population. They obviously were not sharing significantly in the increased production of the nation. In short, the private sector of the economy was not much better off at the end of the war than at the beginning. The Depression was over, but people were not as well off as often is imagined. Of course, if we consider the psychological benefit of fighting and winning the war, overall social welfare broadly defined may have indeed increased. The war provided a new collective purpose, and certainly more people had jobs and the self-respect derived from being employed. Clearly the poorer segments of society were living more comfortably.

Economic Life in Modern America

What Is Income?

Nevertheless, this brings us to the crucial question: What does income really represent? Does it matter what we produce? Can an armored tank yield satisfaction to the general public? In fact, many argue that it is an intermediate good, not a final good—intermediate in the sense that it is used to produce what we call *national defense*. As Adam Smith once said, "consumption is the objective of production." However, since World War II modern politicians seem to be saying that tanks and airplanes are also objectives. Who is right? That depends on one's value judgments. Economics or history cannot answer such a question, but individual reflection will certainly lead most of us to our own conclusions. □

12.

Three More Decades of Business Cycles

The end of World War II saw the formation of the United Nations and a renewed commitment to prevent future conflicts endangering the peace and happiness of the world. The awesome destructive power of the atomic bomb had been amply demonstrated at Hiroshima and Nagasaki. The possibility of worldwide destruction and the end of the human species now truly existed. But, despite the United Nations and the persistent fear of destructive atomic warfare, the three decades that followed World War II were ones of alternating hot and cold hostile actions. Only half a decade was to transpire before American men, women, and machines were again engaged in a conflict—the Korean War.[1] After the truce in Korea it was again barely one and a half more decades before American forces were involved in another costly and, as it appears in retrospect, senseless engagement in Indochina. But all during this time the economy was growing; the per capita income was increasing. This can be seen in Figure 12—1, which shows the rise in per capita real GNP in the United States from the end of World War II until the mid-1970s. Underlying this long-run trend of increasing prosperity, however, were numerous problems of unemployment and inflation.

---

[1] This is euphemistically called the Korean Conflict, in which American forces were merely engaged in a United Nations "peace-keeping mission."

Postwar Inflation and Unemployment

The very strict price controls that were in effect during World War II were lifted almost immediately after the war. Consequently the pressure of repressed inflation that had built up for three or four years was now allowed to vent itself. Prices jumped sharply, and Figure 12—2 shows how the rate of inflation increased dramatically after World War II. Then it slowed for a while due to a relatively minor recession at the end of the 1940s. Once the Korean War broke out, however, prices again shot up at a very rapid rate.

Curiously, this happened despite the fact that neither government spending nor the money supply were increasing at very rapid rates during this period. However, people still vividly recalled the effects of price controls and scarcity during World War II. They feared that the same thing would happen during the Korean War. During the Korean conflict, there was an extraordinary buying spree, particularly for consumer durables and automobiles. The American public bought now in anticipation of shortages soon to come. But few shortages actually developed, since our participation in the war was relatively minor: 5.7 million men and women were engaged during a three-year, one-month period. There were

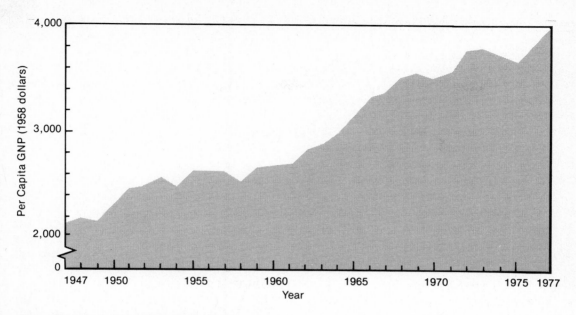

Figure 12-1. Rising Real Standards of Living.

Source: U.S. Department of Commerce

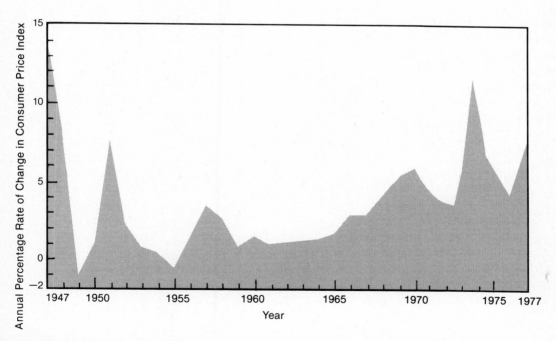

Figure 12-2. The Rate of Inflation.

Source: Bureau of Labor Statistics.

Three More Decades of Business Cycles

157,500 casualties, and the total cost was estimated to be in the neighborhood of $60 billion. The country experimented with a moderate amount of price controls during this war, but the effort was not very extensive, and the effects went largely unnoticed.

After the war, prices rose at very low annual rates—between 1 percent and 2 percent—until things heated up in Indochina. Starting in 1964, the rate of inflation advanced. Not only did this inflation continue, but it worsened as we entered the next decade. President Nixon imposed wage and price controls in 1971, and a modified form of controls were continued for a number of years afterward. Once again, however, they proved ineffective. As suggested by Figure 12−2, price controls will not usually work for long if the underlying forces of monetary and fiscal policies are expansionary. This is exactly what happened during World War II, during the Korean War, and again during the latest period of government wage and price controls. Although since 1971 there have been some periods of monetary and fiscal restraint, the general direction has been expansionary. In such situations, government controls will be ineffective in holding down prices.

Ups and Downs

Increasingly, since 1946, we not only had times of inflation, but also times of inflation concurrent with high unemployment, a situation hitherto almost completely unknown in the history of the United States. The levels of unemployment that occurred since the end of hostilities in 1945 are given in Figure 12−3. There was an immediate but short-lived jump in unemployment soon after World War II, as could be expected with large numbers of

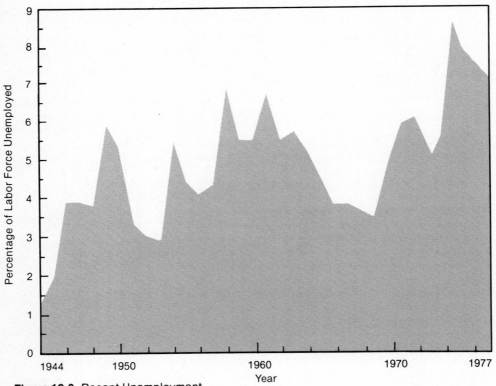

Figure 12-3. Recent Unemployment.

Source: Bureau of Labor Statistics.

Economic Life in Modern America

soldiers being mustered out. There was another period of exceptionally high unemployment at the end of the decade. We experienced yet another recession some ten years later, when the unemployment rate jumped in 1958 to almost 7 percent. Things improved for a few years, but in 1960-61 another recession was encountered. Then the longest twentieth-century period of peacetime prosperity occurred, lasting almost a full decade.

During these ups and downs, numerous attempts were undertaken by government officials, particularly by the Council of Economic Advisors, to enlist legislative help from the Congress. During the presidential campaign of 1960, Richard Nixon ran against John F. Kennedy. Arthur F. Burns, now chairman of the board of governors of the Federal Reserve System, schooled Vice-President Nixon on monetarism. He contended that if the Eisenhower administration failed to encourage the Federal Reserve System to expand the money supply more rapidly, there would be a recession, and Nixon might lose the election. And indeed he did lose, at least in part, over this issue. In 1960, when Kennedy became the thirty-fifth President of the United States, he appointed an activist Council of Economic Advisors, headed by Walter Heller of the University of Minnesota. Kennedy, Heller, and other advisors decided that the best way to pull us out of the recession was to use expansionary fiscal policy by a tax cut. Their ideas were Keynesian, like those referred to in Chapter Ten on the Great Depression.

Rationale Behind Tax Cut

Basically, Kennedy's economic advisors argued that a tax cut would give individuals more spendable income. When people spent this additional income, those who received it would also have more to spend, and this process would continue so that the tax cut would yield a more than proportionate increase in aggregate demand. Increased spending in turn would decrease unemployment, as unemployed workers were hired to produce the additional output demand. By looking at the unemployment record in Figure 12−3, we see that later in the

decade it did fall. The tax cut, however, did not actually occur until 1964, when Johnson was President, after Kennedy's assassination. The results of the 1964 Johnson-Kennedy tax cut seemed impressive. However, when the reverse tactic was used a few years later to quell an overheated economy, the same success did not arise.

The Tax Surcharge

One year after the tax cut, the United States had become heavily involved in Vietnam. By 1965, federal expenditures had leaped ahead of federal tax revenues, and we encountered increasingly large deficits. At about the same time, the money supply was increasing at a rapid rate, except for a slight pause in 1966. Whereas it had increased at 3.3 percent per annum from 1961 to 1965, during the period 1967 to 1969 it increased at 7 percent. In any event, the Council of Economic Advisors told President Johnson that one way to stop the mounting inflation was to increase taxes. The Council presumed that a reverse Keynesian reasoning would hold: Take more income away from consumers and they will be able to spend less, thus causing a contraction in aggregate demand. Prices would stop rising as fast because people would not be demanding as many goods and services as before. The tax surcharge of 1968 was instituted on this basis. But it had little effect on prices, which continued to rise in the next decade.

The Inflationary Recession

Curiously enough, at the turn of this decade, price increases did not slow down, but employment demands did. The unemployment rate rose steadily during the last years of the 1960s and the first years of the 1970s. How can we explain this simultaneous increase in prices and unemployment? In general, our notions about inflation equate it with excess demands—that is, people try to buy more goods and services than actually exist, thus bidding up prices. But with considerable unemployment, we know that there is no excess demand, for unemployed workers imply the opposite. There are basically three popular explanations for what causes an inflationary recession or stagflation.

Monopoly Power Arguments

The first explanation has to do with the power of unions. Presumably, unions become so powerful that they can raise wages high enough to cause unemployment. At the same time, entrepreneurs are forced to raise prices to pay for these higher union labor costs. Thus, we would see increasing unemployment and increasing prices. The second explanation is that business people have large discretionary powers over setting prices, contrary to what would occur in conditions of competition. During the early 1970s, they supposedly desired to increase prices even more in order to increase profits, but consumers balked. Since the law of demand indicates that higher prices lead to lower quantities demanded, entrepreneurs who raised prices found that they did not sell as much as they used to; hence, they laid off workers.

These two theories make only limited sense, however. First, these price rises are triggered by *increases* in monopoly (or union) power, not by their mere existence. Although they exist, there is little evidence that monopoly or union power have noticeably increased in recent times. Moreover, we have no idea when to predict this type of **cost-push inflation**. In what year can we expect unions to gain and assert their monopoly power? In what year can we expect businesses to do this? These theories tell us little and are not supported empirically.

Changing Expectations

An alternative, and perhaps more useful, theory concerns the lag in **expectations** or **anticipations** of individuals. Suppose, for instance, that workers anticipate that the demand for their labor services will yield them a certain wage rate, depending on what they were used to in the past and on what they see their friends and colleagues receiving. Businesses

also have anticipations about what prices they can set on their products in order to maximize profits. In periods of rapidly increasing aggregate demand, such as started in 1965, each year workers and businesses were temporarily fooled. Businesses found that they could raise prices and still sell all the goods and services they had anticipated selling. In fact, at the end of the year they might have found lower levels of inventories than they had anticipated. If so, this told them that they could raise prices even more and make even more profits. At the same time, consumers were buying, because they too anticipated even higher prices in the future.

Workers, on the other hand, were demanding higher wages and getting them or were switching jobs to obtain them. Many discovered that they could find jobs both easier and at higher wages than they had anticipated. In other words, the demand for their labor services was going up faster in money terms than they expected.

A Change in Tactics

In 1969 and 1970, the government's monetary and fiscal policy was suddenly altered. The growth rate of the money supply was decreased, and federal government purchases fell. This led to a lower rate of growth in aggregate demand. But business people, who had no idea that this was anything more than a random occurrence, continued to raise prices because they based their predictions of what they could sell on what had happened in the past. However, at the same time consumers' incomes leveled off. Now they reacted to higher prices by buying less. Inventories started piling up, and layoffs occurred.

Meanwhile, workers still demanded ever-higher wages, for in the past several years they had been accepting wage increases that merely matched increases in the cost of living—inflation. Many union contracts were renegotiated during this period. The union leaders wanted not only to make up for the lost real income of the last three or four years, but also to anticipate future erosions of their paychecks by inflation. Hence, they made demands for higher wages. At first businesses granted them, fully antici- pating that they could pass these higher labor costs on to the consumer while still maintaining their previous sales records. Such was not the case, how- ever, as both laborers and businesses were caught eventually by an unanticipated change in aggregate demand. Hence, we had a period of rising prices and rising unemployment.

Eventually, though, people started learning, so we saw a decrease in the rate at which inflation was growing until mid-1970. In fact, it appeared that the rate of inflation was abating when President Nixon instituted his New Economic Policy on August 15, 1971. The slowdown in price rises was soon to be reversed as the government's expansionary mone- tary and fiscal policies, instituted to pull us out of the recession, reinjected, purchasing power into the economy and started us off on another infla- tionary spiral.

Labor Legislation

We noted that the passage of New Deal legisla- tion fostered the growth of American union activity. However, there was a certain amount of antilabor sentiment after World War II. John L. Lewis' United Mine Workers defied a court order to go back to work after a long and violent strike. The union and its leaders were fined for contempt of court, and the miners finally did go back to work. However, legis- lation against unions was already in the wind, and the Labor-Management Relations Act of 1947 was passed. It is sometimes called the Taft-Hartley Act— and other times called the Slave Labor Act by union people. It allowed individual states to pass their own **right-to-work laws**. A right-to-work law makes it illegal for union membership to be a prerequisite for employment in any individual establishment. In general, the Taft-Hartley Act outlawed unfair labor practices of unions such as "make-work" rules and the forcing of unwilling workers to join a particular union before being hired. But the most famous as- pect of this Act is its provision that the president can obtain a court injunction that could last for eighty

days for any strike that is believed to imperil the nation's safety or health. President Nixon applied this eighty-day injunction to striking longshoremen in 1971. President Eisenhower had done the same thing to striking steel workers in 1959. Other labor legislation was also passed during this postwar period. Some of it involved increases in the minimum wage, and unions strongly supported this particular legis- lation.

Minimum-Wage Legislation

Minimum-wage legislation essentially puts a floor on what employers can pay certain employees. Mini- mum wages have been around for at least three- quarters of a century. This type of legislation grew out of the general movement against "the exploitation of the poor" and the low pay for those toiling under bad working conditions. But until 1912 the movement for a minimum wage produced very few results. In that year, however, Massachusetts passed a "moral suasion" law to compel employers to pay standard wage rates, which were to be set by a state wage board. Any employer who did not comply would have his name published and would therefore be subject to ostracism from the community. A year later, eight more states passed minimum-wage laws, seven of them making the rate compulsory. The laws, however, applied only to women and minors. Most workers were unaffected.

Roosevelt's New Deal and the National Indus- trial Recovery Act in 1933 set up the first federal minimum wage. It started at a rate between 30 and 40 cents an hour. When the NIRA was declared unconstitutional, the Fair Labor Standards Act was passed in 1937, establishing a minimum wage rate of 25 cents for all industries that were involved in interstate commerce. This act has remained the basis for the current federal minimum wage. The national minimum wage went to 30 cents in 1939. By 1950 it was 75 cents. Then it increased in steps up to $1.60 per hour by the start of the 1970s. By 1977, it was $2.30 per hour.

Unions in Favor

Why did unions support and find this legislation so favorable? Although union workers are already making considerably more than minimum wage rates, union labor services at low wages are obviously to some extent substitutable for union labor services at higher wages. If nonunion workers must be paid a higher wage rate than they would be paid otherwise, the demand for union workers will, in fact, be greater. In other words, the high union wage rate will no longer be *relatively* as high if other workers must be paid more than they would receive under competitive conditions.

Who Gets Hurt?

Some people are definitely hurt by minimum wages. Growing evidence from reports by the Secretary of Labor, by Arthur Burns, and comments by such respected economists as Paul Samuelson and Milton Friedman indicate that teenagers and blacks are hurt the most by the minimum wage. In fact, Paul Samuelson once said, "What good does it do a black youth to know that an employer must pay him $1.60 an hour if the fact that he must be paid that amount is what keeps him from getting a job?" Monetarist Milton Friedman called the minimum wage law "the most anti-Negro law on our statute books—in its effect, not its intent." How is this so? Doesn't a minimum wage merely mean that employers have to pay workers higher wages? Yes, it does, but it does not require them to hire the same number of workers.

For example, suppose the wage rate is arbitrarily increased by government edict. Now some workers may become unprofitable to employ. These "marginal workers" are those whose output in value terms barely equals what they are paid. If they suddenly have to be paid more, they will be fired, because now the market value of their contribution to output is less than the minimum wage rate. Employers would lose money by keeping them on. What happens is that those "marginal workers" who lose their jobs do not receive the minimum wage; they receive nothing. They have to find work in sectors of the economy that are not covered by minimum-wage legislation. And in those sectors of the economy, the additional supply of workers will cause wage rates to fall. By eliminating marginal job opportunities, the minimum wage rate actually hurts many of the very people it intended to help.

Some Facts

In 1956, the minimum wage was increased from 75 cents to $1.00 an hour, a one-third jump. Three years later, the Secretary of Labor concluded in a report that after the increase in minimum wage in 1956, "there were significant declines in employment in most of the low-wage industries studied." From other evidence we find that teen-agers are predominantly in the low-wage groups if for no other reason than they have less experience in working and therefore are less productive than older experienced workers. Therefore, they are the most affected by the minimum wage. If we look at white teenage unemployment from 1950 to 1956, it ranged between 6.5 percent and 11 percent. When the minimum wage was raised in 1956 to $1.00, white teenage unemployment shot up from 7 percent to almost 14 percent. Ever since then, it has remained in excess of 12 percent. Even more startling is what happened to black teenagers. In 1956, unemployment in that category jumped from 13 percent to 24 percent. A 1965 study by Arthur F. Burns concluded that "the ratio of the unemployment rate of teen-agers to that of male adults was invariably higher during the six months following an increase in the minimum wage than it was in the preceding half year."

Another Type of War

Throughout the three decades just covered, a new type of war was being waged. It has been called a *cold war* because no overt declarations of war were ever made. But its existence, nonetheless, has created a continuing and growing military establishment in this country. We will look at the accompanying problems of that cold war in the next Issue. □

Definitions of New Terms

Cost-push inflation: The theory of cost-push inflation states that costs are pushed up either by strong unions or by monopolistic businessmen, thus causing prices to rise.

Expectations and anticipations: Expectations and anticipations are formulations in people's minds about what will happen in the future. Individuals have expectations about future rates of inflation, future rates of change in wages, and so on.

Right-to-work law: A right-to-work law is a law deeming it illegal for union membership to be a prerequisite for employment in an individual shop.

HOW WE LIVE WITH THE GENERALS

The Cold War Begins

The uneasy truce between the Allies at the close of World War II quickly disintegrated into what we have long known as the cold war. The United States pitted itself against the communist countries in general and Russia in particular. We were not going to let the Russians "bury us" in economic output, as former Premier Nikita Khrushchev once prophesied to the American people. The U.S. was not going to let communist aggression engulf ever-increasing parts of the world. Whether or not the cold war political philosophy of this nation was indeed correct or valid is beyond the scope of this book. However, we can determine to some extent whether the era of cold war diplomacy brought about the rise of an unmanageable **military-industrial complex.** The question is not new.

FDR Strikes Out

Back in the 1930s, President Roosevelt himself raised the specter of a mammoth military influence in the domestic economy. On the eve of a Senate investigation of the munitions industry, for example, he said very plainly that the arms race was a "grave menace . . . due in no small measure to the uncontrolled activities of the manufacturers and merchants of the engines of destruction and it must be met by the concerted actions of the people of all nations." Roosevelt even had a campaign pledge in 1932 to "take profits out of war."

Eisenhower Bids Farewell to the Nation

During his eight years in office, the former five-star general of World War II experienced firsthand what kind of duress could be brought against him and the other policy makers by the munitions manufacturers. This was the time when Charles E. Wilson, Eisenhower's Secretary of the Defense, said, "What is good for General Motors is good for the country." Eisenhower decided to give the country a solemn and, as he saw it, necessary warning of what could happen if things weren't stopped. On January 17, 1961, he said:

This conjunction of an immense military establishment and a large arms industry is new in the American experience. The total influence — economic, political, even spiritual — is felt in every city, every state house, every office of the federal government. We recognize the imperative need for this development. Yet we must not fail to comprehend its grave implications. Our toil, resources and livelihood are all involved; so is the very structure of our society.

In the councils of government, we must guard against the acquisition of unwarranted influence, whether sought or unsought, by the military industrial complex. The potential for the disastrous rise of misplaced power exists and will persist. . . . Only an alert and knowledgeable citizenry can compel the proper meshing of the huge industrial and military machinery of defense with our peaceful methods and goal, so that security and liberty may prosper together.

Military Expenditures

There is no doubt that at the time Eisenhower was speaking, expenditures for defense (and offense) were increasing. This can be easily seen in Figure XII–1. The big jumps were during the Korean War and the war in Indochina. However, similar to what happened after the Revolutionary War, the War of 1812, the Civil War, and World War I, we did not reduce our military expenditures to pre-war levels immediately at the end of World War II. Today, although the estimates vary, we have a military budget in the United States that may account for 10 percent of total output. The Pentagon, center of all government defense activities, is almost like a country. In fact, it has been called the largest planned economy outside the Soviet Union. Almost 10 percent of all assets in the United States belong to the Pentagon. It owns, for example, around forty million acres of land, and it employs, directly or indirectly, over four million workers. Its budget is only 25 percent less than the entire gross national product of Great Britain! The Defense Department is, in fact, richer than just about any small nation in the world.

The Military and Economic Activity

Although it is not clear that military spending is necessary for full employment, the military is involved in numerous aspects of economic activity in the United States. In fact, at the height of the war in Indochina in 1968, almost 10 percent of our entire labor force was employed in defense-related work. The spending of the military machine is, furthermore, highly concentrated. In 1967, a De-

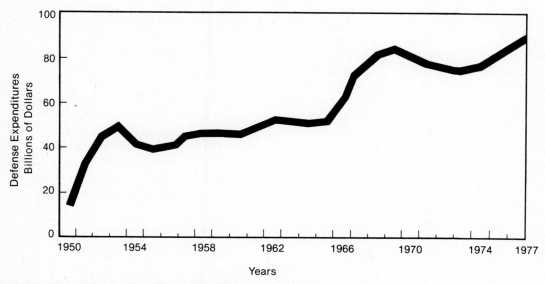

Figure XII-1. National Defense Spending in the United States.

Source: Office of Management and Budget.

Did the Cold War Foster a Military-Industrial Complex?

fense Department study found that seventy-two employment areas depended on war output for about 12 percent of their employment; 80 percent of these employment areas were small communities with labor forces numbering less than 50,000. The impact of any cutback in military spending to these selected communities can obviously be very detrimental. It is not surprising, then, that congressmen whose constituents will be affected lobby vigorously against any cutback in specific spending by the armed services.

When we look at defense employment, it is obvious that it is concentrated among a very specially skilled set of people who are defense oriented, just like the companies they work for. Scientists in specialized companies often have an extremely hard time finding alternative employment if and when the military decides to cut back on spending. Consider what happened to the aerospace industry when the government cut back in 1969. Lockheed almost went under, and Boeing's Seattle employment fell from over 100,000 to less than 30,000 in less than two years.

Military business is big business. The existence of a military-industrial complex seems almost obvious. In fact, if one looks at the workings of a military-industrial firm,

the abuses to which the taxpayer is subjected are indeed disconcerting.

The Military-Industrial Firm

One of the most outspoken students of Pentagon capitalism, Seymour Melman, has presented several propositions concerning military-industrial firms:

Proposition One: The military-industrial firm is not autonomous.

Proposition Two: The military-industrial firm is controlled by the state management.

Proposition Three: The military-industrial firm does not minimize costs.

Proposition Four: The military-industrial firm is not a profit-maximizing entity.

Proposition Five: The military-industrial firms as a group lack flexibility for conversion to civilian work.

Melman's stinging indictment of business practices in defense industries seems to be borne out somewhat by many of the scandals that have so afflicted defense contractors in recent years.

President Eisenhower was aware of this when he cautioned the nation to beware of the military-industrial complex in his famous farewell address to the nation. In 1961, Eisenhower was thinking of a fairly informal group of high

military officers, defense-oriented firms, and congressmen who would be bound together by an ideology of continual expansion of the military machine. If one looks at the way prime government contracting firms have been able to operate in past years, some argument might be made in support of the idea of a "complex."

Approximately 22,000 firms are deemed prime contractors with the Department of Defense. These firms in turn subcontract much of their work to smaller enterprises. When all the contractors and subcontractors are added up, there are perhaps 100,000 firms directly or indirectly engaged in supplying the Department of Defense. There are, however, a few very large firms that supply most of the manufactured goods to the Pentagon. The hundred largest prime contractors supply almost 70 percent of manufactured goods to the Department of Defense. Many of these firms actually employ government-owned capital, such as land, buildings, furniture, office machines, and material.

Military Procurement

There has been much recent criticism of the way defense contractors manage their firms. Headed by Senator William Proxmire of Wisconsin, the Joint Economic Committee of the Congress of the United States looked into the economics of military procurement and made a public report in May 1969. Essentially, the report was a stinging criticism of the problem of "uncontrolled costs." It was attributed to an unmanaged, unshaped military procurement policy. The Joint Economic Committee stated that a set of practices and circumstances exist in the Department of Defense that leads to: (1) economic inefficiency and waste, (2) a subsidy to contractors, and (3) an inflated defense budget.

The circumstances in the Department of Defense that led to these three undesirable results had to do with the following practices:

1. Low competition and high concentration among prime defense contractors.
2. Allowing contractors to use government-owned property.
3. Using progress payments to reimburse contractors for up to 90 percent of incurred costs on a pay-as-you-go basis, even if these costs are greatly in excess of original estimates.
4. No uniform accounting standards.
5. Voluminous change orders and contractors' claims.
6. The absence of ongoing reports to Congress.

7. No incentive contracting.

Some of the results of careless military procurement have been incredible indeed. The original cost estimates of the F-111 jet fighter turned out to be one-third of the actual cost per plane. The cost overruns on the infamous Lockheed C5A jet transport are on the order of $2 billion.

A Symbiotic Relationship

The relationship between prime defense contractors and the Pentagon is close and seems to be getting closer all the time. Congress finally has taken heed of certain practices within industries that lead to some dubious actions by Pentagon officials. Not only does the Pentagon support a large sector of our economy through defense contracts, but it also supplies a large number of key executives to large defense-contracting firms. Senator William Proxmire has criticized the "incestuous hiring" that industry engages in among retired Army officers and high Pentagon officials.

In 1959, a survey was made by Congress. It brought to light that almost 800 retired officers of the rank of colonel, Navy captain, and higher were employed by the largest 100 defense contractors. In 1969, the defense Department made a similar survey that showed that the number of former top military men working in defense industry firms was over 2,000. In 1969, Lockheed Aircraft had 210; the Boeing Company 169; McDonald-Douglas Corporation 141; General Dynamics Corporation 113; and North American Rockwell Corporation 104. You can imagine that something less than hard-nosed business rules would be used in dealings among retired generals and current generals running the Defense Department. Moreover, you can expect that officers looking forward to a cushy retirement job might act differently toward prospective employers than if there were no chance of getting such a job after retirement.

The military establishment also has a powerful political arm. The Department of Defense employs almost 350 lobbyists on Capitol Hill; it maintains some 2,850 public relations men in the United States and foreign countries.

The close relationship between the Pentagon and defense contractors has led one staunch critic, John Kenneth Galbraith, to hypothesize the following:

> Where a corporation does all or nearly all of its business with the Department of Defense; uses much plant owned by the government; gets its working capital in the form of progress payments from the government; does not need to worry

about competitors for it is the sole source of supply; accepts extensive guidance from the Pentagon on its management; is subject to detailed rules as to its accounting; and is extensively staffed by former service personnel, only the remarkable flexibility of the English language allows us to call it private enterprise. Yet this is not an exceptional case, but a common one. We have an amiable arrangement by which the defense firms, through part of the public bureaucracy, are largely exempt from its political and other constraints.[1]

The Trends

That there is a large defense establishment is not really subject to debate. All one need do is look at how many tax dollars go to the Pentagon. However, the trend seems to be, if not

[1] John Kenneth Galbraith, *The Military Budget and National Economic Priorities*, Part 1 (Washington, D.C.: U.S. Government Printing Office, 1969), pp. 5–6.

downward, at least not upward. In other words, the percentage of the U.S. federal budget going to defense has actually declined slightly in the last few years. Whether or not we can establish this as a long-term trend is another matter. Critics of the Carter administration have contended that Carter's pro-human rights posture will guarantee that defense (and perhaps offense) spending will become, once again, a growing percentage of federal government spending. Moreover, in no way could we answer the question in this issue of whether a military-industrial complex actually has prevented us from achieving an enduring world peace.

One can note that by using economic theory, we would predict that if unusually large profits could be obtained by those supplying Defense Department needs, then there

would be an economic incentive for these firms to foster an atmosphere in which hot and cold wars were continuously fought, so that the demand for their products would stabilize or increase. And if they could make higher profits doing defense work than other work, they would be better off.

However, as in all competitive systems, there would be countervailing forces, for those dollars that are spent on defense cannot be spent on improved health conditions, alleviation of poverty, improvement in the environment, increases in higher education spending, and so on. All of those who would benefit by the expenditure of defense dollars elsewhere in the economy would seem to have an incentive to counter the influence that the military-industrial complex has on our foreign policy. □

Definition of New Term

Military-industrial complex: The meshing of the military with the industries that provide its arms and materials.

Economic Life in Modern America

13. Critical Problems in a New Decade

Over two hundred years as a nation, the United States has attained a standard of living that is still the envy of most people in the world. That does not mean that the American economic system has solved all of the problems facing it in the past. As the 1970s end and the new decade begins, this country still faces such diverse problems as high rates of unemployment, environmental deterioration, inflation, labor force discrimination, and others. In some quarters, there is increasing dissatisfaction with how the government has handled some of these problems in the past. This dissatisfaction has extended to government-provided welfare, educational, and medical care services, plus a host of other public endeavors. And political candidates increasingly cry out for streamlining government.

The United States Versus the Rest of the World

It used to be fairly common to read that Americans enjoyed the highest living standard in the world. Advanced American technology and know-how epitomized U.S. leadership and won the envy of other nations. By the middle of the twentieth century and perhaps earlier, technological advance was no longer an autonomous sporadic affair. No longer was it the result of piecemeal individual inventions. Increasingly more and more investment in research and development brought forth a steady stream of new technologies. Like higher and higher levels of investments in education and health, which raised the skills and productivity of labor, mounting investments in research and development—by both government and the private sector—raised productivity. In this way, technological changes became a sustained process. Nevertheless, today, according to many statisticians, the United States no longer leads in terms of per capita income. Official statistics on per capita income in 1975 show the United States trailing many other countries! Table 13-1 shows the per capita income for selected countries throughout the world. The United States no longer seems to be the leader in living standards.

We should be somewhat suspicious, nonetheless, of this conclusion. It is extremely difficult to compare living standards across countries because of the difficulties in standardizing the way in which income is measured throughout the world. We even have difficulty estimating living standards in various regions within the United States, because prices are different for different items in those different regions. For example, a price index for Honolulu may be 20 percent higher than the price index for, say, Phoenix. Does that mean that if you move to Honolulu with the same income you would be 20 percent poorer? Probably not, because you would substitute the cheaper items for the more expensive ones in Honolulu. You would tend to eat less fresh meat and more frozen imports from New Zealand. You would tend to substitute more frequent picnics

Table 13—1. Per Capita Income for Selected Countries, 1975

Switzerland	$8,754
Sweden	8,540
Denmark	7,106
United States	7,099
Norway	6,944
Canada	6,935
West Germany	6,842
France	6,386
Australia	6,168
Netherlands	5,886
Japan	4,425
United Kingdom	4,089
Italy	3,074
Turkey	929

These figures represent 1975 per capita GNP figures. Note that no correction for differentials in the cost of living has been applied.

Source: U.S. Department of State, Bureau of Intelligence and Research, and *Statistical Abstract of the United States.*

on the beach in the sun for more expensive restaurant meals. The same is true when one shifts from country to country. Individuals react to changing relative prices by substituting more of the relatively cheaper commodities.

There is something else that official per capita income statistics seem to miss entirely. Income, properly measured, is not just money income, but includes a host of other things that yield utility to individuals. As an example, consider a household that owns several cars, a boat, a stereo system, a house with a swimming pool, a sewing machine, and a few other consumer durables. Throughout the year this household is receiving implicit income or income in kind from all of these consumer durables. For the most part, the implied income stream of utility received by this household is not counted in official government statistics on per capita income in this country nor in any other. Since United States citizens have a dramatically higher per capita level of consumer durables, the official statistics underestimate the true relative position of Americans in the per

capita income ladder. Nonetheless, it is true that the rate of economic growth in this nation has been slower than at many other periods in U.S. history. If this trend continues, U.S. living standards will continue to be surpassed by other nations' living standards.

The Ecological Mess

Fresh air used to be a free good. We could get all we wanted without taking it away from somebody else; it was not scarce. Clean water used to be a free good. We could go to a nearby stream and fish and swim in that water to our hearts' content. Today things are different. Air quality in major cities has deteriorated. Water is polluted in so many places that we cannot begin to enumerate them. The Cuyahoga River became so polluted that it was declared a fire hazard![1] Ecological problems are not, however, new to Americans or foreigners. In fact, London has had smog problems for centuries, due to the burning of soft coal. Only recently did it decide to ban the burning of that pollution-causing heating source. (And the air cleared up remarkably fast.) There were killer fogs in London many years ago and awesome smog attacks in New York as far back as the 1950s. But today the problem seems worse than ever, probably because we are more aware of it and because we demand more social amenities.

Clean Environment Costs

Like other valued items, a clean environment is a good; it does not come free. But today people are willing to pay more for a cleaner environment because their real incomes have risen. As we become richer, we are willing to pay more to have environmental amenities around us. Whether or not we are willing to pay the price that would be necessary for obtaining a much purer environment is another

---

[1] It even caught fire, causing bridge damage estimated at $70,000.

question. In any event, Congress has passed numerous pieces of legislation aimed at controlling the degree of pollution-causing activities of producers and consumers alike. The Clean Water Act specifies that all rivers and lakes should be swimmable by the year 1985. The Clean Air Act specifies maximum limits of how much pollution is to be allowed in every city, of how much pollution will be allowed from cars, and so on. Individual cities and states have passed their own environmental legislation. The results in some cases are impressive. In others, only the magnitude of the costs seems worthy of mention. From the very beginning, for example, automobile producers have complained about the tremendous costs involved in cleaning up automobile engines. Soon after the passage of the Clean Water Act, there was a relaxation of standards in 1976 because of the fuel crisis.

It may be uneconomical to clean up *all* the waterways and all the lakes in the United States. We have to realize when discussing ecological problems that every clean-up effort involves a cost. And the closer we try to come to purity, the higher the costs become.

Reduce Pollution to What Level?

We obviously have to make a choice, and the rule for maximum economic efficiency is to reduce pollution up to the point where the additional cost of pollution abatement is just equal to the additional benefit, then stop. Of course, this means that the level of pollution desired is not zero. (Finding out some of the hidden costs of pollution may be extremely difficult, however. When such hidden costs surface in the future, they may haunt us with a vengeance.)

Nation-wide standards for automobiles, smokestacks, and factories may be the best ways to control pollution, but they do cause inefficiencies in our economic system. After all, it is not the total physical quantity of pollution that is important, but rather how harmful it is in any given situation. Sulfur oxides are emitted in much smaller quantities than are numerous other pollutants. But they are much more injurious to human health. It would be absurd

to set the same physical standard for sulfur oxide emissions as for, say, particulate emissions. What we have to examine is the actual economic costs of different types of pollution in different types of situations. The billowing, belching smokestacks of New York's Con-Edison electric utility coal-fed steam generators certainly cause much more damage than the same amount of pollution would cause in the middle of the Mohave Desert.

If we are going to be economically efficient in our pollution-abating system, pollution must be reduced more in the heavier populated areas of our nation than in the less populated areas. National standards do not in fact take account of different degrees of population density and, hence, the different degrees of economic damage sustained per unit of physical pollution. That leads up to another seemingly serious problem in the United States—concentration and urbanization.

The Congested City

Now is the age of urbanization. In 1980, it is estimted that 79 percent of the population will be living in urban areas. At certain hours, cities are so crowded that one can barely walk the streets or drive through them in a car. In fact, congestion due to automobile traffic is usually overwhelming in New York, Los Angeles, Chicago, Atlanta, and numerous other big cities. The crowded environment in the cities seems also to be correlated with poverty and ghetto life, deteriorating housing conditions, and deteriorating air. But the urban environment is the one sought by Americans, and people continue to move out of the country into the city in spite of the high costs that are involved in city life. They do this partly because income earning opportunities are higher in urban areas, but also because the urban environment allows for more diversity in life-styles and entertainment. After all, specialization—as we have said many times before—is a function of the size of the market. There are not many symphony orchestras in towns of 5,000 people, nor many movies, either. The list of what does not exist in such towns is long indeed.

The problems of the cities seem at times insurmountable, and, to top this all off, city governments clamor for more money from the federal government to help solve their problems. Cities contend that they are facing a fiscal crisis as their needs rise faster than their revenues.

A Different Urban Perspective

To provide the necessary perspective to see what is actually happening and the trends in urbanization, we cannot look at what has happened in a few major cities. The urban problem must be put in wider perspective, and many of the problems that plague urban environments also exist in the countryside. Even in small towns there is substandard housing, functional illiteracy, hard-core unemployment, drug abuse, veneral disease, vandalism, and violence—perhaps not in the same proportions as in big cities, but there nonetheless.

Now the Census Bureau tells us that by the year 2000, 85 percent of all Americans will live in metropolitan areas. This is a misleading statistic, however, and the term *metropolitan area* is difficult to define. It can mean many suburbs that have a total population of 50,000, or New York, with its millions of people. Actually, the percentage of the population living in cities of 100,000 or more peaked at the start of the Great Depression. It has dropped over time since then. Moreover, it should be realized that most people who live in standard metropolitan statistical areas, or SMSAs as they are called by the Census Bureau and other government agencies, do not live in the center of the city. Most live in contiguous suburban environments. This is not the same thing as being in a congested area. In fact, many suburbanites also work in suburbia and rarely frequent the center of the city they are near. Further, it appears that small, relatively isolated towns are becoming increasingly important for manufacturing employment. One study in Pennsylvania showed that between the beginning and the middle of the 1960s, manufacturing employment grew faster in cities of less than 25,000.

But even if we look at the core areas of large cities, they are not becoming more congested, but less.[2] In the past decade, over half the central cities of every size lost population. Density—as expressed by persons per square mile—in standard metropolitan areas shows a downward trend, as expressed in Figure 13–1.

Also, certain things within central cities are getting better, not worse. The 1950 Census indicated that well over 15 percent of housing units in cities were occupied by more than one person per room. By 1970 the figure dropped to less than 7 percent. Paradoxically, it appears that attempts at urban renewal have caused almost as much harm as good. In 1972, part of a huge public housing project in St. Louis was torn down. Moreover, without any help at all from public housing projects, the poor and the black have been able to improve their own housing environments. Between 1960 and 1968 housing occupied by blacks which the Census Bureau called "not meeting specified conditions" fell from 25 percent to less than 9 percent. They were able to obtain better housing without urban removal. Perhaps that indicates it may no longer be the answer to housing problems.

And Lastly, the Government

If we look at a graph of total government spending as a percentage of GNP, such as depicted in Figure 13–2, we see an unmistakable trend upward. Until the Great Depression and World War II, government expenditures never exceeded 10 percent of GNP (except for World War I) and in general were much less. On the eve of the Great Depression, they were only 8.2 percent. At the beginning of the twentieth century, they were closer to 6 percent. No empirically refutable theories have succeeded in explaining why there has been a continued rise in the percentage of total expenditures accounted for by government—local, state, and federal—in the

---

[2] In fact, now some city leaders are worried about the abandonment of the central city.

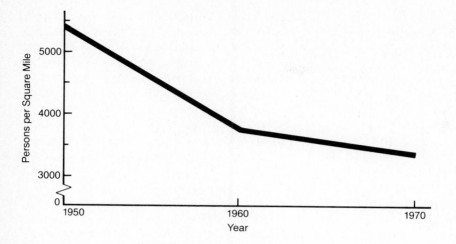

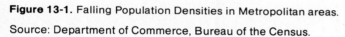

Figure 13-1. Falling Population Densities in Metropolitan areas.

Source: Department of Commerce, Bureau of the Census.

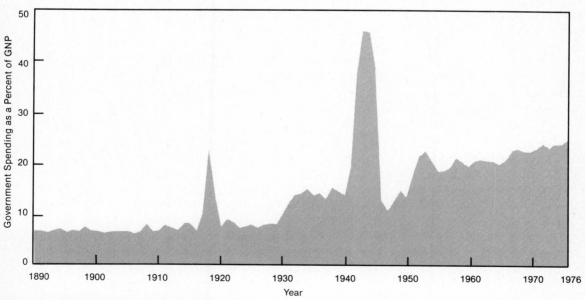

Figure 13-2. Rising Government Activity.

Source: U.S. Department of Commerce.

Critical Problems in a New Decade

United States. It apparently has little to do with levels of GNP, for in other countries we find no correlation between high levels of government spending and high levels of per capita income.

Increasingly over the twentieth century and very evident today, there has been a willingness to turn to government to resolve crises and cure economic woes. The results have seldom proved satisfactory and the last few years have witnessed growing concern with the results of increased government expenditures. Johnson's "Great Society" and Nixon's "New Prosperity" have done little to alleviate the problems they were designed to cure. In fact, it is common knowledge now that much of the money spent on the War on Poverty simply filled the pockets of well-paid government bureaucrats. It is very difficult to predict whether or not the current dissatisfaction with government will actually lead to a reduction in the trend of more and more government involvement. Perhaps such a reduction will become more of a possibility if we ever manage to live in a period devoid of crises. Tomorrow will tell. □

issue XIII: CAN POVERTY BE ELIMINATED?

THE HAVES AND THE HAVE NOTS

The United States is one of the richest nations on earth. That does not mean, however, that everyone is rich and no one is poor. As of 1977, the U.S. Census Bureau showed that some twenty-six million American still lived below the federal poverty line.

The Official Definition of Poverty

In 1959, the President's Council of Economic Advisors originally set a poverty line of $3,000 income, regardless of family size. In 1965, it redefined poverty by taking into account family size. That definition is still used today and was designed by a Social Security Administration statistician who devised a formula for a definition of the minimum adequate standard of living. The statistician took a nutritionally adequate "economy food budget" for various family sizes drawn up by the Department of Agriculture in several of its household consumption surveys. Table XIII—1 shows that the official poverty line for 1977 changes depending on the number of persons in the family. That poverty line is updated annually to reflect cost of living changes.

Is Poverty Absolute?

If the original poverty line of $3,000 is carried backward to, say, 1935, we find that one-third of all Americans were "poor." By 1955, one in five would have been classified as "poor," and today something like one in twenty. Clearly, if we were to keep $3,000 as the limit, even with adjustments for inflation, there would be no poor in a few more years. The poverty line, however, does not remain stable. Poverty is a relative concept. Today's official

Table XIII—1. Poverty Levels for Various Family Sizes, 1977.

Number in Family	Non-Farm	Farm
1 (14-64 years old)	$2,797	$2,396
1 (65 or older)	2,581	2,196
2 (where head of household is 14-64 years old)	3,617	3,079
2 (where head of household is 64 or older)	3,257	2,772
3	4,293	3,643
4	5,500	4,695
5	6,499	5,552
6	7,316	6,224
7 or more	9,022	7,639

Source: U.S. Bureau of the Census.

poverty income would have been considered opulence 200 years ago. Moreover, the poverty line in the United States is greater than the average income level in most other countries in the world.

The fact is that as long as the distribution of income in this country is not more or less equal, there will always be relative poverty, by definition. There will always be some families who earn more than other families. Hence, in a realistic sense, relative poverty is impossible to eradicate.

We have just mentioned inequality in the distribution of income. This topic is linked closely with the problems of the poor and the supposed nonelimination of poverty in this country. Let us take a look at standard income distribution statistics at the end of the 1970s.

Income Distribution

Consider the total distribution of income cut into fifths, the lowest fifth to the highest fifth of income earners and their percentage of total income in the economy. In Table XIII—2, the percentage of national income going to the various fifths of the population is given for this period right after World War II and for 1974. There is relatively little change in the measured

Table XIII—2. Distribution of Income.

Families	Percentage of Money Income Share	
	1947	1974
Top 20 percent	43.1%	42.1%
Fourth 20 percent	23.1	23.0
Third 20 percent	17.0	17.2
Second 20 percent	11.8	12.1
Bottom 20 percent	5.0	5.6

Source: U.S. Bureau of the Census.

money income distribution over that period of time. The bottom fifth of income earners still appeared to earn not much more than 5 percent of total money income. The highest fifth still earn approximately 40 percent of national money income. The conclusion that many critics of government welfare programs reach is that neither the progressive nature of our federal personal income tax system nor the massive money transfers that the U.S. government has engaged in have succeeded in pulling the bottom 20 percent of income earners out of their plight. Indeed, some observers, such as MIT's Lester C. Thurow, believe that the United States is still plagued with relatively large inequalities in the distribution of economic resources. "The richest 10 percent of our households receive 26.1 percent of our income, while the poorest 10 percent receive only 1.7 per-

cent."[1] To Thurow, that means that the top 10 percent of U.S. households receive fifteen times as much income as the bottom 10 percent. He compares this with Sweden, where the ratio is seven, Japan, were the ratio is ten, and Germany, where the ratio is eleven.

Both the Congressional Budget Office (CBO) and a number of academic researchers do not agree with Thurow's conclusions nor with the data on which they were based and on which our Table XIII—2 is based.

The Wrong Measure of Income

The statistics that come from the Census Bureau measure what is called *money income.* The only thing that is included in its distribution of income estimates is the

[1] *Newsweek*, February 14, 1977, p. 11.

actual monetary income (including money transfers from the government) that households receive. The standard of living of a family is not, however, solely a function of money income. If a family receives rent supplements, Medicare, Medicaid, food stamps, and so on, then that household has a higher real standard of living than is indicated by its money income alone. It turns out that much of the emphasis of government transfers to poor individuals in our society has taken the form of these "in-kind" benefits since 1966. The average total of such in-kind benefits for the ten years since 1966 has been something like $40 billion a year. When the CBO took these into account, it came up with some startling conclusions about the number of poor in America in 1977. Instead of twenty-six million, as reported by the Census Bureau, the CBO contends that there are only nine million. The Census Bureau figures show that 15 percent of Americans sixty-five and over are living in poverty; the CBO believes that only 4 percent are. According to CBO director Alice M. Rivlin, "The nation has come a lot closer to eliminating poverty than most people realize." The Rand Corpo-

Table XIII—3. Family Income Percentages.

Family	Percentage of Total Income Share	
	1947	1974
Top 20 percent	42.3%	31.9%
Fourth 20 percent	23.0	20.9
Third 20 percent	16.8	18.4
Second 20 percent	12.6	16.1
Bottom 20 percent	5.3	12.6

Source: Edgar K. Browning, "The Trend Toward Equality in the Distribution of Net Income," *Southern Economic Journal*, July 1976, Vol. 43.

ration did a study of New York City's welfare families and found that their in-kind benefits lifted 80 to 90 percent of them above the poverty line, even though officially, they are still counted as poor.

Economist Edgar Browning has recomputed the Census Bureau distribution of income figures to take account of in-kind transfers to the poor. In Table XIII—3, we see the dramatic changes that take place when such calculations are done. What we see is that the bottom 20 percent of income earners have more than doubled their share of national income to over 12 percent since World War II.

But There Are Poor

Just because the bottom fifth of income earners have dramatically improved their lot since World War II does not mean that poor people do not exist in the United States and certainly there is widespread (high percentage) poverty among certain portions of the population: blacks, single women with dependent children, and others. Nevertheless, to the extent that we accept a *relative* definition of poverty, there will always be some poor people. Whether or not we can go as far as George Washington University economist Sar A. Levitan, who stated that "if poverty is defined as a lack of basic need, it's almost been eliminated," is an open question. We can, nonetheless, point out that the problem of poverty has not been ignored in this country. Better, more efficient methods of transferring income to those who truly need it are certainly available. Perhaps if President Carter holds to his promise, these methods will be found. ☐

Index